PRAISE FOR *Cheesemonger*

"Gordon Edgar, punkster turned cheesemonger, has a knack for telling stories and crams his passion, wry humor, and knowledge into every page. It's such a treat to read that as I neared the end, I started to ration the pages to make it last longer."

—DIDI EMMONS, author of *Vegetarian Planet*

"Smart, compassionate, and fun to read, *Cheesemonger* took me by surprise! Who would expect the memoir of a cheese man to be so fascinating, playful, and refreshing? It's great to hear a voice on food from the punk route, and Gordon Edgar brings a fresh and important perspective that we could all use for handmade foods, those that aren't, and the people who buy them."

— DEBORAH MADISON, author *of Local Flavors: Cooking and Eating from America's Farmer's Markets* and *What We Eat When We Eat Alone*

"Gordon Edgar knows his cheese and aims to please. Unique in the offering of cheese books, Gordon weaves an intricate web of his world at Rainbow Grocery: a democracy of passionate food mavens with a look at social justice and the foibles of the human condition. It's all there. Gordon's expres   d entertaining prose exudes his smiling wit. His ta' light-hearted and poignant. He dares to ask a' questions. Blessed is the cheesemonger."

—ALLISO

V   ᴊe

"Weaving together seemingly disparate worlds, Gordon Edgar takes you on as a passenger in his wickedly funny and insightful memoir. By the time I finished reading, I had learned new things about cheese, for sure, but was more struck by his unique and humorous take on cooperatives, community, and how Americans relate to their food. Cheese may be the focus, but human dynamics, in all our shared quirks, passions, and constructed factions, is really the subject."

—BECKY SELENGUT, chef and author

"All I can say is this: If Randall Grahm, of Bonny Doon, would have discovered cheese before wine, he would have written this book. *Cheesemonger* is witty, insightful, and utterly packed with passion and fine humor. This book now goes on the 'required reading' list for my entire staff!"

— CHARLIE TROTTER, Restaurant Charlie Trotter

"*Cheesemonger* is a deliciously fun read, cover to cover. Gordon gives a knowledgeable and thoroughly unabashed view from the front lines of a surging field."

—MAX McCALMAN, author of *The Cheese Plate, Mastering Cheese: Lessons for Connoisseurship from a Maître Fromager* and Dean of Curriculum at www.artisanalcheese.com

CHEESEMONGER

CHEESEMONGER

A Life on the Wedge | GORDON EDGAR

Chelsea Green Publishing
White River Junction, Vermont

Project Manager: Emily Foote
Developmental Editor: Benjamin Watson
Copy Editor: Laura Jorstad
Indexer: Lee Lawton
Designer: Peter Holm,
      Sterling Hill Productions

Printed in the United States of America
First printing January, 2010
10 9 8 7 6 5 4 3   13 14 15

Our Commitment to Green Publishing

Chelsea Green sees publishing as a tool for cultural change and ecological stewardship. We strive to align our book manufacturing practices with our editorial mission and to reduce the impact of our business enterprise on the environment. We print our books and catalogs on chlorine-free recycled paper, using vegetable-based inks whenever possible. This book may cost slightly more because we use recycled paper, and we hope you'll agree that it's worth it. Chelsea Green is a member of the Green Press Initiative (www.greenpressinitiative.org), a nonprofit coalition of publishers, manufacturers, and authors working to protect the world's endangered forests and conserve natural resources.

Cheesemonger was printed on Natures Book Natural, a 30-percent postconsumer recycled paper supplied by Thomson-Shore.

Chelsea Green Publishing is committed to preserving ancient forests and natural resources. We elected to print this title on 30-percent postconsumer recycled paper, processed chlorine-free. As a result, for this printing, we have saved:

4 Trees (40' tall and 6-8" diameter)
2 Million BTUs of Total Energy
304 Pounds of Greenhouse Gases
1,651 Gallons of Wastewater
111 Pounds of Solid Waste

Chelsea Green Publishing made this paper choice because we and our printer, Thomson-Shore, Inc., are members of the Green Press Initiative, a nonprofit program dedicated to supporting authors, publishers, and suppliers in their efforts to reduce their use of fiber obtained from endangered forests. For more information, visit: www.greenpressinitiative.org.

Environmental impact estimates were made using the Environmental Defense Paper Calculator. For more information visit: www.papercalculator.org.

Library of Congress Cataloging-in-Publication Data
Edgar, Gordon.
  Cheesemonger : a life on the wedge / Gordon Edgar.
    p. cm.
  Includes bibliographical references and index.
  ISBN 978-1-60358-237-7
  1. Edgar, Gordon. 2. Cheese industry--United States--Biography. 3. Cheesemaking--United States--Biography. I. Title.

  HD9280.U62E34 2010
  381'.4173092--dc22
  [B]

                              2009035968

Chelsea Green Publishing Company
85 North Main Street, Suite 120
White River Junction, VT 05001
(802) 295-6300
www.chelseagreen.com

MIX
Paper from
responsible sources
FSC® C013483

For the farmers, the cheesemakers,
and all the cheese workers.

CONTENTS

PREFACE

There are plenty of great cheese guidebooks out there. This is not one of them.

However, in writing a cheesemonger memoir, it seems a little unfair to the reader to not include some helpful hints for cheese-curious people and some descriptions of the cheeses I use as examples in this book. At the end of every chapter there are profiles of a couple of cheeses that sum up some of the subjects I discussed in that chapter. I have included approximate pricing as well, though who knows what things will cost by the time this book is published. So, if only for comparative purposes:

$ = under $10 per pound
$$ = $10 to $20 per pound
$$$ = $20 to $30 per pound
$$$$ = $40 per pound and up

I've also included a glossary and a "Cheese Buying for Beginners" section at the end of this book that will help you get what you want out of your cheese purchases. I didn't want to bog down the book by going over those definitions and tips in the main chapters, but I bet even some of you cheese-experienced people may find something interesting in there.

—GE

ACKNOWLEDGMENTS

It's a punk rock tradition to have a "Thank You" list that takes longer to read than it takes to listen to the album. I can't quite do that in this medium, but no work like this is a solo endeavor. This simply wouldn't have been possible without the people listed here.

First off, big thanks to my coworkers in cheese: Mariah Sparks, Jenny Glazer, Pete Weiss, Kelly Parrott, Anna Costa, Andy Levi, Sarah Reed, Liz Ramos-Jajeh, D'louie Snyder, Jean Kwan, Pat Seguin, and everyone who has ever worked in cheese even for one shift. Thanks for putting up with this project, even when it's meant more work for you. I also owe appreciation to all my other coworkers (past and present) at Rainbow Grocery Cooperative, the country's biggest worker-owned and -run retail store—there are way too many of us to name. Thanks to all the people who've bought cheese from us at Rainbow over the last fifteen years, especially the ones who had the patience to let us get our act together way back when.

Some other co-op folks deserve note, too: the Cooperative (the band). All the workers at the Cheeseboard Collective in Berkeley for raising the worker co-op cheese bar so high. All the worker co-op folks across the Bay and the country whom I have missed organizing with for the last couple of years, as I tried to finish this book. Melissa Hoover and the US Federation of Worker Cooperatives. Also, sorry to the Network of Bay Area Worker Collectives where I flaked on my BOD membership when I got serious about writing this book. That should probably go for Brahm and People's Grocery in Oakland as well, since they had to deal with a distracted Gordon over the last year or so. Also, I want to acknowledge all the 1980s anarchists, "Outrage" collective members, anti-apartheid activists, and Epicenter punks who helped push me down the co-op path.

This work clearly would not have happened without the cheese buddies, mentors, cheesemakers, distributors, and dairy scientists who inspired me and taught me so much (I'll let you guess who is who): Sheana Davis, Andrea London, Jessie Schwartzberg, Raymond Hook, Brad Dube, Kathleen Shannon Finn, Molly Brownson, Steve and Patty Ehlers, Judy Creighton (the first cheese person to befriend me), Jeanine Creighton, Rachel Ennis, Jennifer Bice, Steven Schack, Dee Harley, Ig Vella, Ricki Carroll, Donna Pacheco, Mandy Johnston, Mark Todd, Tim Pedrozo, the Boersma family, everyone in the Rossi family, Joel Fanfelle, Hans Kunisch, Dannie Ray, Jim Yonkus, Diane Sauvage, Debra Dickerson and everyone at Neal's Yard, Susan Patton Fox, Steve Giambalvo, Maxx Sherman, Catherine Donnelly, Cara Ching, Lenny Rice, Becki McClure, Rachel Cohen, Sue Conley, Peggy Smith, Dennis Yashar, Bob McCall, Janet Fletcher, Mary Keehn, Sue Worthman, Terri Rowley, the Beehive folks, the Sierra Nevada folks, Franklin Peluso, the Giacomini family, the Little family, the Kehler families, Juliet Harbutt, Moshe Rosenberg, Gianaclis Caldwell, Paul Kindstedt, Soyoung Scanlan, Paul Haskins, Jeff Jirik, Ray Bair, Julianna Uruburu, Alma Avalos, Laura Martinez, Kate Arding, Andy Lax, Allison Hooper, Sid Cook, Joe Widmer, Cindy Major, Mariano Gonzalez, Daphne Zepos, Dan Strongin, Cassy Adamson, Marie Schmittroth, Richard and Karen Silverston, Marci Wilson, David Grotenstein, Sarah Marcus, Jeanette Hurt, Bryce Canyon of Cheese, and everyone from the California Artisan Cheese Guild.

I'm sure I've left someone out here, so let me praise all the reps who loved the cheese more than unit-moving, all the dairy workers, especially the ones whose names will never be known to the public. All the cheesemakers and dairy farmers, especially the ones who let me visit. And to all the other cheese workers out there, I hope I've represented us well. Also, I want to take this space to acknowledge the late Patrick Rance for writing the best cheese book ever. *The French Cheese Book* is long out of print and the only book I've ever paid over $100 for. I never regretted that decision.

Certain people encouraged me early on and/or provided me with feedback when I was most desperate for it. Special thanks go to: Eliani Torres, Nick Mamatas, Liz Jones, Joan Meyers, Amanda Piasecki,

Chloe Eudaly, Erik Farseth, Amy Hundley, Christina Drumm, Sarah Dentan, Daphne Gottlieb, Steve Dabrowski, Khristina Wenzinger, Alexa Guerra, Soumeya Bendimerad, Vikki Karan, Max McCalman, Michelle Tea, Sarah Fran Wisby, Sarah Katherine Lewis, Lauren Wheeler, Cas McGee, Sara Ryan, Steve Lieber, Casey Ress, Mark Haggerty, Kristen Connolly, Kim McGee, Chewy Marzolo, Jen Angel, Bruce Anderson, Barth Anderson, Chaia Milstein, Laura Fokkena, Gabriella Lanyi, Susan Stinson, Sarah Shevett, Laren Leland, Leah Lakshmi Piepzna Samarasinha, Karen Eng, Joan Hilty, Ericka Baile-Byrne, Taryn Hipp, Kelli Callis, Julie Burton, Jenn Laughran, Calvin Crosby, Lori Selke, and all the folks who befriended me on LJ.

Thanks to Todd Stadtman and Keith Morris for letting me use their song lyrics and providing part of the soundtrack for my punk rock youth.

Thanks to my wonderful agent Elizabeth Wales, her assistant agent Neal Swain. Thanks to everyone at Chelsea Green, especially Joni Praded, Ben Watson, Laura Jorstad, and Emily Foote. It's great to work with people who put out such awesome and important books.

This book also would not have been possible without my parents, who have always encouraged me to write and helped give me the skills I needed to make it in this world. Thanks, Mom and Dad.

Extra-Special Thanks for extra-special help: Bee Lavender, Frances Varian, and Cindy Emch. You all know why.

Most of all though, I want to thank Laurie Jones Neighbors for all the editing help, emotional support, patience, and the love I needed to help me get through this process and my daily life. No one else did more to make this book a reality and I honestly don't know if I would have finished this book without her help. Hey, Laurie (and Schnitzel), thanks for making everything better.

CHEESEMONGER

o n e

Cheese Dreams, Cheese Nightmares

Every year during the holidays I have the same nightmare. I'm in the store's walk-in cooler, but instead of the cheese area being twelve feet by sixteen, it's warehouse-sized. Boxes of Fromage de Meaux, Vella Dry Jack, Valencay, Vacherin Mont d'Or, Reblochon, and every other cheese I could ever want—legal or illegal—are stacked to the ceiling on shelves, on milk crates, and in every nook, cranny, and corner.

They're rotting before my eyes.

Mites are turning the Gruyère into nasty tan dust. Orange stinky washed rinds are liquefying and dripping onto the cheese below. White bloomy rinds are yellowing, browning, and spotting. All the beautiful cheese is going concave—hardening or disintegrating—and I am helpless. When I look more closely, I see that the few remaining beautiful and snowy white cheeses don't have rinds at all; instead, they are covered with seas of maggots.

While I try to stop the cross-contamination of decaying cheese, the delivery drivers continue to wheel hand trucks, loaded over their heads with cheese, into the cooler, yelling out, "Where do you want this?"

The produce workers are angry. They can't reach the broccoli because my stacks of cheese are in the way, and the cheese mold is starting to infect the salad mix. I grab at the good bits, trying to hold on to what's still edible, when I notice the display coolers are full and there are no customers in the store. My cheese coworkers stick their heads in and scream, "It's your fault!"

It is my fault. I am the Cheesemonger, and I have failed them. I have failed the store and the customers. I have failed the cheese.

No matter how organized I am, it's a rare year when I don't have this nightmare during the Thanksgiving to New Year's rush. I wake up, startled, and have to force myself not to rush down to the store at 3 or 4 a.m. The stress is always at its worst in the several days leading up to the holiday week, when I'm surrounded by more cheese than can fit in the cooler, and the buying pace hasn't picked up to full craziness. I swear I can hear the cheese dying over the rumble of the cooler fans.

While cheese is a more forgiving perishable than produce or some other refrigerated foods, its short and finicky life span can give nightmares to those of us who buy it for a living.

I'm the cheese buyer for Rainbow Grocery Cooperative in San Francisco. We are the Bay Area's largest independent natural foods store, the country's largest retail worker-owned cooperative, and one of the most democratic workplaces you will find anywhere. My job as a "cheesemonger" gives me specific responsibilities: It's my job to judge the quality of cheese and to decide which cheese our store should carry. I set prices, sales, and promotions and make contacts with distributors or cheesemakers. I figure out the best method to get cheese to the store and decide when cheese is ripe enough to cut. I determine when a cheese has gone over the hill and how to get credit for bad or damaged cheese from the distributor who sold it to us.

Referring to myself as a "cheesemonger" elicits snickering from some, but those who don't laugh often tell me, "You have the best job ever." I love it. I've been working in the cheese mines for fifteen years and counting. Maggots, mice, and misanthropes haven't been able to cut into my love for cheese.

People might imagine that a cheesemonger visits peasants in France or haggles over prices in Italy, but cheesemongering is mostly retail work with some credibility and a better title. Most of my work is accomplished inside the store, which is surrounded by freeways and homeless encampments. Our neighborhood is not the part of San Francisco that appears on postcards. The cheese discussions are not all glamorous, either. While I love to expound on the discovery of a barely legal raw milk cheese, or an exciting new local cheesemaker, the conversations I have with sales reps trying to sell me a subpar product remind me that I'm at work. As with any trade, there are many liars, exaggerators, and fast talkers out there, but almost all have a portable cooler full of samples, and a good cheesemonger knows that the cheese always does the talking.

Cheese is an old food riding a wave of new popularity. Consumption of cheese has exploded in the years I've been a cheese buyer. The average American has almost tripled his/her consumption in my years on this planet, now eating over thirty pounds a year.[1] One reason for this vast change is that a greater selection is available, particularly among American handmade cheeses, which boast varieties that thirty years ago would have been unimaginable. We are in the midst of a cheese boom.

Almost every day at work a customer asks me how I ended up as a cheese buyer. The answer comes as a surprise to most folks: Punk rock made me a cheesemonger.

When people ask me how I became a cheesemonger, they probably expect to hear one of the typical origin stories: I went to the culinary academy or I apprenticed with a well-known cheesemaker or I grew up in a dairy family. No, no, and no. I hung out with the anarchists and freaks. I was a member-volunteer at Epicenter Zone, a not-for-profit punk community center and record store, just a couple of blocks from Rainbow Grocery. Collectively we created a place where people could hang out as long as they wanted without being pressured into buying things. Political groups, zines, and undercapitalized music projects could be found there, and we had movie nights and social events, conferences and performances, support groups— even a political library. Despite the lack of coherence guaranteed by a group of ever-changing, unpaid volunteers living in an expensive city, the Epicenter Zone was a home base designed to incite others to political education and action.

Still, after a few years in San Francisco, the revolution hadn't found me, and since I couldn't seem to find it, I started imagining how I could make a living that didn't make me hate myself and everyone around me. I had never liked office work, and I figured out quickly that I wasn't very good as the type of outsider organizer that so many activist campaigns need. Rainbow Grocery Cooperative, where I had shopped, always seemed like a good place, but I didn't have a lot of interest in being a grocer. I did have an interest in environmentalism and collectives, though, so I put in an application.

I will admit that I fudged my interest in cheese when applying for my job in the cheese department at Rainbow. I wanted any job I could get at the most nonhierarchical large co-op in the country, and that job just happened to be in cheese. I hope this confession doesn't anger any readers out there who are looking for that perfect cheese job and who are doubtless much more qualified now than I was back then. But let's remember that a decade ago "cheese worker" was not the glamorous job it is today. And it was even more subject to mockery.

I was nervous during the interview, and I almost blew the opportunity when my future coworkers asked, "What are your favorite cheeses?" We were upstairs in the old, smaller, more hippieish store location. The tiny meeting room had big industrial warehouse windows and no chairs. We had to sit on pillows. Actually, most of the current cheese workers who were interviewing me were reclining while I was trying to sit as upright as possible. I didn't think it would look good to lie down on the job before I even got it. They awaited my response.

I scrambled for the right thing to say. Monterey Jack would have been uninteresting. Brie would have sounded pretentious. I am not always the quickest thinker, but luck was with me that day when I remembered the cheese in my fridge at home. I had bought this cheese from the very store where I was interviewing.

"Uh . . . ," I said, pulling the few buzzwords that I had just learned out of my ass before thinking about what they meant. "Anything raw and rennetless?"

Oh man, I lucked out. It was the perfect answer for the time and place. If you want to define hippie cheese, those are the two words to use. To this day the most common questions I get are: "What does it mean when it says a cheese is raw?" (It means it's not pasteurized.) And "What is rennet?" (Traditionally, an enzyme taken from the stomach of a dead calf and used to coagulate milk. Cheese made with vegetarian versions is colloquially called rennetless.) I sounded like an expert and I didn't know a thing. I had just read it on the packages of cheese, which, I soon discovered, is a good skill to have if you're going to work with the public.

At the time of the interview, I was working at a crappy job cleaning buses for hippies, and this is where Rainbow called to offer me the job. I had chosen to work at the bus-cleaning gig so I could quit without notice and take a job at a worker cooperative when one presented itself. It's odd to think a job can make you feel free, but the call from Rainbow was one of the happiest moments of my life: I would never have to deal with Gatorade bottles full of piss ever again. I let out a whoop when I got the news.

"What's up?" an office worker asked.

"I got a job at Rainbow. I won't be in tomorrow. Or ever again."

The office manager started talking about his feelings, and the company being like a family, and being let down, but the wonderful thing about passive aggressives is that, unless you're dating one, they are easy to ignore.

As enthusiastic as I was on my first day at Rainbow, I soon realized that I was entering a demoralized department. We only had a three-door cooler with rusty shelves hammered not quite into place and held together with duct tape. We could occasionally sell a couple of pieces of specialty cheese: a Roquefort, a handmade Brie, a local chèvre, before the rest turned on themselves like hunger strikers, shriveling in protest of their conditions.

I had no idea how much I had to learn. Concentrating on keeping the forty-pound blocks of Cheddar and Jack cut and stocked occupied hours of my time, as did reading about the cheese our customers asked us to carry. The idea of attending a cheese conference—or that this sort of gathering even existed—well, let's just say that if someone had told me I would soon be speaking at one, I would have laughed.

Those of us who didn't grow up with fancy food are often expected to have a transcendent food moment. A gasp of joy at our first noncanned peach, our disbelief that avocados or artichokes are not only edible but enjoyable. Weird-smelling sauces, meat eaten in other cultures, and spices that don't smell like home alter our appetite forever. For a food professional, these experiences are transformative: They are the moments when the true purposes of lives are revealed.

I grew up on Velveeta and Kraft singles. When I moved three thousand miles away from home to upstate New York, my mom brought Monterey Jack when she visited because she wasn't sure if I could get it there. Of course she also brought sourdough bread, which actually was unobtainable in upstate New York at the time.

When I moved back to San Francisco, along with my worldly, urban-raised, culturally different lover, we shopped at Rainbow long before I got hired there. Much to her dismay, I would resist the factory-made, triple-cream blue Cambozola she liked so much. We'd often settle on smoked Gouda, which was about all that I could handle. It wasn't even the natural kind, but pieces cut from the cooked and emulsified processed logs.

I didn't really *get* cheese back then. How hard it must have been for her to be involved with a non-food-lover. Ironically, in 1994, at almost exactly the same time she became lactose-intolerant, I got my job in the cheese department. Life can be so cruel.

Eventually, I would have my transcendent moment, but it didn't arrive on my first day working with cheese. I knew that I would either learn to love cheese or have to find another job. I convinced myself that I was game. I would try every cheese and be open-minded. I steeled myself for the nastiness because, contrary to the cliché that food folks are ever excited to try new experiences, I wasn't that culinarily curious.

Luckily for me, when I first started Rainbow did not have a huge cheese selection, so I could pace myself. Sure, I ate more Brie and blues than I ever had before, but many of those cheeses, beyond some basics like Jack and mild Cheddar, we don't even carry anymore. Slowly, I learned to appreciate these cheeses—how to cut them, and what they were commonly used for—but I hadn't yet fallen in love.

I grew scared that I was one of those people who simply can't feel the cheese love. There is nothing wrong with not loving cheese, but I liked my job and my coworkers, and I didn't want to leave.

I was voted into the position of buyer six months after I started working at Rainbow, but my new title involved little more than doing inventory and checking off grid sheets. Our specialty cheese selection was almost nonexistent, and the cheese knowledge required was minimal.

Regular shoppers, however, were dismayed by our selection and didn't want to go elsewhere just to buy cheese. They would make mysterious suggestions: Basque sheep cheese, Goat Gouda, handmade French Brie. The names were all new to me in those days.

We tried to sell some of these seemingly exotic cheeses, and the experience was certainly important in my development as a cheesemonger. There is no substitute for working hands-on with as many different cheeses as possible.

While bringing in new and unfamiliar cheeses was a necessary step, in our case it was a pathetically executed one. It takes a while for a store to build a good cheese reputation, and the people who bought our fancy cheese were just experimenting or in a rush. At that time I did not fully comprehend the daring it takes for customers to buy the lone fancy piece of cheese on a dimly lit shelf, but I am thankful to those folks now.

What you need to run a quality cheese department is turnover. Cutting a wheel of Ossau-Iraty (a traditional Basque sheep's milk cheese) or Fromage de Meaux (the pasteurized version of the classic French Brie) into twelve or sixteen pieces can be intimidating. The product is expensive, and cutting a wheel open meant we would have to identify sixteen people who wanted to take a chance on buying it from us when nothing else in our department signified that we knew anything about cheese.

And we didn't really know anything about cheese. I didn't know who to believe in the world of ignorant or misleading pitches from unethical sales reps and the sometimes exaggerated claims from customers about the cheeses they desired. One customer told me that we could sell hundreds of pounds of dry-curd cottage cheese (which tastes just like it sounds) if we sampled it to our customers.

The bigger problem was not knowing what a cheese was supposed to taste like. I ordered my first Taleggio because a customer had requested it. At its best it can be a little intimidating to uninitiated cheese eaters. While not a strong cheese, it is stinky and often slimy. It's a washed-rind cheese, and the paper wrapper sticks to it to such an extent that my coworker, who goes by the cheese name Anarqueso, refers to the process of removing the wrapper as "skinning the zombie."

Before we moved a lot of cheese, our options were limited. I couldn't order from every distributor in the area as I do today because we simply couldn't buy enough to make their minimum order. In the case of the Taleggio I figured, *Hey, Italian American company, they should do okay with the cheese of their people.* But let's just say I found out the hard way that companies have their strengths, and that this one does better with Jack and Cheddar.

In retrospect, this cheese was the nastiest Taleggio I have ever seen. At the time I had no way of knowing, since it was also my first. Too-old Taleggio can present in different ways. Usually it's dried out and less smelly than usual, desiccated, and has too big an inedible-rind to edible-inside ratio. But not this one. Sometimes the bacteria that ripen the cheese go crazy, liquefying and intensifying the cheese. That's what I got for my first Taleggio: an oozy puddle of nasty, pink stink.

I didn't know what to do. I opened the box gently because cheese was dripping out the seams. I carefully pulled back the paper wrapping (which was easy, since the cheese was so wet) and looked at what might, at one time, have been a nice cheese. The pink rind, with green mold in the grooves, was cracked into so many small pieces that it no longer held together. Bits of rind floated on top of the oozy cheese so that it looked like a color-coded aerial shot of a flood disaster. Flies began swarming around, and it was still the dead of winter.

I looked at the cheese. I pondered the cheese. I meditated on the cheese. I phoned the distributor and described the mess they had sold me. Their response, which I soon realized would always be *the* response, was, "Oh it's fine."

They made suggestions. Just wrap it. Sample it out. Cup it without the rind and sell it as "Taleggio cream." There is always going to be variation in handmade cheese; that's what sets it apart from the commodity blocks—cheeses like Jack and mild Cheddar, which always taste the same, are made in huge quantity, and have their prices set by the commodities market in Chicago. Blah, blah, blah. To my shame, I considered all this.

I worked up the nerve to taste the Taleggio. I had spent too long on the phone, and the cheese was flattening. More cheese ooze dripped from the box seams onto the counter. I had read in books about what Taleggio, often called the Italian Brie, was supposed to be like: rich and creamy, but also nutty. Smelly, but also mild and milky. The cheese in front of me was smelly, that was for sure. I doubted this one would be mild, especially to my palate, which only a couple of months before thought smoked Gouda was a stretch. I was scared.

Today I certainly would have sent the cheese back within a few seconds of looking at it, but exploration is an important part of the educational experience. That day, I prodded it with a knife. The cheese gave but bounced back into shape. I scraped off a bit of the yellowy paste, brought it up to my nose, and smelled it. That didn't tell me anything. I had been warned that Taleggio was supposed to smell, but there is a wide range of possibilities contained within the word *smell*. It smelled, all right. So far so good?

I scooped a blob off with my finger and smelled it again. I almost brought it to my lips. Once. Twice. Okay, this time for real. When the cheese hit my tongue, I immediately knew something was wrong. Sweetness was the first thing I tasted. But not a good sweet. Sweet like blood, death, and putrefaction. I have never pulled my car over and tasted an animal I saw rotting on the side of the highway, but this is what I imagined it would taste like.

After the flavor of sweet rot came bitterness. I am one of those folks who can taste bitterness fairly easily, and this sensitivity has helped me tremendously in my cheese tasting and buying. I would go so far as to say that I can sense when a cheese is going bad before most other people. This was not a gift that paid off when I tasted this Taleggio. It wasn't a snappy little bite that awakens the taste buds. It was an ice pick to the tongue. I felt like a cheesemonger Trotsky.

My introduction to Taleggio was an important moment in my development as a cheesemonger, though I didn't realize this as I spat the cheese into the garbage and searched for something benign to take the awful taste out of my mouth. I had returned cheese for obvious defects like mold, but this was the first time I returned a product against the distributor's wishes, because it just wasn't right.

Despite the disaster of my first Taleggio, I was still hoping to find my true cheese love. That love eluded me. I tasted many different cheeses, in no particular order or fashion, and my taste broadened to be sure. I especially got into the rich and creamy ones because, as everyone knows, fat tastes damn good, but I was also playing the field, looking for the cheese that would send me over the edge.

Following in the footsteps of other great love stories, I found my true cheese love by accident. Every store sells Gruyère, but our store, and most supermarkets, bought what is known as Gruyère "cuts." Reputed to be from the center of aged wheels of Swiss Gruyère, they were all we could handle in the small cutting area of our old store. Full wheels of Gruyère run seventy to eighty pounds, and you need some room to work. I didn't know enough to know then that there was a difference between the cuts and the full wheels—I just remember thinking the cuts were strong. And they were, compared with, say, mild Cheddar.

But the cuts had none of the stink, nuttiness, and power of a full wheel of Gruyère. The cuts are only guaranteed aged one hundred days, and they are a sad replacement for the tremendous and distinct variety of smells and flavors that older wheels develop. Then one day a distributor pleaded with me to buy wheels of Antique Gruyère that they had received by accident from their importer in Chicago. I agreed because I got a good desperation price that would cover the added cost of labor and the cheese we would give out for free. But I was wary.

I wasn't prepared for the actual cheese, which was hard and crystally, but also sweet, nutty, and pungent. Aged cheese develops hard crystals that crunch when chewed. These little nuggets are made of calcium and salt or amino acids, and they show up in a number of different well-aged cheeses. This Gruyère was fragrant enough that people from the other side of the store came to check it out. It was a whole new world for most of our customers—and a whole new world for me.

Taleggio: Cow's milk cheese from Northern Italy. Sometimes called the Italian Brie because it is oozy and rich, this is actually a washed-rind cheese—meaning it is brushed with salt water, which makes it pink and smelly. It's a gateway cheese for people who want to learn to love the stink. Not only is it generally a good price compared with other European imports, but though it smells strong, it is more milky and fruity than strong and pungent. [$$, Similar cheese: Meadow Creek Grayson (US), washed-rind Robiola (Italy).]

Swiss Gruyère: This is the raw milk Alpine cheese that changed my life and allowed me to see the glory of cheese. If you are buying a well-aged one, it will be nutty, oniony, and spicy.

Gruyère is a cheese that will range in flavor and color depending on where the cows were grazing in the mountains, but when it's more than a year old it should always be a fabulous cheese. It's probably the best cooking cheese in the world, but equally good on a cheese plate. [$$, Similar cheese: Comte (France), Beaufort (France), Appenzeller (Switzerland), L'Etivaz (Switzerland).]

t w o

Becoming a Cheesemonger

The week that we sampled out the Antique Gruyère changed my life. I had bought two eighty-pound wheels, one to cut and one to display. Typically, we went through about a ten-pound box of cuts a week, so the quantity I had ordered seemed reasonable. Within about six hours we had to cut into the display wheel because we had sold so many pieces. I emergency-called my distributor and asked her to bring more cheese as soon as possible. Because the Gruyère had been a desperation sale for them, they were happy to oblige. Soon the owner of the company was there—on his day off—wearing tight, out-of-style shorts instead of his usual suit and asking me where I wanted the next four hundred pounds of cheese.

What hooked me weren't the sales—though I admit it was fun to watch cheese fly out faster than we could cut it—but the complexity of the cheese. I kept discovering new flavors. *Long-lasting* is an over-used phrase among foodies, but a year-old Gruyère is the epitome of a cheese that grows more interesting the longer it stays in your mouth. For the first time, I understood why people get so passionate about food and go to ridiculous lengths to describe their passion to others.

When I tasted the Antique Gruyère, the first thing I noticed was the strength. There was a pungency that, had it increased, would have been too much to take. But it didn't. It just awakened my senses.

Next came the nuttiness. Then the sweetness. Then some oniony undertones. Finally, a satisfying residue of fat and milk. At the time, the Gruyère was the best food I'd ever put into my mouth.

I knew I needed to find more cheese like this. More cheese that would blow my mind. Cheese that would help me understand why people obsessed over food. In that spirit I sought out further resources for cheese professionals. One of the biggest and best is the American Cheese Society (ACS), a trade organization that supports American cheesemakers by lobbying to prevent the banning of raw milk cheese, providing services to cheesemakers, raising the awareness of American-made cheeses, and much more.

I joined the ACS in 1999, imagining the fabulous tastes in store for me, yet the most helpful aspect to my development as a cheesemonger turned out to be meeting the actual people who made some of the cheeses I sold. Before I began meeting cheesemakers, I hadn't given any thought to what the animals ate, the different characteristics of their milks, or the techniques involved in the various styles of cheesemaking.

Once I've met a cheesemaker, it's also easier to call and say obnoxious things like, "I think the humidity level in your aging room is off because the cheese I got from you this week is oozing like an infected wound." In reality, I wouldn't say that because, as a group, cheesemakers don't respond well to similes or metaphors. But I never have any trouble with the cheesemakers; they're usually down-to-earth rural folk. Other retailers tend to be okay, too, for the most part. Even the one at the ACS conference drunkenly waving his penis at a group of Italians in the men's room and yelling, "I got your provolone right here!" provided a much-appreciated spectacle.

The first cheese conference I attended revealed two important things. The first was how much I didn't know about cheese. The second was how much I did. Despite my limited knowledge in the late 1990s, simply tasting the amount of cheese I had up to that point meant that I already knew more than most of my customers—even if I knew deep down that there was so much more to learn.

In a crowd that contained the best minds in American cheese, I knew that I couldn't even raise my hand in certain seminars. I had nothing to say about the chemical reactions in cheesemaking, the properties of different cheese cultures, or how the seasonal composition of milk would affect the finished product. Seminars set up for mongers were dominated by louder cheese people than me, arguing over cheese industry details that I knew nothing about. I was still getting a grip on the local California cheeses and the basic European ones when suddenly I was thrown into a much bigger world. The Festival of Cheese, a tasting with every American cheese entered into the judging competition, introduced me to hundreds of cheeses I'd never encountered before.

This conference, my first, was too expensive for my co-op to cover, but luckily I had made a cheese friend. Sheana Davis, a cheese educator, chef, and cheesemaker who worked for a few local dairies, needed some help receiving and organizing cheese for the annual judging competition, so she set me up with a volunteer gig. My conference fees were waived and I crashed in an extra bed reserved for a local cheesemaker who couldn't attend. I was so excited to be part of the professional cheese world that I pored over the conference schedule before I left, debating with coworkers which panels would be the best to attend and how best to bring the information back home after the conference.

I knew before I left that I had a lot to learn. But if I'd known just how much, I might have been scared off completely.

Volunteering at the conference, however, helped me to realize that some of the impressive-sounding people were full of crap. Faking it for retail customers was one thing, but faking it in front of a room full of cheese professionals takes nerve. Obviously, I was pretty low on the cheese food chain, so I decided to bide my time and figure out who was who. Much like the punk scene and the political activist world, there were poseurs on one side, and then there were people to listen to and learn from.

The moment in which I learned the most took place in the walk-in cooler where I was doing my volunteer work. Most of my day was spent organizing cheese for the cheese competition. I was teamed with another cheese punk, the only other person I know with a cheese tattoo. Fate brought us together. Or at least the promise of cheaper out-of-pocket expenses.

He'd been a cheese buyer longer than I had and referred to himself as a cheesemonger. "Tommy, how do you define *cheesemonger*?" I asked.

During the course of the day we hashed out the definition and connotations. Obviously, *cheesemonger* was a title that meant "one who buys and sells cheese." We both liked the history associated with the word *monger*. Fishmonger, warmonger, whoremonger, et cetera: Clearly it was a serious title, and one to be earned.

Cheese lovers sometimes get confused and call themselves cheese-mongers. I try to be understanding. After all, who wants to be called a "turophile"? It sounds like you have a fetish for molesting out-of-town visitors.

Unfortunately, sometimes I've heard cheese workers use the title *cheesemonger* after they've been at the job for about five minutes. In doing so, they ignite in me a visceral distrust. Policing this definition cuts both ways, and I'm sure some folks would question how appropriate it was that I applied the term to myself. And while my new cheesepunk friend and I talked about the definition and what years of experience, gross sales, and ratio of factory to artisan cheese should be required, he had a few additional rules.

"You can't call yourself a cheesemonger unless you've killed a rat in the walk-in cooler, kicked a sales rep out of your store, and bled from a cheese wound," Tommy declared.

We argued about the rat qualification both on humane grounds and based on the fact that his urban store might have been in the food business for a hundred years, but mine had just been a St. Vincent De Paul thrift store and Mack Truck showroom before recently becoming a grocery store. I'd had no opportunity for that kind of vermin killing. That I had killed many defenseless animals in my hunting-oriented youth convinced Tommy to give me a pass on that qualification. My dad was right: Those freezing predawn mornings spent up to my waist in ice-cold water putting out duck decoys really did pay off.

I never saw Tommy again, but his words have guided me ever since.

It wasn't all smooth sailing from there. Everyone who talks to the public on a consistent basis is bound to occasionally make a mistake. Take, for instance, the particularly bad incident in which I confused the names of Epoisses and Vacherin Mont d'Or (two of the best cheeses made anywhere, but not very similar), the brash comments I made about raw milk cheese that ended with someone's personal story of a miscarried baby, or just the many regrettable misphrasings ("Oh, you like those big mozzarella balls, don't you?"). Not to mention the information that distributors taught me early in my cheese life that turned out to be just plain wrong and took me a while to unlearn. "Facts" like: To make blue cheese, mold is injected into the cheese during the aging process.

This cheesemonger learning process took time, as did finding a customer base for the new (to us) cheese we were interested in carrying. But a year or two after we started building our specialty cheese selection, other people began taking notice. We had never been a place people went to for cheese. Our cheese sales, until we began sampling, were more of an afterthought and convenience than inspired dairy desire. Then, in a discussion on cheese retailers in the city, I saw a post on a local food Web site that made me realize we were making a name for ourselves. Someone had raved about our cheese department, calling it the best in the city. Another reader responded with the following comment: "The kids who often work the cheese counter at Rainbow do not know the first thing about the rare cheeses carried there. Perhaps it's because I do my grocery shopping on the weekend and the 'real' buyers have the weekends off." At the time this was posted I was certainly working the weekends, but I also looked more punk rock and had fewer gray hairs. Mostly because they were all dyed pink.

Customers, when looking at me, were always searching for the "real buyer," until I hit thirty-five or so. It's not the worst problem to have, certainly. There are very few punk rock cheesemongers.

You learn to defend your territory while handling food—and not just from truckers and customers. Soon after that first ACS conference, I fulfilled Tommy's Cheesemonger Qualification Number Two. A local distributor, now out of business, had its importer visiting San Francisco from New York. My local sales rep brought him to our store, and before he even introduced himself he started telling me our cheese was terrible. He started throwing things around the case. He picked up an Epoisses: "Garbage!" Valencay and Sainte-Maure: "Awful!" Vacherin Mont d'Or: "Crap!"

That's when I stopped him. One can reasonably have a preference for one Vacherin Mont d'Or over another, but none is "crap." It's just the best cheese in the whole world. Oozy, rich, woodsy, beefy, milky sweet, a touch pungent, wrapped in spruce bark. Amazing. I took the cheese out of his hand before he could pitch it to the other side of the cooler and lovingly placed it back in its spot.

My local rep looked sheepish. Local reps are often assigned to chauffeur higher-ups, importers, and/or visiting cheesemakers during food show times. Sometimes they visit to sell product. Sometimes to put a human face on something mysterious. Sometimes it's just one of the ways that those folks justify the expense of their trips. Often these visits are extremely valuable and can lead to a better understanding of the history of a particular cheese. Even if I have little interest in the product, I generally indulge out-of-towner visits as a favor to my sales reps, so they don't get in trouble with their bosses. Visitors are relatively painless and usually polite, except for the time lost forever in the avalanche of self-aggrandizement and buzzwords. Usually, however, they are polite.

This visiting importer went on about how the Vacherin he imported was better and how I should get serious and start buying from him. I was getting serious. The cheese conference had crystallized my desire to carry the best cheese I could find. But it also crystallized my belief in not dealing with jerks.

The importer was from New York, so I defaulted to California slang: "Dude, shut up and get the fuck out of our store." My use of expletives didn't faze him; he continued talking about how everyone else carries shit and his company imports the only decent French cheese available in the United States. The local rep tried to push him toward the door, and, as they disappeared down an aisle, I told her, "Don't bring him back."

Later that evening, the rep called to apologize. Of course she tried to claim New York–San Francisco cultural differences as the cause of the problem, not the fact that the importer was obviously a bully and a jerk. Then again, since he was higher up in the company, she had to limit what she said. Some people definitely practice a sale-by-cutting-you-down technique. You can't let them get away with it. You need to defend your turf if you are going to be a cheesemonger.

Without realizing it, I had amassed cheesemonger qualifications. I had experienced my transcendent cheese moment. I had learned more than I thought possible about the process of cheesemaking. I had tasted hundreds of cheeses and had replaced most of the imposters I had inherited with the higher-quality originals. I had completed one of Tommy's qualifications by kicking a rep out of our store. And then, I'm honored to say, the most classic cheese of all gave me my first serious, bloody, work-related wound.

I don't want to assume that people comprehend the mass of a wheel of Parmigiano Reggiano. Each weighs eighty-five pounds, but a dense eighty-five pounds. In the warehouse-sized aging rooms of Italy, Parmigiano Reggiano is rotated by machine. Folks who handle this cheese, and who are not used to moving the wheels, will almost always say, "Fuck, that was heavier than I thought!" If the cheese has been out of a cooler, which they often are since they are easier to cut if they're set out a day or two beforehand, the wheels start exuding a thin film of greasy moisture that makes them slippery, like an incredibly sharp, fruity, nutty, greased cheese pig.

Parmigiano Reggianos are workers' compensation claims waiting to happen. Even though I would usually ask for help lifting the large wheels, the cheese isn't big enough to give two people a good grip. I'd rather know where all eighty-five pounds are headed than think I have forty pounds and suddenly have it all. Luckily, I have a belly big enough to fit the cheese perfectly in the crooks of my arms while balancing it against my tummy. I can then waddle it the eight feet to the cutting area. I have noticed in cheese books that Italian cheese-mongers often have large bellies like mine. I am proud to uphold this tradition.

We have two large cheese displays clogging up the small aisle in front of our coolers. One is for whatever we are sampling to our customers. Usually it has some full wheels of cheese, our plastic, health-department-approved mini sneeze guard, a plate of sample-sized cheese bites, a toothpick holder, and a ton of cut and wrapped cheese for easy purchase. The other display is an upside-down barrel that once housed a mammoth Cheddar. That Cheddar looked impressive but cutting it almost killed us, and, beyond the aesthetics of being huge, it was overpriced. The barrel serves us much better as the permanent home of the Parmigiano Reggiano display. No samples here, just a pile of two or three full wheels and, again, lots of cut and wrapped cheese.

I was rotating the Reggianos one day, when we were first becoming a specialty cheese section and we thought it would look classy to have fake hay all around. Very rustic. You know, the way you used to find Parmigiano Reggianos piled around haphazardly in Grandpappy's barn. Anyway, we had enough space to pile the Reggianos two-high and it looked impressive. Everyone loves a big cheese.

I took the top wheel off and carried it to the cutting area. I removed all the cut pieces and piled them in a milk crate. I then placed the bottom Reggiano on a rolling cart so that I could position a new one on the bottom. *Rotation of stock* is the grocery worker's mantra.

I left the hay where it was, since it created the backdrop for our ode to the myth of artisanal pastoral production. When I took the new cheese off the cart, I found it refreshingly cool and not slippery since it had just come out of refrigeration. I struggled with the eighty-five-pound cheese monster, rolling it from the cart to the barrel. Once I had the back side placed correctly, I slipped my fingers out as I let the cheese drop onto the hay-covered barrel, something I had done many times before.

Unfortunately, this time one of our customers had left a sample toothpick in the hay. I doubt the toothpick was intentionally placed to inflict maximum injury, but intentions were the last thing on my mind when the sharp tip entered my finger. As I tried to pull the injured finger away, the Parmesan wheel landed on top of it.

Since the first day I used a razor blade to cut the heavy plastic off my first commodity Cheddar, I've had nicks and cuts on my hands. When you work with knives, you quickly learn that you don't feel a cut the moment it happens. Maybe a hot sensation, then moisture from the blood, and then an ache. This sensation, however, I felt right away. My brain went into survival mode and, like the urban legend describing people who lift Buicks with superhuman strength to save their trapped children, I lifted the Reggiano back up instantly, using just my other hand in the crevice created by my trapped fingers.

I don't remember how I conveyed my situation to my coworker—probably with a loud scream. Regardless, I made it to the worker bathroom very quickly, dripping blood along the way. It wasn't until I was inside, holding my hand over the sink, that I actually looked at my fingertip. The toothpick, which had once resided in some customer's mouth, was sticking all the way through my middle finger. The toothpick had also broken in the middle so that both ends were pointed down, like a blood-smeared smile on an unhappy face.

My coworker, who had followed my dripping trail, cleaning it up, arrived at the bathroom with an adhesive bandage and hydrogen peroxide. I asked her to get my box knife from my back pocket and open it up. I don't carry a thin cheap box cutter, but the sort you have to unscrew with a coin. The cutter holds the blade in use on one side, and also has a little compartment for extra blades, which I had just refilled. I knew those blades were fresh and sharp.

I know that I should have found a needle and sterilized it, but I wanted that toothpick out of my finger right away. Blood pulsed from both sides of the wound and from underneath both ends of the toothpick. It dripped into the basin of the just-cleaned, white porcelain sink, forming deep red, bubbly ovals that oozed toward the drain. Plop, plop . . . plop, plop . . . plop, plop . . . I felt like a character in a war movie or a western. I looked at my coworker. "Cut it," I said.

She had grown up in a rural area and was a mom so she wasn't squeamish. She took charge, slicing my finger directly above the broken toothpick. My wounded finger went white, then darkened, the blood pouring out as the toothpick came free. The blood buried my finger so that I couldn't see it until I applied direct pressure to ease the flow. I thought I might pass out from the pure ugliness of the wound and because I'm a wimp at heart. The relief I experienced when the toothpick popped out was one of the greatest feelings I had ever felt. When the bleeding slowed, I drenched my finger in hydrogen peroxide. It burned and I didn't care.

I looked down at the sink and steadied myself. The blood was diffused by water and fizzy with peroxide. The basin swirled dark red and pink and bubbly white and a broken toothpick was caught in the sink stopper. The cheese was testing me. I taped my finger, put on a vinyl glove, and returned to the counter.

Finally, I claimed my hard-won title: cheesemonger.

Vacherin Mont d'Or: **One of the most complex cheeses in the world. Another Alpine cheese, made on both sides of the French–Swiss border. When ripe, this cheese is so ready to ooze that the bark on the outside holds it together like the walls of a dam after weeks of rain. Beefy, earthy, pungent, creamy, rich, milky, grassy, and almost fermented fruity. A seasonal cheese: People get on waiting lists for this cheese, which is available, roughly, from late October until March. Some places may sell you a cut of one of these wheels, but** treat yourself to the whole thing: Cut off the top rind and dig into the treasure below. You won't be sorry. [$$$$, Similar cheese: Besides Chaux Doux (Switzerland), honestly not much is similar. Pasteurized versions like L'Edel de Cleron (France) look similar but have a lot less character.]

Parmigiano Reggiano: The name-controlled, real Parmesan that everyone wants to copy. Made in eighty-five-pound wheels and aged for glory, this cheese can only be made in the zona tipica areas of Italy's Emilia Romagna region. Sharp, nutty, fruity, salty, a touch sweet, and just all-around big flavor. It amazes me how much we sell of this cheese and how many people I meet who have never tried it. There's a reason so many inferior cheeses try to ride the coattails of this great cheese by stealing its name. If there were seven Cheese Wonders of the World, this would be on the top of the list. If you were trapped on a desert island with only one cheese—this would be a top choice. If you had to explain to a Martian why humans steal the milk of other mammals, add stripped stomach linings of cute baby calves, form it into shapes, allow it to biologically alter over time, build robots to flip it, ship it halfway across the planet, and pay good money for it, this would be a perfect place to start. [$$, Similar cheese: Grana Padano (Italy), Trentino (Italy), but definitely not the "Parmesan" produced in the United States or Argentina.]

---

three

Grass, Farmland, and Where
My Cheese Love Story Begins

I was called to jury duty last year. When we walked into the courtroom for selection, each potential juror had to inform the court of his or her name, neighborhood, and occupation. When my turn came (and, like a punch line, I was last), I said, "My name is Gordon Edgar, I live in Duboce Triangle, and I work at Rainbow Grocery Cooperative as a cheesemonger."

Everyone laughed. The lawyers laughed. The potential jurors laughed. Even the judge and the court reporter snickered. Only the eighty-five-year-old plaintiff, who had been run over by the defendant, didn't crack a smile—but she had an excuse since she only spoke Cantonese. Her lawyer recovered, and then asked me, in open court, for any cheese tips I might have.

Like everyone else ever in the history of jury duty, I was frustrated by the glacially slow jury selection process. We were in our second day, and since the plaintiff's attorney was getting paid quite well, I didn't feel like sharing my professional knowledge for free. "Don't get me started," I replied curtly.

After we were chosen, the remaining jurors asked if I could bring cheese to the deliberations. I brought chunked pieces of four-year-aged Gouda, Bravo Silver Mountain Cheddar, and Italian Piave in clear, compostable, sixteen-ounce bulk containers for the lunch breaks. I brought doughnuts to our two-hour deliberation because it started at eight thirty in the morning.

I often get asked my opinion on the relationship Americans have with cheese, usually by a customer who has a pet theory about how society works. Often these theories are pessimistic: Processed American Cheese symbolizes soulless suburban white-bread culture; commodity block Cheddars are emblems of Americans' disconnect from their cultural roots; the relatively small number of choices we have (outside of a few urban centers) when buying cheese reveals how much control factory farming has over the food supply. Jury duty provided a good amount of time to think about this question: How do Americans relate to cheese?

When conversing with me over the counter, customers often declare that Americans, excluding themselves of course, don't appreciate cheese. Yet every American, on average, consumes over thirty pounds of cheese a year. That's less than half what the people of Greece, the world leader, consume, according to the International Dairy Association. Still, it's good enough for seventh place in the world.[2] In 2005 the United States produced over nine billion pounds of cheese. Clearly Americans love cheese.[3]

An oft-spoken critique is that Americans don't appreciate "good" cheese. If we assume that "good cheese" means cheese in the $10-a-pound and up range, we have to remember that, in the more fancy-cheese-friendly nations, cheese is much cheaper. In Berlin I once visited a department store with a huge cheese selection. There was no American-made cheese there, but the same European cheeses we carry in San Francisco were about a third of the price. And this was a very high-end place. Ten thousand fewer travel miles, and a smaller number of people with their hands in the pie, make a difference in pricing, to be sure.

Holding a huge bag of cheese and trying to find an exit, I stumbled across the US food section. Imported Pop-Tarts were about $10 a box. Small plastic jars of Skippy peanut butter were even more. When

American foodies mock other Americans for not appreciating fine cheese, they should remember that the US equivalent to French Brie is a forty-pound block of commodity Cheddar.

Of course it's ridiculous to generalize about "Americans." But I find there's a default reaction—amusement—among most people when I tell them what I do, a fact confirmed by my experience in one of the most diverse civic gathering places of all: the jury room. The reason for their bemusement is simple: Most Americans think cheese is funny.

Don't get me wrong. I love the cheese. I'd like to think it loves me back. But there is a certain absurdity associated with my job that I've become immune to noticing, and it's helpful to get an outside view every once in a while. Cheese is funny to almost everyone except dairy farmers and cheesemakers. I have a great job: full benefits, worker-run store, decent pay for eating cheese all day long. I'm not complaining in the least. But when I say that cheese is funny, I mean funny in the sense that when I tell strangers what I do, as in the jury room, they tend to laugh.

Fancy cheese might be funny to most Americans, even if the individual ingredients aren't amusing. Most cheese is made of milk, starter culture, rennet, and salt, and I'll go into great detail about all these ingredients. But where's the amusement here? Nothing funny about milk. In fact, before chemical companies began messing around with the recombinant bovine growth hormone (rBGH), milk was looked upon as a symbol of purity. Starter culture determines certain chemical reactions in the cheesemaking process and the overall finished flavor, but starter culture is often used in breadmaking and no one laughs at bakers. Rennet, traditionally an enzyme from the lining of a calf's stomach, used to coagulate milk, is not in any way funny. Gross yes, funny no. Salt? I can't think of a less amusing basic ingredient.

As a whole, only fancy cheeses get mocked. Nobody, except elitist foodies, really laughs at processed cheese. Forty-pound blocks of commodity Jack, Cheddar, and mozzarella demand a grudging respect because they are honest and relatively cheap. They go on pizzas and nachos. They are useful.

But moldy, stinky, fragile little cheeses? People love to come to our store and laugh at them. I had to make a special sign for the Le Farto brand of French Reblochon because I got tired of hearing the same attempts at humor every day. The sign starts off by saying, OK, FIRST OFF, WE DON'T WANNA HEAR YOUR "CUTTING THE CHEESE" JOKES. People, people! I assure you. I beg you. Your cheesemonger has heard that fart joke you are contemplating. Just move on.

The need customers have to make fun of the Le Farto puts a visible strain on their faces. I get to observe people physically trying to hold their comments to themselves, nudging their friends, pointing at the sign. The sign also gives us cheese workers free rein, if someone actually does attempt a fart joke, to just stare back at them and say, "Excuse me sir"—and 90 percent of the time it is a sir—"did you read the sign?" Shaming customers is not something one is supposed to do in retail work, which makes the technique all the more effective.

Of course, the occasional actually-French-from-France customers often say, "I do not und-air-stand. What iz zee meaning of zis sign?" And I have to explain what *fart* means. This can be quite embarrassing, depending on how much English they speak. Pantomiming a fart and a bad smell to a customer would probably get me fired at another job, but when the non-cheese-workers at our store see stuff like that they just shrug.

There are things to laugh at, of course. Whenever people invest their self-esteem in whose-provolone-is-bigger battles citing specific arcana, outsiders will mock. It doesn't matter if we're talking about record collectors, D&D wizards, or cheese fetishists. I guess the question is, why do I sometimes think of myself as an outsider?

I have spent more than forty hours a week for well over a decade hanging out with cheese folks. I have argued with cheese folks, drunk with cheese folks, attended their weddings and funerals, been on panels with them, even slept with some of them. I have a cheese tattoo for Christ's sake. Who am I trying to kid?

The cheesemonger life still strikes me as rather absurd, and I try to keep an emotional distance, because while I once debated whether or not the Paris General Strike of 1968 was a truly revolutionary moment, now I discuss the goats of Périgord and know, against my will, that Mimolette—a French cow's milk cheese, often aged until riddled with cheese mites and acquiring a caramel-sweet, sharp flavor—was de Gaulle's favorite cheese. If I knew what student leader Daniel Cohn-Bendit's favorite cheese was, perhaps I could claim I was working on a clear continuum. I did, briefly, sell Slow Food pioneer and McDonald's dismantler José Bové's cheese before he went to jail. I'm just not sure that's enough.

I try to maintain this continuum. Since French cheese is ubiquitous, it seems appropriate to look to their revolutionary movements for inspiration. The Situationists, a loose political group who created much of the revolutionary art in Paris 1968 through the reuse and captioning of everyday images, might appreciate my reuse, unaltered except for lamination, of a graphic I cut out of a trade magazine. I like to leave it on our table of cheese samples. It's a picture of a goateed hipster from the mid-1990s who might be putting on his flannel shirt and going to see Nirvana after work. He wears latex gloves and is caught in the act of happily doling out food. The caption reads GEN XERS LOVE SAMPLES. I think it's hilarious to remind people that they are being marketed to, but it is doubtful that the Situationists would appreciate that the image is used to sell cheese.

Like an aged cheese, the path of my life was determined by many factors. It would be a mistake to discuss any life as simply the product of one experience or action. Certainly one event, say childhood trauma in humans or massive change in humidity in cheese, can have a long-lasting effect. My love for cheese, however, went through a natural maturation process.

When cheese lovers talk about cheese, they often start with milk. The cheesemaking process begins with what their mammal of choice is eating. Are the cows grazing up the French Alps with the seasons like those that make the Beaufort Alpage possible? Are they eating fresh clover and grasses that are only available in a certain part of the world? Are they eating fermented grasses (silage) instead of fresh forage? Have they gotten into a patch of wild garlic or onions that will ruin the flavor of the milk completely?

Cheese is a product of its milk, and the milk is a product of the feed. I don't want to overemphasize this point because there are many steps between feed and the finished cheese where the process can get messed up. But when you taste one of the great cheeses, you know that this first part is crucial to the finished product.

I wish I could create a linear narrative, one that describes a key interest or hobby in my youth that led directly to my adult occupation. Unfortunately, there was no particular love of the cows we'd drive past on Highway 101 near Novato, no sneaking out of bed at night and drinking all the milk in the fridge, no ongoing mold fixations or udder obsessions. Cheese was functional. It came in a green can for spaghetti, pre-sliced for sandwiches, or sometimes in a bug-yellow Velveeta box for melting or cooking. I didn't think much about it, to be honest.

On family trips to the beach we'd often stop at the Cheese Factory. I'd love to claim that this family tradition somehow influenced me, but the only memories I have of the Cheese Factory (aka Marin French Cheese Company, aka Rouge et Noir) are that it smelled, and that the geese in the pond outside were really mean, but still preferable to the smell of the actual Cheese Factory. If I had known I was going to end up a professional cheese worker, I would have paid more attention to this coincidence: the fact that I was growing up only miles away from the United States' oldest continually operating cheese plant.[4] Instead, I fixated on the fact that the mailing address of the "Marin" French Cheese Company located it in Sonoma County rather than Marin County. That childhood memory seems more suited to the memoir of a fact-checker, not a cheesemonger.

To suggest that there was a direct connection between my love of cheese and the experiences of my childhood would be too simple. However, I would say that the nature that surrounded me in my childhood influenced me, albeit not as intimately as it influences an

Alpine cheese. We made those visits to the Cheese Factory because it was a handy bathroom stop on the way to and from the beach. I didn't realize it at the time (I knew no other place), but the Northern California coastline is one of the most beautiful areas in the world. In the 1850s Portuguese dairy farmers began jumping ships and grazing cows as San Francisco grew into a real city. It's easy to see why: Many places offer the cows million-dollar views of the Pacific Ocean. You couldn't really take a trip to the beach without passing by a field dotted with cows.

I grew up in a suburban setting, not a rural one, but we were close to farmland. There was a lot less sprawl and a lot more farmland back then. The fact that the country's longest-running continually operating cheese plant is in California might seem odd, historically speaking, but the dairy business was the first economy to take off in Marin and Sonoma. When I drive in Marin and Sonoma now, I see the names of the dairy families everywhere in the towns, on the street signs, and in the other, nondairy businesses. I had always seen them; I just didn't know they were dairy names.

One of the things I love about living in San Francisco is its proximity to nature. I make a point of going to the beach at least once a week, even though I love the concrete and the concentration of people in my everyday life. Driving out of the city and into the brown hills gives me a sense of peace. And if it's one of the winter months when we've had some rain and the hills are actually green, my breath catches from the beauty and from the feeling of being home.

The cows love the green hills, too. Though almost no farm in this country counts on grazing as the sole source of nutrition for its cows (indeed, at last count only about 11 percent of US dairy cows grazed, according to the US Dairy Forage Research Center), the sight of cows eating their way through spring grasses excites me as a cheese eater. This is why people talk about seasonality and cheese. Grasses, herbs, and flowers bloom at varying times of the year in different parts of the world, and therefore the milk that animals produce can be unique both in taste and chemical composition depending on what they eat.

There are differences in the components of feed-based milk and pasture-based milk. Feed-based milk is higher in protein and fat because those are desirable properties in milk, especially milk for cheese, and the animals are fed accordingly. However, recent studies have shown that grazed cows have two to five times more conjugated linoleic acid (CLA) than other cows.[5] Some preliminary studies have shown that CLA may be an effective cancer inhibitor.

CLA is such an important area of study—to both human and animal health—that an international conference on the subject brought together more than twenty-five dairy scientists and veterinary professors who presented a wide array of papers on many aspects of CLA and its effects. Though more research is needed to determine exactly how the different forms of this natural trans fatty acid work, the scope of research is impressive and encouraging. The Dairy Council of the United Kingdom summarized the meeting with the statement, "CLA may have the capacity to influence a broad range of different aspects of health and food production."[6]

The more a ruminant—a mammal that digests its food twice in order to ensure thorough breakdown and digestion of the plants it eats—is grazed, the better the ratio of good to bad fats. Grass-fed milk is almost equal in omega 3 (good) and omega 6 (bad) fatty acids. The more commercial feed the ruminant consumes, the more the bad omega 6 fatty acids increase. Studies have shown that the ratio of good to bad fat changes dramatically and almost immediately when a cow is moved from a grass-based diet to one that is grain-based.[7]

Not only does the dairy they produce become healthier in terms of fat with increased grazing, but some research shows that the cows themselves are healthier on a pasture-based diet. Illness spreads less readily among cows that have room to move. Often, dairy farmers who decide to let their cows forage instead of using feed also have them producing fewer months out of the year, concentrating on the months when the grasses are at their best. In this way, not only do pasture-fed mammals have the potential to create unique cheeses, but pasture-based farming—unlike large-scale automated production—is based on quality, animal health, and on the variety of nature, not solely on maximum efficiency and production and standardized flavor.

Jessica Little of Sweet Grass Dairy in Georgia grew up in a dairy family. However, she and her husband decided to switch from more conventional dairy methods to forage-based ones, including rotational grazing. Little has been extremely happy with the results. She notes:

> Quality as defined by dairy farmers is low bacteria and low somatic cell counts [in the milk]. By that standard of quality, the biggest difference that I have noticed between the two [systems] is the happiness of the animals. It is a scientific proven fact that, the more stress that is put on the cow, the lower in quality the milk is going to be. Imagine several hundred cows in a barn living on concrete and eating grains. They cannot run, enjoy the sunshine or eat any green grasses like they were designed to do. Instead they lay on either rubber mats (like at my parents' conventional dairy) or on composted manure, sawdust, or straw and are kept cool by big fans and sometimes sprinklers. The lengthened life span of the cows alone was enough for me to say, "Wow, this is really how it is supposed to be."

Retail customers are no longer used to being told they can't have a product they want. Large-scale production and international "free trade" has added to the expectation that what once was seasonal can now be had on a whim if one can afford it. Yet if customers want to really taste the differences among various seasonal cheeses, they must first understand that they can't always get what they want.

Unfortunately, as of this writing, there is no clear definition of what a *forage-based* dairy is. Because of environmentalists and writers like

Michael Pollan, I encounter more and more customers who want to know on which dairies the mammals are "grazed." There is currently no legal standard for designating terms related to what dairy animals eat. If a cheese is marketed as being from milk produced by "pasture-fed" cows, there is no standardized definition of what percentage of their feed is forage. As demand increases, I imagine a lot of "pasture-fed" cheese will come on to the market, but it will be unclear as to whether the percentage of forage is 5 percent or 95 percent. As with the problematic nature of USDA organic dairy laws, which state only that dairy animals must have "access to pasture" (rather than a specified number of days of the year, for example), ill-defined catchphrases create nothing but skepticism and cynicism in the end. There's a reason that the dairy in-joke on "access to pasture" is, "Yeah, they walk 'em through the field on the way to the slaughterhouse."

Some cheese sellers get kind of squirmy when I try to pin them down on what they mean when they use the term *pasture-based* or *grass-fed*. I may buy the cheese, but I won't promote something as pasture-based unless the sellers are willing to talk about their cows' grazing patterns or the percentage of supplemental feed. Tim Pedrozo, a dairy farmer from Orland, California, gained my everlasting respect when he came into our store with his Pedrozo Dairy and Cheese Company Northern Gold. He put a big sample on the table and the first thing he said was, "My cows eat 90 percent forage and 10 percent other feed." I wish everyone made it that simple.

Of course, one of the reasons that most dairies are not pasture-based is that many dairy states are mud- and snow-bound for a good portion of the year. The irony is that more cows, percentage-wise, have access to real pasture in snowy, cold states like Wisconsin and Vermont than in certain large-scale, feedlot-possible areas of California (the "Happy Cows" commercials notwithstanding). This is just one of many tensions that bubble beneath the surface at cheese conferences.

What the dairy animals eat is so important to the taste of the finished cheese that, in an article about grass-based dairy farming, Alice Beetz of the National Sustainable Agriculture Information Service wrote, "Think of the milk as a means of marketing the forage."[8]

With factory-made cheese, effort is taken to counterbalance these seasonal differences in order to make as identical a finished product as possible every time. Indeed, the history of factory cheesemaking is not only about the Fordism of the dairy industry in terms of efficiency, but also about attempting to guarantee that consumers know exactly what the cheese tastes like, regardless of where they purchase it, whether it's in June or December. With handmade cheese, the seasonal variations come through in the final cheese, and they are the very thing that excites some customers and compels them to seek out artisanal (handmade) cheese. People love to discuss the variations between this wheel and the last one, the spring versus summer versions, the cheese they ate in its home country as compared with the imported version we get here. Vermont Shepherd, a small sheep dairy in Putney, Vermont, actually encloses a card in every box of cheese that states when the cheese was made, what the weather was like, where the sheep were hanging out, and anything else that seems pertinent or interesting. While there isn't always a huge effect on the milk at the micro level, it reminds cheese eaters that their food comes from actual farmers and actual animals, all with their own personalities. And it's fun.

Emphasis on seasonality, however, can be taken too far. Slightly subpar batches can sneak into the production process at any time of year. Fluctuations in the humidity level while aging, wheels overheating on loading docks, slow sales, distributors misrotating stock, retailers mishandling cheese and selling it anyway: All of these factors have effects on the cheese before the consumer buys it. Those concerns aside, I can talk, talk, talk on the variations among spring, summer, and fall Parmigiano Reggiano, to the point that I run the risk of boring people. But the fact is, they're all amazingly good, and 90 percent of our customers are just going to grate this cheese on their pasta and won't notice the difference anyway. While customers will likely notice the difference between grating Parmigiano Reggiano as opposed to a Pecorino Romano, an aged Asiago, a Dry Jack, or a crappy factory-made domestic Parmesan on their pasta, the distinctions among the richness of spring milk, the grassiness of summer, and the fruitiness of fall can easily be lost depending on how a cheese is used.

Rather than focusing on seasonality, I find concentrating on certain farms or regions, identifiers that are branded into every wheel, and making sure that the Parmigiano is not too old are the best ways to maintain quality. In fact, unless the Parmigiano was specifically intended to be aged longer, its wholesale price generally starts dropping when the wheels hit three years because of the loss of subtlety and the higher rind-to-paste ratio. Yet some distributors and stores use the fact that it is so old as a misleading selling point.

Cheese eaters need to decide for themselves which quality differences really matter to them; then they need to factor in the cost of those differences in making their purchases. Snob culture may demand a pedigree for every purchase, but every plate of pasta doesn't need a story behind it. If the rent is due, raw milk and/or artisanal credentials for your family's mac-and-cheese casserole may be optional. Some people are snobby for snobby's sake, but there are definitely times when, for my own kitchen, I buy a cheese I know is not as good as another for a specific purpose.

One of the world's greatest cheeses is Beaufort Alpage. Beaufort is a Gruyère-type cheese from the French Alps and, like the Parmigiano Reggiano, it also comes in monster-sized eighty-plus-pound wheels. This cheese, while sharing similar properties—raw cow's milk Alpine cheese, nutty taste, and great for cooking and melting—will blow away any I've ever had if it is designated as Alpage. The Beaufort Alpage is made only in summer when the cows, which are grazed up and down the mountains following the fresh growth of forage, are at their highest elevations and giving their richest milk. Beaufort Alpage has all the characteristics I named above, but they are intensified with a richness, an earthiness, and a sweetness that is bigger than the sum of these descriptions.

Beaufort is not the strongest Gruyère-type cheese. Rolf Beeler's Hoch Ybrig is more intense, Le Maréchal more herby, Antique Gruyère sharper, and good Comte just as sweet and nutty, but a Beaufort Alpage puts the characteristics of those cheeses together in one bite.

What I often do when Beaufort is available is plan some elaborate casserole or potato dish, something that calls for about two pounds of Gruyère. Then I buy two pounds of the Antique and half a pound of the Beaufort Alpage. You might imagine that I mix them together, but no. I use the Antique Gruyère for cooking and eat the Beaufort right off the block. I know the Beaufort is made for cooking, but for me it's just too good. Some people laugh when I describe a cheese with the phrase, "You can taste what the cow was eating," but this is one instance where the location of the cows on the hillside really determines the flavor of the cheese.

Another way to "taste what the cow ate" is to buy cheeses labeled *farmstead*. This means that the cheese is made on the same farm where the ruminants live and that the milk for that cheese is limited to that herd. In the dairy industry, milk is typically collected from many dairies and pooled. Thus, any particular flavor attributes one location might contribute (through the local vegetation and microclimate) will be diluted when mixed with milk that may be conventional-feed-based.

While *farmstead* means there is more control over the condition of the animals and the quality of the cheese, it is good to remember that it, too, is only part of the picture. A cheese can be farmstead, but the cows could live on packed dirt and never see a growing blade of grass. One of the best cheeses in the country is farmstead Cheddar, but it is created from the milk of ungrazed cows. Clearly, the farmstead dairy farmer's ability to control factors such as using feed that results in high protein levels in the milk can make for good cheese, but it's also a testament to that cheesemaker's considerable abilities that a truly exceptional cheese can be made with nontraditional methods of dairy farming and without the benefit of the flavor of the natural flora.

Most of the hills on which I spent my youth drinking are now topped by multimillion-dollar homes, but there are still many open spaces left in the Northern Bay Area. For such a large urban area, the Bay Area's local farms are remarkably accessible. Most of the food sold in grocery stores these days is not from anyone's local area, of course— no matter where you live—but from within 250 miles of where I grew up you can still find miles of farmland, hundreds of dairies, and some of the country's best cheeses. Sure, there's less agricultural land each year, but the amount that remains is impressive indeed.

Not that that kind of thing happens without a fight. Much of the land preserved as farmland in Marin and Sonoma is due to the work of people like the late organic dairy farmers Ellen and Bill Straus. Seeing the lure of developer cash and the internal logic of suburban sprawl as too powerful for agriculture families to overcome individually, they helped set in motion a land trust that has preserved more than thirty-five thousand acres of land for agricultural use. For this the American Farmland Trust, a nonprofit farmer organization set up to help preserve farmland, gave the Straus family a Steward of the Land award in 1998.

Indeed, one of the biggest problems dairy farmers everywhere in the United States face is urban sprawl. Land that was once unquestionably rural has now become suburban, as people are willing to commute farther and farther to work. It's ironic that at a time when farmer's markets in urban areas have achieved a new popularity and there is more lip service paid to buying local than ever before, the same urban areas that demand local products are forcing out their local producers by pushing them off the land.

According to the American Farmland Trust, the United States loses a million acres of farmland a year, and seventy-five percent of the produce and dairy is farmed and produced near urban areas, and therefore in constant danger of being sprawled out of existence.[9]

The problem is particularly tricky for both urban people who want to buy local products and farmers trying to make handmade cheese. As urban sprawl expands, consumers of local goods have less variety to choose from, and cheesemakers continue to lose both dairies to buy milk from and pastureland for grazing their own animals. I've talked to quite a few dairy farmers who are thinking of either moving away from their family's farming region or getting out of the business altogether.

While a pastoral landscape may actually be appealing to those escaping the city, the newcomers don't exactly welcome certain smells and noises that are part and parcel of dairy production. Much like what happened during the dot-com disaster in San Francisco, people invest their money in an area and then decide that they need to regulate or shut down the very activities for which those areas are known. In the old industrial and transient part of San Francisco, known as SOMA, people bought the newly developed condos in what had been established as, basically, a nightlife and public sex district, and were shocked—*shocked*—to find out that their new neighborhood was noisy. To be fair, those folks probably had invested their life savings into what was obviously, for them, a horrible mistake, but when they tried to take political action in getting bars and clubs closed down, they ended up forcing out a lot of the longtime residents and businesses.

In agricultural areas, manure smells and slow-moving tractors have become issues of litigation and road rage, respectively. However, in many instances, the county supervisors increase taxes to build infrastructure to attract the developers and newcomers, forcing the farmers to contribute to the enticements that will eventually force them off their land. It's a neat trick to make the agricultural community pay for its own eventual demise.

California's Central Valley, for example, is not only the World's Fruit Basket, but also the World's Meth Syringe. It's a so-not-funny-you-have-to-laugh problem that toxic materials from the local meth labs get dumped on Central Valley farms all the time. Whether stories of farmers getting charged (as much as $50,000!) for toxic cleanup by the county if they report such illegal dumping by others on their own properties is rural legend or the truth, such fears lead farmers to collect the dangerous drug refuse and, in turn, dump it on county property.

California, of course, is not the only state in which dairy farmers are losing their ability to farm. Even in Vermont, land use is a growing problem. I was shocked the first time I visited Vermont to find that the state's whole population was less than San Francisco's. It was head-turning for a Bay Area kid like me to see so much rural land, beautiful landscapes, and low population density—especially on the East Coast, which my West Coast brain always sees as built up and packed full. At one cheese conference I saw a dramatic slide show by Jon Wright of Taylor Farms detailing areas in his hometown that traditionally had been farmland but now were being used in other ways. Wright once had grazing rights all around his land, but slide after slide showed housing developments, soccer fields, and businesses. Not only does this make the area potentially less agriculture-friendly, it also leads to added costs when farmers have to buy more feed instead of grazing their animals. Down the line, then, such land-use tensions adversely affect the flavor as well as the cost of cheese.

In recent years the establishment of land trusts has proven one highly effective way to preserve farmland. Land trusts—often called agricultural easements—differ depending how a given state or county organizes its program, but basically they allow a farmer to sell off development rights that would change the nature of the property. The state, county, or a nonprofit trust pays farmers to not sell their farm off to a big-box store or housing developer, and legally binds the land to agricultural use in perpetuity. The Farmland Information Center, a clearinghouse for information about farmland protection and stewardship run by the USDA Natural Resources Conservation Service and American Farmland Trust, defines a conservation easement as a deed restriction landowners voluntarily place on their property to protect resources such as productive agricultural land, ground and surface water, wildlife habitat, historic sites, or scenic views. They are used by landowners ("grantors") to authorize a qualified conservation organization or public agency ("grantee") to monitor and enforce the restrictions set forth in the agreement.[10]

These types of agreements now cover more than 1.1 million acres of farmland throughout the country.[11] That's a lot when you consider what these farmers have done: Not only have they agreed *not* to sell to the highest bidder, but in most cases they've empowered a government agency to check up on what they're doing on their farms. It may be a cliché, but I have found it to be mostly true that rural folks don't generally jump at that type of oversight.

Agricultural easements have their limits, too. They cannot stand in the way of eminent domain (the taking of property by the government to create a freeway, for example), nor can they guarantee that the farmland saved will actually be farmed. Also, I have heard farmers in areas near cities with high costs of living complain that where housing is pricey and sprawl is fast, many developers are willing to pay more than the appraised value—something the trusts can't or won't match. Obviously, political action to save farmland remains necessary.

There is much debate over what constitutes effective political action for the maintenance of small, individually owned farms. Many folks, both farmers and urban consumers, offer up the solution of only buying from small-scale local producers. On an economic level, this makes some sense, and I support people doing it as much as possible. However, consumer action cannot be the end of food people's political effort. Any political tendency that bases itself on what purchases people make has inherent limits—it practically ensures that the people with more money to buy goods will be the people with more political power. The self-righteousness of people who can buy themselves out of political responsibility tends to be off-putting to everyone else.

At a national conference a few years ago, one cheesemaker gave an impassioned speech about political action. He pointed to the success that farmers had found in partnering with nonfarming allies to defeat an anti-farming measure. In a once agricultural and now largely suburban county, he found that they could form a coalition where the newcomers understood the importance of the rural economy. It was enthralling and inspiring. I congratulated him, thinking he was talking about the defeat of eminent domain on a local dairy farm that had been on the ballot. Oops, he was talking about defeating the proposed ban on genetically engineered crops. Heh. Some politics overlap, some don't.

A different farmer talked about the ridiculousness of the scientifically proven idea that cows give off more hazardous gas than cars, asking, "Shut in an airtight garage with a running car or being stuck in that garage with a cow . . . which would you choose?" It seems like a commonsense assertion, but the fact is that methane and nitrous oxide from cow belches, cow farts, and cow manure contribute to global warming at a much higher rate than carbon dioxide.[12] If you are wondering why, with so much scientific proof, there is still so much US opposition to the concept of global warming, it's good to remember that there are many interests other than the oil companies, including those of Big Meat and Big Dairy, which would surely be impacted by initiatives to reduce greenhouse gas emissions.

Attempts are now, finally, being made to develop technology to capture those cow-produced gases for energy use. There's even dairy industry talk of developing power plants with huge dairy farms to provide the raw material. It's good to remember that early experiments with this technology, like the early attempts at saving family farms through land trusts, were pioneered on small, pasture-based dairy farms like Straus Family Creamery in my old backyard.

Traveling through Marin these days, it's hard for me not to keep count of the hills that used to be empty and the tract houses that used to be fields. It seems unfathomable that Marin County was rural enough back in my teen years that, when Dead Kennedys played Novato the first time, rumor had it that the punks, both from the immediate area and from the city, were greeted by conservative farm kids with ax handles. I went south or east for my punk shows, not north, so I'm not sure if that story is true, but it was a realistic enough premise back in the early 1980s to be accepted wholeheartedly by those of us who cared about such things and those of us who also feared for our own health and safety.

Ironically, the "rednecks" were the bogeymen of my youth, and I now spend my time selling rural products. Not a rural person myself, my friends and I used the word *redneck* as a general insult for the violent and reactionary kids who would attack punks (and people they suspected of being gay, or any kind of "freak" or "weirdo" really). Those kids certainly existed, and other reactionaries sometimes claimed the word *redneck* as a title for their stupidity, but it wasn't until many years later that I realized that the word could also have a positive connotation. Rather than bigots getting drunk at a 7-Eleven and waiting for "fags" to show up so they could start a fight, *redneck* used to, and in some places still does, mean someone who works hard all day outdoors doing jobs that I certainly wouldn't want to do. Not with my soft cheese hands.

In an odd way, cheese has brought rednecks and punks together. Many wayward punks have ended up in the cheese business, even working as cheesemakers at established dairies. At the first cheese conference I went to, I was standing around sampling cheese with my coworkers. We were dressed extra punk, even the nonpunks, because that's how we liked to deal with fancy-schmancy events. This was fancy to us, being held at the Culinary Institute of America at Greystone in St. Helena. As we minded our own business, with our leather jackets and freshly dyed hair, all of a sudden someone slammed into us yelling, "Let's start a pit!" It was a cheesemaker from an established Sonoma County cheese company who used to run a Santa Rosa punk label. We are everywhere.

Black Butte Reserve, Pedrozo Dairy and Cheese Company: **Let's be honest, this is basically an aged Gouda. When cheese of this style sits around, it starts to become sweet, sharp, and salty, almost like cheese candy. It's one of my favorite styles of cheese. The Pedrozo Dairy and Cheese Company makes the Black Butte seasonally, and it represents some of the most traditional cheesemaking in the country: pasture-based, raw** milk, farmhouse cheese. When we get our allotment for the year, it's an event. [$$$, Similar cheese: Aged Goudas like Saenkanter and the Essex St. L'Amuse (Holland).]

Maple Smoked Gouda, Taylor Farms: Look, most smoked Gouda is crap. Those round, sausage-y logs you see all over the place? Those are the processed remains of Goudas that didn't work out for whatever reason: cooked, emulsified, processed, plasticized, and "smoked," sometimes with chemical flavor. They give smoked cheese a bad name. The Taylor Farms Smoked Gouda, though—even though it's made in Vermont, not Holland—it's the real deal. Maple-smoked on a century-old farm. The Wright family may have less room to graze their animals these days, but their cheese is still fabulous. [$$, Similar cheese: Naturally smoked, unprocessed Gouda (Holland, US) is the obvious choice, but really I'd think another maple-smoked cheese like the Grafton Maple Smoked Cheddar (US) might actually be a better choice.]

---

four

Herd Animals, Farmers, Foodies, and Co-op Workers

My coworker was visibly upset. "The goats are all crammed into such a tiny space. They're falling all over each other."

We were on a tour of Redwood Hill Farm, a local dairy in the rolling hills of Sonoma County. There are many things I love about cheese-mongering, but one of my favorites is meeting the farmers and cheese-makers. We're a very urban store, and getting out to the country for visits to dairies and organic farms is the first time some of my cowork-ers have ever seen agriculture up close. The forage, typically, is just starting to change from the dark green that always surprises me when I leave the city during the winter. I grew up with the golden-brown, California-summer beauty of dormant grass, so when I look over the land that's what I expect to see, not this soft, moist, welcoming stuff. It always makes me want to jump on the ground and roll around.

Making trips to dairies is something I try to do as often as possible. It's not that I think I'm going to stumble on any dangerous or illegal practices when I visit, even if I have expressed dismay at potential health hazards on occasion. No, a farm/dairy tour is mostly an oppor-tunity to see how things really work, observe the slight differences in cheesemaking style and equipment, pet some dairy mammals, and look for things that I don't understand so I can ask questions. Often

I have no idea what I don't know until I'm confronted with it. Also, once you've visited a farm or seen a cheese being made, explaining it to customers is much, much easier.

The only thing marring the beauty of this dairy was the vineyard on the next hill. Nothing is uglier, agriculture-wise, than a vineyard during most months of the year. The empty support stakes and lack of vegetation make them look like barren wartime graveyards. Still, while most goats crammed themselves together in the barn, others were grazing, bumping one another, jockeying for position. One in the distance was trying to knock down a tree with her head. Another was trying to eat some newspaper that had blown onto the property. A third was poking her head through the fence, looking for our attention. It was a beautiful sight.

My co-worker was not enjoying the show. "Why did you bring us here? This is so sad."

"Do you see how they're not fenced in?" I asked. "That they have acres of land?"

"Yeah . . ."

"They like each other's company. That's why they're called herd animals."

I didn't mean to mock. Well, that's a lie, I love to mock. But it is understandable that people who haven't had exposure to agriculture don't know what farms look like and how animals might behave. We were at one of the roomiest, nicest goat farms I've ever been to, but unfamiliarity and legitimate fear of factory-farming methods can color people's views.

I have my own issues. When visiting farms, I always feel better when the milkers are named and the dairy workers know their distinct personalities, because that surely isn't the case at large factory farms. There's a danger to romanticizing practices like naming animals. Certainly, life-and-death decisions will be made based on an animal's production, not an animal's personality quirks, but while farming can be a brutal business for both the farmers and the farmed, at most farmstead dairies I have visited, the love was obvious. Love for the animals, that is.

I wouldn't make too big a point of this, but many dairy farmers seem to have decided long ago that animals are better company than most people. These folks tend to interact more with their mammals than with humans since there may not be a hundred people in the closest town, but there will be fifty cows or a hundred goats on the farm.

Conversely, working in an urban, worker-run cooperative pretty much demands that you enjoy the company of other humans. We have 230 coworkers and between two and five thousand customers coming in each day. The lines at the register are, at busy times, just as packed as the barn with the herd-loving goats. Hopefully with less nuzzling and bumping.

I never had the rural fantasies that other political activists have. I don't like the idea of buying communal land, getting off the grid, creating an isolated, alternative world. When I was in my early twenties and politicos around me started having those conversations, I wanted nothing more than to continue living in the city surrounded by people.

I am such a social person that when I got hired, my job didn't even seem like work for the first six months. Working crappy jobs for not only hands-on but hands-clenched-tightly-enough-to-leave-bruises bosses left me drained and depressed. Cold-call temping drove me close to insane in a matter of hours. The bus job—cleaning up after other peoples' vacations—was hands-off but demoralizing. I knew I couldn't last there very long.

At Rainbow, not only were there, at that time, one hundred other worker-owners to get to know, but there were also customers who were part of my community—friends doing their shopping, and even anarcho-tourists and touring bands stopping by to replenish on natch food for their journey to the next urban center.

Beyond all the people to meet, I had to get used to the way the cooperative operated. I had collectivist skills already: the ability to facilitate meetings, an understanding of different voting procedures, and a skin thickened by group evaluations. I'd worked in a million political groups with collective structures. Rainbow operates collectively, which means that the ultimate power in the store resides in the hands of the workers. It's divided up into departments that autonomously oversee almost every aspect of their daily work. I was hired into the cheese department, which is in charge of deciding which cheese to sell; how to merchandise, price, cut, and wrap; when to schedule, hire, and evaluate coworkers; when to decide on individual raises; and how to deal with any necessary disciplinary action. The near autonomy of the departments keeps work on a meaningful level, sometimes creating a feeling of fourteen different collectives working together instead of just one large mass of people.

We think of it as *near autonomy* because departments can't do things that go against larger collective decisions. Our department could change the brand of cream cheese we carried, but not add, say, pâté, because the whole store had already voted not to carry meat. In fact, since many cheeses have animal rennet, we were already pariahs to some.

Many businesses these days try to portray themselves as "teams." Though the grocery business is traditionally unionized, many of the new chains that have started selling natural foods are not. Thus there's a gap between how these stores portray themselves as having a certain unity of cause and how they offer less money and fewer guarantees for the future than the businesses they are competing against. In a normal large business, the idea that workers and owners are on the same "team" is laughable, but one can hardly market food as a lifestyle and political issue and brag about being anti-union.

Rainbow started at a very different time in San Francisco. Before the downtown area was built up, before the rents went crazy, before the industrial base was completely turned into clubs and then condos, and before the working class was mostly forced out, San Francisco was a much easier place to live. Food, as it always is, was a big political issue in the Bay Area. The Black Panthers created breakfast programs and the Diggers were giving away free food in the parks. Many people sought to change the way that food was grown, distributed, and sold.

In an era well before government-legislated "organics" and a natural foods "industry," people, most of them countercultural types or leftists, wanted more natural, less packaged, cheaper food than was available at the local stores. San Franciscans, unlike residents of any other US city except Minneapolis, organized themselves in this food movement that shifted from a consumer cooperative (owned by the customer) model to a worker cooperative (owned by the workers) one. In the mid-1970s many San Franciscans were involved in creating the People's Food System, which attempted to create an alternative production, distribution, and retail network, one that prioritized people over profits.

The People's Food System spread to nearly a dozen neighborhood stores throughout the city. It consisted of a warehouse/distribution center, a trucking collective, and some producer cooperatives. Its history has never been adequately written, but it grew to serve thousands of customers before collapsing in sectarian battles and an actual gunfight not long after its birth (and unfortunately before the chicken farm that was to be called Left Wing Poultry had a chance to get off the ground). Rainbow had opted out of the system before its death, which, according to some of the old-timers, was due to the increasing polarization and non-food-oriented political battles.

We are workers and owners of the store, traditionally skeptical of the top-down management structure and wary of outside experts. Though started by an earlier counterculture, Rainbow certainly exemplifies the do-it-yourself spirit of punk, since the original members, and many other folks who started this food movement, envisioned a project that would make their neighborhood a better place, and just went ahead and did it. Since I, along with much of the political punk scene, devoted a lot of energy to creating and maintaining alternative institutions including collectively run record stores, political info shops, and all-ages venues, it is no wonder that Rainbow attracted me. Rainbow is a concrete example that these projects can succeed, even in a sometimes hostile and expensive world. Since Rainbow had opted out of the Food System before its untimely demise, it survived the aftermath of its collapse, eventually growing into a $50-million-a-year business that shares almost every penny of profit with the people who work there based on how many hours they work in a given year.

As a worker-owned cooperative, the people who work in the store hold the power to make important decisions. Any change in hiring, firing, pay, or benefits, or any "significant change in business practices," must go to a vote by the entire membership. The membership is made up of those workers who have worked a thousand hours, completed a series of orientations, and bought their voting share. While different workers may have different amounts of money invested in the store, we operate on a one-worker, one-vote system for decision making.

No matter what the job, all new workers also start at the same rate of pay. Workers receive raises on a regular basis, so the longer one is employed, the more money one makes per hour. The level starting wage ensures the tangibility of the concept that we value, and need, all the work done for us to stay in business. While almost anyone walking into the store would assume we value organically grown food and environmental sustainability, the other cornerstone of our unity is operating our workplace as a democracy.

As I mentioned earlier, I was hired into the cheese department not knowing much about cheese but very interested in learning how to create and work in alternative institutions. Although it wasn't easy to get hired, Rainbow seemed like a great place to see a large collective in action, to test the possibilities of radical change.

Some types of people, like the goat butting her head on the tree, jump right into places like the co-op, trying to move things that may or may not have deep roots. As for me, whether it's lack of ambition or a different philosophy, I tend to check things out first. After I got hired, I kept my head down a little. I made sure I did my work well, learning the difference between the basic Cheddars and Bries we carried and how to cut and wrap them, but I also kept an eye out for hidden power. I wanted to see if this dream was sour before committing too much to it. I wanted to see, despite proclamations to the contrary, if someone was really the boss in disguise.

Despite that plan, a few months after I was hired I ran afoul of some in the larger collective. Even as a customer I had noticed that the labels on the cheese were horrible. Some not-very-well-done-in-the-first-place-but-now-incredibly-dated splashes of color struggled to represent a rainbow and failed. I asked a produce worker who was then doing a comic in the *SF Weekly* called "Electric Maggotbox" to try a new design. His odd is-it-a-cow-or-is-it-a-rat creature looked great, and our department voted to change the labels. It wasn't until after they arrived that some workers in other departments told us that we had killed the store logo.

Oops.

Now, that logo needed killing for sure. And since it wasn't used for anything except cheese, we had no idea anyone would care. We had no real marketing strategy for the store at this time, no personalized shopping bags, no T-shirts, not even a real sign out front. Certainly, I never thought of the sad little arcs of color as the store logo and neither did the other department members, even the one who'd been there since the 1970s.

Luckily, any vote that recorded the faded color splash as the official logo had been lost in the piles of handwritten co-op policy books, and it was so undeniably ugly that it failed to spark action among most of my coworkers. But this accidental logo-killing introduced me to one of the cornerstones of co-op life: discussion.

In my previous collective experience, I had checked in, processed, and gone over group decisions with other folks, but those were in smaller, more homogeneous groups, where we knew one another pretty well. They were also more conducive to my default style of youthful punk rock bluster and exaggeration. Clearly, I needed to learn some more skills.

Since this was my first collective job, being told it was a priority to discuss things felt almost like paid therapy. If something happens that upsets you, not only is it okay, but it's actually encouraged to go and talk about it on the clock. While in almost all cases our decisions are majority rule, people try not to be all "Ha! Fifty-one percent in your face!" about it. Since we don't have bosses and highly paid CEOs, our "administration" costs are our meetings and conversations. In my previous jobs, trying to talk about such things was met with ridicule or contempt. I had been shut up more than once with the phrase, "What is this, a coffee klatch? Get back to work."

Discussion is great as long as it doesn't become never-ending, of course. It's good to work things out and to say things rather than resent them until they become that dense pit of anger deep in the stomach that ceases to have a rational cause. That was pretty much the way it was at all my previous workplaces. Everyone at Rainbow seems to have different issues that they need paid discussions to address, but as long as one acknowledges that we all have our pet peeves, those conversations become exercises in coexistence and cooperation. You know, good stuff.

Contrary to what I would have thought, while we may fight over bigger business decisions like moving the store or spending millions on a construction project, we talk about those so much in structured and unstructured gatherings that by the time they are decided there is a general agreement and people are talked out. In general, the store is a model of nonfactionalization; people will agree on one issue, disagree on another, and unlike volunteer, not-for-profit collectives, people don't quit when something doesn't go their way. It's too good of a job.

Surprisingly, people can go completely batshit crazy over the little decisions. I once had to help break up a fistfight between two workers who were rallying people to their vision of what color to paint the outside of the store. Color and art were so controversial that there was a little sarcastic song some of us were singing when we moved into our current location in 1996. To the tune of "Frère Jacques": "Terra-cotta! Terra-cotta! Paint it green! Paint it green! What about the mural? What about the mural? It's obscene! It's obscene!"

But I'm getting ahead of myself here.

The discussion I had with the upset coworker about the logo was about important issues: the decision-making process, how we represent ourselves to the customers, the way different images can appear to different people, et cetera. I came away from the conversation with an awareness of potentially delicate situations that I didn't really have to worry about in my punk or political-action-oriented groups. Thank God the label was so hideous that almost no one wanted to bother getting riled up about it. I think my coworker came out of the conversation happy that I wasn't planning to come into the co-op and five minutes later try to change everything.

A lot of things did need changing in the cheese department, though. I came into my cheese job wanting to make sure I didn't fuck it up. At my last retail job I had been a photographic printer who at busy times would get called upon to sell cameras. Since it wasn't my official job, I never had time to study the differences among the various models, so I usually had to fake it. They were point-and-shoots, and I could usually work out how they operated as I was talking to a customer. But I hated the anxiety of having to stay one step ahead, of spewing a cloud of words big enough to provide cover while I figured out the selling points.

I promised myself that I wouldn't do that with cheese. Not only because I really wanted to work in this co-op and do a good job, but also because I didn't want to have such an anxious work life. Remember, I knew nothing about cheese when I got hired. I also wanted the basis of this job to be honesty. Can one work retail without telling lies? I wanted to find out.

I tasted every cheese I cut, from the Jack to the awful goat blue we carried at the time. I read all the cheese books the store had, even the one we had somehow acquired from a national cheese store chain that gave great advice like: "Instead of buying 200-pound wheels of Emmenthal, buy the precut blocks." Why? "They weigh 12 to 14 pounds. And can be easily handled by a woman clerk." Since that book had other advice that was actually good, I hid that page for a while to prevent its burning and to keep my credibility when I pushed other, reality-based suggestions from that source on, say, altering the cheese display.

In this way, I began taking my first stumbling steps toward becoming a cheesemonger. I learned from my coworkers. I took a lot of advice, good and bad, from sales reps. Mostly though, I had a lot of attitude when it came to selling cheese. My punk rock scene had taught me that I could learn whatever I set my mind to and shouldn't be intimidated by pretentious people who stood in my way and claimed to be true experts. In my own DIY way, I was teaching myself about cheese. This was years before I could imagine "cheesemonger" as being an identity, and years before Tommy outlined for me what people need to accomplish before they should be able to call themselves cheesemongers.

Over the years I've learned that the people who don't last at my workplace are those who don't get along well with other humans. At a multimillion-dollar-a-year business, with no top-down management and as little hierarchy as possible, where people are supposed to make plans and work out issues with their coworkers, a desire to interact with others is a pretty big requirement for the job. The workers here are like herd animals in that way.

We could choose to work in more private, less crowded settings. We could work where we didn't have to talk to the public. We could work where there's one boss to talk to. We could try to start a business and be that boss.

I don't want to imply that I believe in some kind of free-market fetish porn, where anyone can easily do exactly what he or she desires. Our job has good pay and great benefits, and some folks are undoubtedly attracted to that. But if you're a completely antisocial person, you're going to have a hard time dealing with the level of communication and intermingling necessary to deal with so many other people and their needs, desires, and opinions.

Do we, as co-op workers, have more in common with herd animals than the farmers who sell us food?

My coworker who became upset at the imagined mistreatment of the goats that herded themselves together underscores the fact that nonrural Americans are alienated from the food they eat and that consumers looking to avoid inhumane practices can over-anthropomorphize a situation. A couple of acquaintances, for example, had what they thought was a great business opportunity based on a trendy new retail food niche: running a humane chicken farm.

"Have you ever spent any time around chickens?" I asked them. I have no real farming experience myself, but even I know that chickens are often regarded as the smelliest, nastiest beasts in the barnyard.

"Yes," she replied. "I stayed with a friend up in Mount Shasta who had five or six."

Oh, no no no no no.

It's not that there's not a market for free-range, nonhormone eggs from chickens that retain their beaks. I have been shown repeatedly that a fair amount of people in the Bay Area will pay $7 a dozen when our store can get them from the two farms in the area that commercially produce them. It's just that there's a reason that only a couple of farms produce them: Land is expensive for your free-range chickens to wander around with enough space so that they don't peck one another to death.

Also, farming is extremely hard work. I think a lot of nonrural "entrepreneurs" envision an idealized farm with happy chickens, consensual egg-laying, and lots of time to enjoy pastoral nature. They probably won't plan ahead and realize that they need to hire someone to shovel out the pile of chicken shit in the barn. More likely, one day they will be, *suddenly,* confronted with a huge pile of chicken shit and have to figure out what to do.

Farther into the discussion of the realities of farming, this person said, "I only want to eat animal products from farms that let the male babies live."

"Oh yes," I replied, "I've visited that farm. It's the Impossible Dream Ranch over in Fantasyland County, right?"

Then I realized one of the big issues really at play here: whether it's rural/(sub)urban, blue state/red state, rich/poor, many of the people who want "humanely" raised food really believe that farmers are purposely being cruel and heartless rather than simply trying to survive and stay on the land. In nonrural areas with organic markets, there is the perception of a battle between noble small farmers ("family farms") and evil, over-mechanized agribusiness. That battle is real and this perception is mostly true, but it's the way of farming to focus on what supports you and not on what wastes resources. Anyone who believes that small farmers can afford to live in some sort of barnyard paradise where every life is celebrated equally must have never actually been to a working farm, at least not one close to an expensive urban area.

I saw another example of the culture divide between urban and rural when I visited a goat farm a few years ago run by hippie back-to-the-landers. They were attempting to go fully organic and to have a permaculture project going up on their land. They named all their goats, et cetera. The perfect feel-good-about-supporting-them farm. And hanging from the deck of their modest built-it-themselves house were goat hides drying in the breeze. They were going to sell or barter them for food from other farmers. They were going to eat or barter the meat. Why? Because that's what they had.

For most people this represents a harsh cultural difference. It's tricky to understand that one can truly love animals and still make necessary or pragmatic decisions about their lives.

When I started meeting farmers and cheesemakers, they turned out to be a mix of old-school dairy people and hippie back-to-the-landers, though sometimes they were both, as in the case of Steven Schack and Jennifer Bice of Redwood Hill Farm in Sebastopol, about an hour north of San Francisco.

Jennifer's a prizewinning goat breeder who grew up in a more isolated Sonoma County than exists today—with more goats than neighbors—taking the traditional agricultural route to a career in farming by being a teenage 4-H Club member. Steven was an urban countercultural guy who wanted to live a more fulfilling and meaningful life with nature. Together they saw a way to make a living on the land, raising and breeding award-winning goats and making goat cheese, milk, and yogurt.

Though Steven died from cancer in 1999, Jennifer and Steven symbolized the merging of new and old dairy styles. Creating a market for goat cheese and selling raw goat milk (though Redwood Hill doesn't do this any longer) were visionary endeavors at the time. Caring for goats and doing the hard work necessary to make it as farmers was something a lot of other folks couldn't do. Visiting their farm always made me return to my store and sell more of their cheese because their love for the goats, the cheese, and the land was so apparent.

I don't want to over-mythologize this, but there is something about having a connection with the people who make my food that makes me feel good in an urban, alienated world. This is one of the reasons for the popularity of farmer's markets, especially now that a lot of urban areas have fancy ones that aren't much cheaper than going to the grocery store. Because of the abundance of local dairies in the Bay Area, cheesemakers sample directly to customers and answer questions about how cheese is made and how they treat their animals. This practice has gone a long way toward making cheese the trendy food item it is today.

The counterculture movement of the 1960s and '70s created new kinds of eaters. They fall into two basic camps: the Food Is Functional people and the Food Is Pleasure people. Since our co-op is a full-service grocery store and not just a cheese shop, I deal with both kinds. In fact, historically, the biggest source of tension in the natural foods world has been the battles between those factions, at least since the debate over we-must-educate-the-masses-to-eat-healthily versus the-masses-want-Twinkies-so-we-will-sell-them-Twinkies-which-will-bring-them-into-our-revolutionary-organizations was won by the health food people in most co-ops.

In some ways the new battle lines are a modernization of that argument, with the Food Is Pleasure folks recognizing that many traditional foods are not only healthy, but also tasty. Food Is Functional folks see good-tasting food as suspect. While it's a more individual-ist political line than The-Masses-Want-Twinkies people, the Food Is Pleasure camp also see eating traditionally produced food, including new cheese made in nonmechanized ways, as a means to help save small farms and counterbalance agribusiness. And what a reward it is to eat a triple-cream Brie or a fresh goat cheese and think of it as a political act! That's a political line that anyone who can afford it will be happy to support.

Not that everyone who desires good cheese is rich. I see people budgeting for good cheese, eating cheese instead of going to the movies or bars. I see regular folks—bike messengers, Volvo mechan-ics, teachers, poets, administrative assistants—prioritizing cheese in their shopping budget because it makes them happy.

One friend of mine from Detroit, who is also in the fancy food busi-ness, once talked about how much she misses her hometown. She told me about how her friend, a part-time waitress, managed to buy a big house. She said, "I'd go back there in a minute . . . but there's nothing to eat there."

As cheese sellers and cheese lovers, my coworkers and I have been riding this foodie cheese wave, but none of us came from a legacy of fancy cheese eaters. While the process of cheesemaking is at once incredibly simple and frustratingly complex, the act of selling cheese requires just a few simple taste descriptions, some modifiers, an occa-sional intensifier, and the ability to remember cheeses well enough to compare them with one another. However, some in the dairy world, those not coming from either the old-school dairy or the countercul-ture dairy camps, would like cheese to become the new wine, and their faction is on the rise. You can recognize their influence when you hear anthropomorphic descriptions, words borrowed willy-nilly from other languages, and pretentious obsessions with only one ingredient of the cheesemaking process. All of this probably makes sense from a marketing standpoint. Unfortunately, as the language gets more exclusive and specialized, it also creates barriers among people from different backgrounds. Dairies need to be able to "tell their story" in the right words with increasingly rarefied terminology. Sometimes they accomplish this internally, but more often they facilitate the process by hooking up with the right distributor. They may also hire a marketing person to do it for them. I admit that I prefer heartfelt, if awkward, phrasing to generic trendy terms like *artisan* or *terroir*. I also think it's almost always a mistake to follow some marketers' ideas for rebranding company logos and repackaging for color. I hope they don't hate me for saying this, but a homely label like the old Bravo Farms' military-stenciled logo above a basic drawing of a cow endears a farm to me. Inside every box of their amazing Silver Mountain Cheddar there were care and handling instructions that ended with the sentence, "The cows say hi." I melted a little every time I read the message.

Sometimes I feel like the only cheesemonger who still wants to stay down-to-earth and keep cheese simple. I try to keep in mind that we are selling old fermented milk at a grocery store to people who work for a living, and I remind customers of the real work that creates the food we eat. The contrast between the snobbery of a lot of the new language of cheese and the people who are up to their elbows in udders or curds is mighty stark sometimes. It is easy to rely on the familiar concepts of the honorable family farm and of the magical cheesemakers without getting into what farm work is really like.

I'm sure this reliance on cliché and selling points has to do with the focus of retail work. Even though I can be judgmental about the cheese snobs, I don't think about the animals too much in my daily cheese life. Sure, it's always fun to have some pictures of cute goats up along with the foreign peasants and big blocks of cheese, but as a cheesemonger, I don't need to know a lot about herd maintenance. I know that, say, Jersey milk is higher in fat and protein than Holstein milk but that Holsteins give a bigger yield. I know that Guernseys are fucking huge scary monster cows, but they seem very sweet. I know that Nubians are considered the "Jerseys" of the goat world, and that goat eyes can hypnotize you and make you do crazy things like try and open up a dairy farm if you stare at them too long. And I love the concept of sheep, and the dairy products they are responsible for, though they tend to remain somewhat aloof. Truthfully, I have the luxury of only needing to know the final product.

Visiting farms, however, makes things more clear. Brushing cows with metal barbed combs that look like weapons, being gnawed by baby goats, watching the dairy farmers feed the newborn calves and calm the milkers before they attach the udder sucker—there is so much love in the air that it really does make me want to go back to the city and do my job better.

I'm not one of those people who thinks it's cute to put "love" on a product ingredient list. In fact, I think that if "love" is listed, people should comply with the federal labeling guidelines and list the possible allergen warnings along with nuts and milk. Still, there's something about healthy, well-cared-for, seemingly happy animals from small dairies where the farmers refer to the animals by name that makes me think the milk, and the cheese, will be better.

Hillis Peak, Pholia Farm: **Milk from Nigerian dwarf goats on a solar-powered and off-the-grid farm in Oregon. I tried Hillis Peak at a regional tasting and thought it was the best aged US goat cheese I had eaten in a long time. It has the fruity, sharp, full flavor of a Basque goat cheese. In this chapter I mocked urban fantasies of an idyllic dairy farm, but if there is one dairy in the country that is a cruelty-free utopia, it's Pholia Farm. They don't cull the males, but instead find pet homes for them and their retired milkers. Their Web site, with its goat obituaries, actually made me cry. I can't say that for any other cheese Web site. (Poor little Cloud . . . you never had a chance.) Pholia is a small, sustainable dairy and you're unlikely to find its cheese outside local stores, but if you do, I would grab it. Not just the Hillis Peak. [$$$$, Similar cheese: Aged Basque goat tommes like Val d'Aspe (France).]**

Ocooch Mountain, Hidden Springs Creamery: This is one of my favorite cheeses and very few people have heard of it. Ocooch Mountain is a washed-rind, raw milk sheep cheese from Wisconsin. Aged on wooden boards, as it would be in the Basque country, this cheese is nutty, smooth, and—if aged long enough—a tad pungent. Brenda Jensen of Hidden Springs uses mostly her own sheep's milk, but also that of the ewes that belong to her Amish neighbors. When I visited, the sheep were grazing in green, grassy hills and seemed as satisfied as sheep ever get. Not many US farmers raise sheep for dairy, despite the fact that their milk is rich and contains more solids than cow's or goat's milk. This occurs in part because sheep are notoriously hard to raise. One sheep farmer put it to me this way: "Sheep are born trying to find a way to die." Harsh. The Hidden Springs sheep—frolicking in the Wisconsin rolling hills—and the great cheese that Brenda manages to make with their milk help you to understand why some farmers still take chances. [$$$, Similar cheese: Ocooch Mountain has a very distinct flavor, but similarly made raw sheep's milk cheese like Abbaye de Belloc (France) and Ossau-Iraty (France) would be the closest.]

five

The Milk of Human Neurosis

As I waited on the dangerously sunken couch at the San Francisco Tenants Union, one of the counselors yelled out to me, "Have you had a lot of landlord problems? You look really familiar."

"Nope, I haven't been in here for years," I replied. The house I lived in was being sold, and, worried about eviction, my housemates and I wanted to be sure of our rights in the crazy-expensive city that is our home. But although I'd paid dues, I hadn't been inside the Tenants Union since an issue with a particularly nasty smell in a Mission Street apartment in 1991. We waited for our drop-in turn.

My housemate was quicker on the draw. "Do you eat cheese?" she yelled back at the counselor.

"That's it!" the Tenant Unionist said excitedly. "You're the cheese guy! I just hope I can help you like you've helped me in the past." Then she called out to the whole room, "Do you people eat cheese? He's the Rainbow cheese guy. This is like having a celebrity here." At that point someone else rolled her baby into the room in a stroller. "This is my beautiful baby," the mama said, "and I ate raw milk cheese during the entire pregnancy."

I get befuddled when people recognize me from my job. I guess I shouldn't. I see at least a couple thousand people every day I work. After nearly fifteen years I've seen kids become adults, seen people go through multiple shopping partners, watched people leave the city and come back, and mourned people who've left forever: sometimes because they departed this life, sometimes because they moved to Los Angeles.

In the last chapter I made rash generalizations about dairy farmers and co-op workers, but it's impossible to do the same for the customers at a store like ours, which has a hundred thousand products, an urban setting, and, as a cooperative, a mandate to serve not just the wealthy, but everyone in the community. Though I work in cheese, we have many committed customers who have never set foot in our section of the store. In fact, they'd prefer that we weren't there at all.

One of the best examples of this sentiment was a customer with the funniest shirt I've ever seen. The image was of a human down on all fours sucking on a cow teat. The slogan? GO VEGAN YOU COW-SUCKING PERVERT!

I don't want to spend a lot of time bashing vegans, and obviously I have no desire to spread their propaganda, but there's no denying where milk comes from and to whom it's supposed to go. Mamas feed their milk to their babies. Humans farm mammal mommies to feed themselves. A certain percentage of that milk is used to make amazing cheese. While I have issues with the mistreatment of dairy animals, I have no real problem with the concept of consuming milk from other mammals.

Appropriately enough, the people who are most concerned with cheese milk seem to be pregnant women. When I first started hawking cheese, this wasn't the case, but now according to some, it seems that eating raw milk cheese is yet another horribly selfish thing women can do when they are a vessel for new human life. Luckily, I have heard of no cases where Child Protective Services or local authorities have locked anyone up for endangering their fetus by eating a Parmigiano Reggiano, but you never know what the future will bring.

Many common cheeses are made with raw milk, and people eat them all the time without even realizing it. For the most part, it shouldn't be thought of as a frightening experience. Besides Parmigiano Reggiano, raw milk cheeses you can find in many regular grocery stores include Gruyère, Emmenthal, Raclette, Morbier, aged Cheddars, and many types of blue cheese, including Roquefort. Some of those must be made with raw milk, some vary by producer, but anyone who has done any experimenting with fancier cheese has likely eaten some raw milk bits without even knowing it.

What are the real dangers of raw milk cheese? Often pregnant women who come into the store have received conflicting information from their friends and family, and even from their health care providers, about raw milk cheese. One day, after being confused by what the FDA warning actually said, I decided to do some research. Given how many people come in talking about the warning, I assumed it would be easy to find. Naively, I assumed I could just go to the FDA Web site and at least know what the government was saying about raw milk cheese. Whatever my personal opinions, I owe it to my customers and coworkers to know where I stand legally before making any recommendations.

I'm a cheese professional. I know how to search for things online. I know people in the dairy business, and I know some prenatal-oriented health care workers. But it still took me days to find the real information.

First the basics: Raw milk is milk that has not been pasteurized. Pasteurization is the process of heating milk to a certain temperature for a certain time period prescribed by law (these range in temp/time from 145 degrees Fahrenheit for 30 minutes to 212 degrees F for 0.01 second). Pasteurizing kills food-borne pathogens like listeria, *E. coli,* and salmonella. Pasteurizing milk affects the taste of the cheese, making it milder. Cheese made from raw milk is illegal to import and, in most states, to sell unless it is aged for over sixty days, at a temperature not lower than thirty-five degrees Fahrenheit. These strict regulations are in place because unpasteurized cheese has a higher level of bacteria and/or pathogens than pasteurized cheese.

To make things even more confusing, there is also a third heat treatment for milk. Thermalization is a process in which milk is heated enough to kill many of the bacteria, but not all of them. This process allows the stronger flavor that approaches the taste of raw milk cheese to remain, while gaining many of the food safety benefits of pasteurization. Technically, the milk used is not raw, but since it is also unpasteurized, it falls under the prohibitions mentioned above.

These processes are important because what gives cheese its flavor, chemically speaking, is the interaction of the enzymes, proteins, and bacteria. This interplay can be affected by heat, the acid-to-base ratio in production, and the humidity levels at which cheese is aged, but without cultures and bacteria there would be no cheese. Then again, there are good bacteria and bad bacteria.

Most of the controversy surrounding raw milk cheese has to do with food safety issues. Anti-raw-milk-cheese folks often see themselves as defending public health and saving lives by eliminating unnecessary risks. Pro-raw-milk-cheese foodies often see themselves as characters in those old Fruitopia commercials, demanding flavor in the face of stodgy, gray government bureaucracy.

What I found while trying to Google the information was an incredible number of conflicting advisories and risk assessments put out by the government, which made it nearly impossible to figure out what they were trying to say. For a long time I had been blaming doctors for the misunderstanding and/or misexplanation. But now, happily, I know I can blame the government. Thanks to Colorado State University's Cooperative Extension, I found the FDA's final advisory, which now lists only "soft cheese such as Feta, Brie, and Camembert cheeses, blue-veined cheeses, *queso blanco, queso fresco,* and Panela, unless it is labeled as made with pasteurized milk," as cheese to avoid. They then add, "The recommendation not to eat soft cheese unless it is labeled as made with pasteurized milk reflects a change from previous consumer advice for at-risk consumers not to eat soft cheese at all. Newer data about the contamination of cheese indicates that the risk doesn't appear in all soft cheeses, but specifically in cheese made from unpasteurized milk. This reflects the efforts of the dairy industry and FDA during the past several years to develop effective programs to control Listeria."[13]

Simple enough, right? Avoid soft raw milk cheese. However, the trouble is that the government agencies don't seem to communicate with one another, since the USDA (at the time of this writing) offers guidelines that, while nearly identical to the FDA's, continue to recommend that pregnant women avoid all the soft cheeses listed above, regardless of pasteurization. Still, most newly pregnant women come in the store telling me, "I can't have any raw milk cheese." Somehow most of these women seem to never have heard the part of the warning that, until December 2003, both government agencies had agreed upon—that certain soft pasteurized cheese was to be avoided.

My anecdotal experience may be skewed because we tend to serve fancy cheese lovers who may have asked their health care providers specifically about raw milk cheese. Or maybe because the Bay Area has a large "foodie" culture, the "no raw milk cheese" part is stressed more here. Still, customer concern about raw milk cheese for pregnant women is an everyday occurrence that has been increasing in our store since the late 1990s—a common enough occurrence that when a friend came into the store a couple of years ago I freaked her out. She asked for a cheese recommendation, and I gave her one. Then she asked, "Is this a raw milk cheese?"

"Oh my God, are you pregnant?" I exclaimed. I wouldn't have said this to a regular customer, but I had known her for years.

She screamed and made me promise not to say a word because she hadn't even told her fiancé yet. The cheesemonger is always the first to know.

But does the government warn against consuming raw milk cheese in general, whether you are pregnant or not? The USDA and FDA both warn against drinking "raw (unpasteurized) milk" or eating "foods that contain unpasteurized milk."[14] I'm not trying to get into semantics when I ask whether or not raw milk cheese "contains unpasteurized milk," but, chemically, the process of cheesemaking changes milk. For example, I would strongly discourage anyone against consuming two-year-old raw milk, but I wouldn't hesitate to advise anyone—after reminding them that I am not a doctor or scientist—to go ahead and eat Parmigiano Reggiano, which is made from raw milk. Since specific raw milk cheeses are warned against, it would appear that government agencies are much more concerned with raw fluid milk and raw milk soft cheeses than aged ones, which is good since you can't get pasteurized milk Parmigiano Reggiano, Gruyère, or Swiss Emmenthal: They just don't exist.

It's not that I believe pasteurized soft and high-moisture cheeses are actually dangerous. But I will say they are relatively more dangerous than aged raw milk cheeses such as Parmigiano Reggiano or a nine-month-plus-aged Gruyère because food-borne pathogens much prefer a moist, low-acid environment. In fact the FDA's own research shows that hard, aged cheese, including some types made from raw milk, had the lowest risk for listeria of any of the twenty-three food types researched. That was lower than fresh fruit and nowhere near the associated risk for food items like deli meat or hot dogs.[15]

The Institute of Food Science and Technology researched an "information statement" about the food-borne illness risks of cheese. In a table examining outbreaks of illness and death due to cheese from 1983 through 1998, less than one hundred reported deaths worldwide can be attributed to cheese in those fifteen years.[16] But not all of these are attributable to raw milk, and half were from a single manufacturing process so egregious and illegal that it shocked a room full of hardened cheesemakers. I was in a lecture about milk safety when this story of a certain manufacturer mixing pasteurized and raw milk together and making a high-moisture cheese was detailed. The cheesemakers in attendance were speechless. Pins dropped. Mouths hung agape. Hairs stood on end. This is also what accounts for a lot of the warnings specifically mentioning Mexican-style cheeses.

Why are soft cheeses riskier (even if the risk is pretty small) than aged, hard raw milk ones? Because of the chemical properties of cheesemaking. The reason that cheese made from raw milk must be aged sixty days has to do with the fact that dairy scientists used to believe that this is how much time it takes for the acidity level within the cheese to rise high enough to kill food-borne pathogens such as listeria, which can make you ill. But this rule is not foolproof, since the sixty-day rule was developed with different food-borne pathogens in mind than the more virulent strains of listeria or *E. coli* that we talk about today.[17] Even though aged cheese, raw or pasteurized, has very rarely caused any illness, I do remember sitting next to Dr. Moshe Rosenberg, professor of dairy engineering and technology at UC Davis, on a public panel on raw milk cheese,[18] where he reminded me that even with aged cheese, "There have been a few bad apples."

Not all cheese is the same, chemically speaking, even among the young cheeses. Camembert, for example, has extremely low acidity when ripe due to a combination of high moisture and the specific cultures and bacteria added during the cheesemaking process. This means that Camembert's bacterial activity actually rises as it ages, and if there is a nasty critter in there, it will find fertile ground. Of course, since Camembert is overripe at sixty days, it's illegal to import raw milk Camembert that you'd actually want to eat.

But pasteurization does not remove all the dangers. While it kills the food-borne pathogens and other bacteria that give cheese flavor, pasteurization also creates a petri-dish paradise for pathogens if there is post-production contamination, since none of the other naturally occurring properties of milk are left to combat pathogens introduced accidentally. While pasteurized milk cheeses vastly outnumber raw milk ones, almost all the cheese recalled for listeria in my twelve years of cheese buying were pasteurized, fresh, high-moisture ones.

The warnings are garbled by the government because the people writing the public statements simply don't seem to know a lot about cheese. One FDA warning says, "All consumers should not eat cheeses made from unpasteurized milk." Besides the twisted syntax, let us remember that raw milk cheese is legal when aged more than sixty days, so the agency should either be more specific about the warning or also state, "All consumers should not eat deli meat." Other government warnings contain teeth-gnashing information, like the conflation of feta and goat cheese (not all feta is made from goat's milk, not all goat cheese is feta), but I admit that such errors are relatively minor in terms of consequence.

The private Web sites with food safety information for pregnant women have been even more confusing. Half-understood issues combined with poor editing created some real head-scratchers for those of us trying to soothe panic in the aisles. Pregnant women have brought articles in to our cheese department that they've printed from the Internet, and the bad advice comes in three main flavors: 1. Unclear syntax ("avoid raw milk not . . . unpasteurized cheeses"). 2. Lack of basic cheese knowledge (Mexican-style cheese such as *queso fresco* consumed in the United States is usually made in the US). 3. Lack of understanding of the law ("cheeses made in the US must be pasteurized"). These examples were from Web sites listed as some of the most popular Internet sources for pregnant women in the FDA's internal analysis of the effectiveness of their listeriosis education work, so it is clear why people are sometimes confused about cheese and food safety. However, even with these bumps in the road, private informational sources like magazines and Web sites have improved tremendously over the last couple of years, and they get most of the story straight in the end: Young raw milk cheese is riskier than pasteurized soft cheese, which is riskier than hard cheese.

However, in addition to those customers asking about raw milk cheese because they feel they have to avoid it, we get just as many customers asking about raw milk cheese because they are seeking it out. Generally, there are two types of people who ask, "Where's your raw milk cheese?"

Raw food has been the biggest food fad of recent years. Like any of these nutritional trends, there are kernels of truth in its ideology that are understood less and less as the trend grows more popular. There are many interesting ideas in circulation about raw dairy, including, for instance, suggestions that it has the potential to bolster the human immune system. There has also been speculation that mandatory pasteurization contributes to making people more susceptible to illness.[19] I'm not totally convinced, but I find the arguments intriguing, even if they are of the some-will-have-to-die-so-the-rest-of-us-will-be-stronger variety.

Raw foodists have replaced the macrobiotic folks as the neediest customers. My evidence is anecdotal, but I bet food store workers across the land would back me up. Raw foodists are food missionaries who are often frustrated that other people, including the food producers themselves, haven't yet realized that the discovery of fire was evil. One raw foodist demanded to know why I didn't carry a cheese from a certain raw milk dairy. I told her that I didn't carry the cheese because it didn't exist. She got very upset and insisted it did. Luckily, this exchange occurred during business hours, so I called up the dairy, put them on speaker phone, and proved that I was right.

She then went to the freezer section and demanded that we carry a certain sorbet, which also didn't exist, from a local ice cream company. When the freezer worker, a working-class punk metal drummer from Chicago, tried to explain this, she said, "Well it should. Raw foodies are taking over the world."

He let her walk away and then muttered, "That'll be a short war."

Many raw foodists are dismayed to discover that cheese made with raw milk is not necessarily a raw food. Though made with raw milk, the curds of cheeses such as Parmigiano Reggiano and Gruyère are cooked during the cheesemaking process. Raw foodies tend to buy for function, not taste, so I try to convince them to stick with the basic raw milk cheddars, which are rarely heated above 110 degrees F.

Some foodies, however, come in seeking raw milk cheese for the opposite reason. They ask for raw milk cheese as if there were two kinds of cheese: raw milk and cheap crap. I think this notion is a result of the lobbying my trade organization, the American Cheese Society, had done to save raw milk cheese when it appeared that the FDA was thinking of making more of it illegal. Obviously, because cheese predates pasteurization, raw milk cheese is the most traditional version available. Foodie culture craves the original.

I know it's my contrary nature, but when I think of "artisanal production," I think of feudal muck and lack of sanitation à la *Monty*

Python and the Holy Grail. I am definitely not saying that pasteurization makes superior cheese, but fetishizing the traditional has its drawbacks, too.

I will now write something that often gets me in trouble when I say it at work. Raw milk cheese is usually better than pasteurized milk cheese of the same type, but not always; because the larger an operation, the more homogenized the flavor gets and, for safety and economic reasons, the less likely producers are to use raw milk. But people unwilling to give cheese a try simply because it's pasteurized are missing out. While an airline ticket to France is still the more expensive option for finding traditional raw milk cheese, even there you'll have to work harder and look farther afield to seek out the traditional stuff. While the heating or nonheating of milk is a crucial step, it is not the only factor in the taste of a cheese.

Take Manchego, the most common Spanish cheese in this country. Manchego is a sheep's milk cheese made in the La Mancha area. It's milky and nutty and, depending on its age, can also be caramelly, sharp, sweet, and/or salty. I must have sampled fifty different producers' cheeses. The pasteurized ones aged between six and twelve months are almost universally better than the raw ones. Though I recently found a good one, most raw Manchegos get too gamy, are often too salty, and are usually way overpriced. I acknowledge that these are the imports, and that there might be better cheese in Spain. But hey, our store isn't in Spain, and there are better options available. As raw Spanish sheep's milk goes, both Roncal and Zamorano are similar, but better and cheaper options than raw milk Manchego.

The other funny reaction I get from customers who refuse to believe I'm not nod-and-winking them is when I tell them some young French cheeses are pasteurized for importation. Really. I'm not just lying to hide illegal cheese smuggling. French producers actually do pasteurize for the American market, increasingly so. In fact, traditional, name-controlled cheeses made by longtime cheesemakers have had to be renamed because they are now made with pasteurized milk. Selles-sur-Cher, an amazing ashed, ripened goat cheese that is one of my favorites, is now pasteurized and known as Tradition Jacquin. An ironic name considering that the reason they had to change it is because Selles-sur-Cher is a name-controlled cheese and, by breaking with tradition and pasteurizing it, they could no longer use that name.

Because there is some degree of added risk involved in some raw milk cheese, cheesemongers are often advised to know their producers. This is a time-honored myth among specialty retail. We're always told to "tell their story" in order to support the cheesemakers and to increase sales. We're told that knowing them will guard against inferior products.

Sure, I've met a lot of the cheesemakers and farmers. They seem nice. I feel I know some of them fairly well. But how the hell would I know if they're gonna do some shady stuff to pay the mortgage? I don't think anyone I deal with would go to that length, but in a world where family friends and lovers have committed some serious crimes, saying that I "know" any business associates well enough to guarantee everything about their product is disingenuous. The specialty food world often sells food as if the customer were part of a personal (not business) relationship with these stewards of the land. Most of the time, however, that's just a myth of capitalism.

After all, things happen. One longtime cheesemaker I know has an incredible amount of integrity. I would never doubt his word. He would never engage in shady activities. But he also had no idea that workers at his cheese plant were using the cheesemaking vats weekly for drunken Jacuzzi parties with women they picked up at the local bars. If they hadn't gotten a little too drunk one night and been discovered passed out when the morning milk arrived, I would never have heard this story. Of course, there's little actual danger to the cheese in this scenario since the first thing any reputable cheesemaker does before making cheese is clean and sanitize everything. But I believe my point is clear.

Without raw milk cheese we would be missing out on a lot of amazing food. Pretty much all my favorite cheeses are made from raw milk, even if we can't get many of them legally: true Camembert, Reblochon, Valencay, Pouligny-Saint-Pierre, Cathare, and any number of fresh, young chèvres. But as consumers and retailers, we have to acknowledge that we are eight to twelve thousand miles from the home(s) of most traditional cheesemaking. Sometimes, sadly, we have to take what we can get.

Luckily, some American cheese producers are starting to make incredible raw milk cheese. To make raw milk cheese, you really need to become obsessed with cleanliness and milk safety. You need foot-baths between the outside and the cheesemaking room. You must carefully screen visitors and make sure they are properly clothed. Milk must be used quickly. Leaving the fluid milk sitting unrefrigerated for a relatively extended time simply cannot be allowed because this practice adds tremendous risk and, in a worst-case scenario, possibly fatal consequences to the production. Raw milk cheese producers must also conduct more tests on the milk and cheese in order to look for potential food-borne pathogens. Everyone making raw milk cheese knows that one mistake will probably end their business and potentially that of other raw milk cheesemakers, too—forever.

Since people ask me almost every day what I think of the safety risks of raw milk cheese, I'll tell you, with the caveat that this is my opinion and that I am not a doctor or scientist. If you aren't pregnant or immune-compromised, there is such a statistically small chance of getting ill from US-legal raw milk cheese that you shouldn't even worry about it, unless you already don't cross streets or live in a home with such dangers as electricity.

Catherine Donnelly, one of my favorite dairy scientists, is a hero to many US citizens who care about amazing, traditionally made cheeses. In a 2001 issue of *Discover* magazine she was quoted in a paragraph that has become a hard-to-argue-against mantra of the pro-raw-milk cheese folks: "Ironically, the cheeses that have caused illnesses have often been made from pasteurized milk and then contaminated during processing. Pasteurization may actually create a more dangerous situation, in that you knock out the competitive flora. The good bugs that help keep the bad bugs in check in a raw-milk cheese are destroyed by pasteurization."

At the American Cheese Society conference in 2001, Donnelly spoke about studying the FDA's consideration of banning all raw milk cheese (not just the ones aged less than sixty days, as the current law states). She described her approach to the study as that of a typical food science person, looking to minimize health risk, assuming there was some kind of reason behind the proposed tightening of the laws. What she found was very little evidence that aged raw milk cheese posed much of a health threat. She reviewed cases of food-borne illness over the past thirty years or so and found very little evidence of aged-raw-milk-cheese-related illness or death. She then started questioning the basic concepts relating to raw milk cheese and food safety held by the regulatory agencies of the US government.[20]

That post-production contamination in pasteurized cheese causes more illness than raw milk cheese is not debated (though there is also not much raw milk cheese eaten, statistically speaking, in the United States). But this gets to the heart of the issue: Large-scale factory production has unintended risks. To destroy traditional chee-semaking in the name of food safety is an idea born of false comfort.

Illegal raw milk cheeses, those made with raw milk and aged less than sixty days, are statistically the riskiest cheeses[21]—but man they taste good, if you can find them outside Europe. I would certainly eat them myself, even if I can't sell them.

What about women who are pregnant or people with compro-mised immune systems? Honestly, I try not to add to all the "advice" these folks get already. Pointing out that women in France, for exam-ple, are not advised to forgo raw milk cheese is not a useful strategy, especially after someone who practically wanted to fight me told me that his relative miscarried because of raw milk cheese. The scold-ing tone with which pregnant women are addressed in much of the advisory literature is unnecessary, and I don't want to add my never-gonna-be-pregnant voice to that clamor. Certain foods do carry some risk during pregnancy, and avoiding that risk can make sense if you're accommodating a temporary condition. Friends of mine have drawn different lines in different places, and I don't get involved in those decisions.

As for the issue of the legality of raw milk cheese, it's kind of hard to take this hoopla seriously in a country without universal health care. The only people who eat legal raw milk cheese are in general upscale urban folks. Poor and rural people may eat a lot more illegal (that is, homemade) raw milk cheese, but it's hardly likely that this cheese is going to be labeled *raw milk* when someone makes it in the bathtub. Doesn't it seem like guaranteed preventive health services would prevent more deaths and illnesses in the long run?

But surely one can pick on almost any individual bit of health advice and counter with that argument. There is a zero-risk ideology in the food regulatory world that I do understand. The regulators' job is not to discuss flavor, which is subjective, but safety and risk, which are statistical. They are unimpressed with food lovers' claims, partly because, demographically speaking, they usually aren't the ones who die if something goes wrong.

You can't really eliminate risk from eating. I mean, a lot of what we eat grows in the ground, and the ground tends to be dirty. Science kills some microbes and others develop into resistant super-strains. Many of the regulatory agencies are the same ones that propose irradiation of foods in the name of safety and legalize rBGH/rBST (the genetically modified bovine growth hormone) despite the many concerns that have kept it off the market everywhere else in the world.

Every year some people die from eating food. You could become one of them. That would be very unlikely, but it could happen. But given the underfunding of the Food and Drug Administration, and the recent issues with *E. coli* in fresh foods, concentrating on the dangers of cheese instead of, say, factory-farm-produced bagged lettuce seems odd. Early death is not likely to come as a result of eating fancy cheese. Raw milk cheese is a food that statistically has more risk than similar pasteurized milk cheeses. Act according to how much that scares you.

Recent food recalls of beef, spinach, and even pet food have led to customer wariness about the food we buy. Anecdotally, there does seem to be more fear nowadays about the food supply than at any time since I started working in a grocery store. Trade journals have discussed the risk of terrorists poisoning milk tankers. Environmentalist worries about factory farms and the safety of the food produced there (or downstream) have probably helped a tremendous amount to increase our business and the number of people who want to shop at a natural foods store.

Food may be scary to some customers, but sometimes the customers scare us. The day before Thanksgiving instills a lot of fear in grocery workers' hearts. It's the busiest US grocery store retail day of the year, and many of the customers are borderline aggro because they're stressed by competing for that perfect bunch of celery, or are buying unfamiliar yet desperately needed ingredients—not to mention the jostling and bumping of other customers, the impending cooking hassles, and the underlying torment of a visit with one's family.

It's the only day that I sometimes fear the customers might turn on us.

The produce department on that day often reminds me of a riot scene. Small affinity-group-looking gangs of people, possibly related, try to move swiftly and with purpose through a stubborn mass of shoppers. It's impossible to take in all the action at once. I can only focus on bits of the crowd at one time, keeping my head on a swivel, wary of any new motion in my peripheral vision.

I'm usually just happy that they're racing one another to the registers and not organizing among themselves. Still, I wouldn't want to be there if, God forbid, we run out of tofurkeys.

The day before Thanksgiving is not a day to be obnoxious to grocery workers. And usually the customers don't behave badly, because they are so concentrated on getting out of the store as quickly as possible. Even the regular customers, who like to spend a long time at the store chatting with everyone, know that it's not the right day for that.

One Thanksgiving, though, I had a customer who was so confusing that I started looking for hidden cameras.

At about 9:30 p.m. (we were closing at 10 p.m. because of the holiday), this customer approached the cheese counter needing attention. Not help or advice, but attention. The other cheese worker and I had been there about nine to ten hours each. We were just trying to get started on mopping and trash-emptying since the twelve-hour, all-day rush had just ended. Since we usually close at 9 p.m., only a few stragglers remained.

"I need some creamy cheese for Thanksgiving," he declared.

"Do you want a goat cheese? A Brie? A—" I tried to respond.

"I don't want a Brie. That's what they eat in the Marina. Are you catering to Marina people now?" he said aggressively. *The Marina* (referring to the city's Marina District neighborhood) is often, rightly or wrongly, used as a shorthand expression for trendy, yuppie San Francisco. I was too tired to fight so I didn't attempt to tell him that Brie was thought of as too boring and commodity-priced to be trendy anymore. I tried dodging his attempts at conflict. It was no use. After he tasted a bunch of cheese, he asked a produce question.

Jokingly, I said, "I'm sorry, sir. I'm just the cheese worker."

He stopped short. "Did you call me sir?" he asked. "What's your name? I want to speak to a manager." He was still using a strange tone and had a weird smirk on his face. It was unclear whether he was joking.

"We don't have managers but you can talk to someone at the front desk," I said. "But let me get this straight, you're going to file a complaint because I called you sir? That's not going to appear very incriminating in your complaint."

"Well, I'll just make something up then." He stormed away without any cheese. I still couldn't tell if he was joking.

Five minutes later I realized that I needed to buy beer before the registers closed. As I paid the cashier I realized that the joking-or-serious customer was in the next line over, being rung up by my lesbian buddy Bruce. Joking-or-Serious wouldn't let it go. He yelled out at me, "I made a complaint, you know. You'll be hearing about this I'm sure." Then he laughed. I laughed. He stopped laughing. "Go ahead and laugh. It's really funny isn't it?" Confused, I walked away.

A few minutes later Bruce came up to me as I was mopping out the cheese floor. "What was with that guy?" she asked.

"I have no idea," I said, and then told her the whole ambiguous story.

"He told me the same thing," Bruce said. "When he got to the 'sir' part, I said to him, 'I'm very, very sorry that happened to you . . . ma'am.' Then he called me a bitch and walked away. I still don't know if he was kidding."

Co-ops attract nuts like Taleggio attracts flies, so this isn't odd in and of itself. While arriving at work one day and walking up the aisle to the cheese department, I had to jump out of the way of someone trying to run through the store followed closely by our uniformed guard and the front end coordinator. I write *trying to run* because while he was making running movements, he was moving in slow motion. Total Lee Majors, *Six Million Dollar Man* flashback, except without the sound effects and matching tracksuit. Instead, we just heard his raspy breath and noticed something wrong with his long, wet hair. Was it soapy?

Six Million obviously thought he was playing it cool, but everyone else was staring. It reminded me of the time I was walking home past the edge of the Valencia Gardens housing project and some old, frazzled junkie had attracted the attention of the cops. I was waiting for the light to change and he had just noticed the police cruiser tailing him. He quickly stumble-walked around the corner and attempted to drop a plastic bag in the sewer grate, but he missed the grate by a good five feet, and his motions were so exaggerated that he might as well have yelled to the cops, *I'M THROWING AWAY DRUGS NOW!* The teenage girls standing next to me mocked him, "Ooooh, you are smoooooth." Even the cops were laughing.

Six Million was so out of it that he actually tried to get one last free sample as he was getting chased out. When he was refused the kombucha, matte energy drink, or whatever it was, he tried to make a big deal about it. "You won't serve me because I'm homeless?!?!"

I eventually found out that Six Million had entered the store and immediately went for the cheese samples, picking up the whole bowl and cramming half in his mouth and the rest down his shirt for later. When a cheese worker yelled out to him and went to retrieve the bowl, he fled to the bath and body area, where he started washing his hair in the sink. By then security was on him so he headed toward the entrance, dripping bubbles as he walked. Evidently, after he was kicked out he stood in front of the store saying, "They had no reason to kick me out. I wasn't doing anything wrong. I was just conditioning."

The folks I mentioned above are outliers to be sure. Like food-borne pathogens in milk, disruptive people can travel through the store most days and their presence doesn't really affect much. It's only when their neuroses, craziness, or drugged-out behavior gets especially virulent that it causes problems.

Most customers who come to shop are somewhere in the continuum of unnoticeable to awesome. Like milk, they can vary in their smell, their composition, their richness, and even in their chemical properties, whether they are natural or artificially produced. Most people, however, are nothing to worry about.

Hopeful Tomme, Sweet Grass Dairy: **Here's a cheese story for you. The Sweet Grass Dairy folks, pasture-based cheesemakers from Georgia, had a problem. Due to technical difficulties, their milk holding tanks weren't functioning. What would they do with all that milk? Better make cheese and make it quick! They regularly make Thomasville Tomme, a buttery, grassy cow's milk cheese, so they decided to throw all the milk together and hope for the best. Thus, the Hopeful Tomme was born, probably my favorite of all their cheeses. Raw cow's and** goat's milk mixed together in the style of a Pyrenees mountain cheese, which makes a distinct and new southern cheese classic. Incredibly grassy and floral. This cheese shows off the pasture. Sweet Grass is a family-operated cheese company. In fact, they still buy their milk from Jessica Little's dad, who lives nearby. [$$, Similar cheese: Sweet Grass's Thomasville Tomme (US) is the same cheese without the goat's milk. However, the floral, earthy qualities of a good Pecorino Sardo (Italy) or Flor di Capra (Italy) may be even more similar.]

Pleasant Ridge Reserve, Uplands Cheese Company: This Wisconsin cheese is so good that it's the only cheese to twice win the American Cheese Society Best of Show (in both 2001 and 2005). It truly shows off the forage. Seasonal, it's a grazed-cow cheese that manages to be fruity, rich, nutty, and grassy. It is also a hand-washed-rind cheese, which gives it a slight pungency. It's one of those cheeses that you taste and the longer the taste is in your mouth, the more you appreciate it. The Uplands Cheese Company is run by two families committed to pasture-based dairying who want you to taste the difference between their cheese and more mass-produced ones. Their Web site even proclaims that "producing food slowly, deliberately, and with pride is a value worth preserving in our hurried, industrialized society." [$$$, Similar cheese: It's a smaller wheel, but any well-aged, hand-selected cheese in the Gruyère (Swiss) and Comte (France) families would be similar.]

six

Cheese Culture, Punk Subculture, and Reagan Cheese

When I told my political friends that I attended a workshop titled "Working with Indigenous Cultures" at the 2003 American Cheese Society Conference, they were impressed. They were surprised that a conference for such a Eurocentric food would devote time to the issues of native peoples. Some even asked about attending. I almost didn't have the heart to tell them that that wasn't what the organizers meant.

To the consuming public, culture is the least understood ingredient of cheese. Most cheeses use a bacterial culture that is added to the milk in order to produce chemical reactions that affect the finished cheese in some desirable way. Cheese cultures affect everything. Of course their use is intertwined with all the other ingredients and processes, but they are the start of the chemical reactions that make the cheese magic happen. They determine the acidity level of the milk, the way the milk coagulates, the texture of the curds (and therefore the cheese), the taste, the moisture level, and the way the cheese ages.

In the old days dairies made their own cultures by leaving out buckets of milk to spoil (sour), then adding them back in when making cheese. As you can imagine, this process was risky and unstable: If some microscopic critter got into the mix, the starter could transform or be killed off entirely. While this process lent itself to the creation of unique flavors, cheesemakers risked wasting milk and, worse yet, the production of bad cheese and possible financial hardship. The tradition of homemade culture disappeared for most cheesemakers in this country with the advent of commercial culture houses that could create and sell consistent starters. For many years in the United States, though, all you could buy were the basics: Cheddar, Swiss, or Parmesan. This lack of diversity, of course, homogenized the taste of US-made cheese while lessening the chance of financial ruin (due to inconsistent or inedible cheese) for the cheesemakers. However, many cheesemakers these days are experimenting with making their own cultures as a way to create distinctive, yet reliable, cheeses.

But is culture reliable? Beyond the bacterial cultures that go into forming the actual cheese, there are so many cultures and subcultures involved in the cheesemaking process. Farmers, hippies, dairymen, foodies, I've-lived-in-France-ers, corporate sales reps, family businesses, and cheese punks, just to name a few. Sometimes they clash. Sometimes they sustain one another. Sometimes they're symbiotic, sometimes parasitic.

There are so many subcultures and microcultures that I could use to describe myself, but I suppose I should set the groundwork with the overarching ones, even if they're obvious. I never thought of myself as particularly American until I left the country for the first time in my midtwenties, but then I found it undeniable. I don't mean that I discovered my *U-S-A! U-S-A!* identity (because when confronted with imperialist wars and jingoism I tend to be un-American in a HUAC kind of way), but I've lived my entire life in the United States, and it's marked me in ways both good and bad.

I'm a white American from a family where white ethnicity wasn't anything beyond a vague part of a coming-to-America story. I also grew up middle class and suburban, but not with old money or trust funds. Because my family moved to the Bay Area when I was still very young, and because I am the youngest child, I consider myself the only real Californian in my family, which is probably why I'm both more touchy-feely and lefty.

California is rich in subcultures, and I ran with a few. In high school I hung out with some of the jocks, the writers, the future queers, the politicos, and the punks. I wasn't the only one who overlapped, mind you, but in the Reagan years standing against the cultural death march to the right was the most important way I defined myself.

Reagan was a cultural revolutionary above all else. There was no mistaking this if you were growing up at that time. Sure, there were specific policies he wanted to enact, certain unions he wanted to bust, certain people he wanted to bomb, have murdered, or let die, but his real power came from getting Americans to feel good about their greed and power again. All around, people were seeing a kindly old man speak friendly common sense. Yet many of us saw a horrible monster who wanted to push back every positive political gain made in our short lifetimes and kill us in World War III. We tried to fight this by creating our own culture. We loved not only the music but being banded together in a punk community.

I turned thirteen in October 1980. Three weeks later Ronald Reagan was elected president. The year I got into high school my formerly sort of groovy Northern California high school began eliminating elective classes, got rid of free periods, assigned detention for absences, and rang buzzers for the first time since the 1950s to announce the end and beginning of classes. The particulars are less important than the fact that a certain type of social control was being re-implemented, that a cultural change was occurring. It was clear in my teenage mind: All the petty fuckers who run schools (and other, similar institutions) had been on the defensive, but not anymore. They wanted their power back. Sit down. Shut up. There will be no more questions.

Reagan led a right-wing offensive whose goal was to make (among many other things) respect for authority fashionable again. Many of us in the punk scene became politicized in that era in the face of a mass movement going in the other direction. This of course directly affected the formation of our culture. Through Rock Against Reagan, War Chest Tours, and the anti-nuke movement, we became very good at loudly and flamboyantly saying "NO!" Going to punk shows was kind of like our 4-H club. Instead of going to FFA (Future Farmers of America) meetings, and doing agricultural projects, the punk rockers listened to JFA (Jodie Foster's Army)[22] and protested in the streets.

And besides the growth of the punk scene, what was one of the other things that era was famous for? The thing that would eventually, in an indirect way, lead me to a life of dairy work: Reagan Cheese.

> Soup lines, free loaves of bread, 5 lb. blocks of cheese, bags of groceries. Social security has run out on you and me. We do whatever we can. Gotta duck when the shit hits the fan.
> **—Circle Jerks, "Shit Hits the Fan" (1983)**

What poor family or anarchist squat didn't feed on surplus cheese in the 1980s? It was nasty to be sure, but it was ubiquitous and kept people from being hungry. It is a cultural artifact, a time-and-place bit of history. Government surplus cheese was even memorialized in song, albeit a certain type of song sung by a certain type of band.

What was Reagan Cheese and where is it now? It was mild Cheddar or processed American Cheese that was the end result of price supports for the overproduction of milk. By the US government's estimates, some fifteen to eighteen million people received free food every month during a commodity giveaway program set up in the 1980s to distribute unpurchased commodities like cheese, milk, and rice. As much as four hundred million pounds of cheese were given away at the height of the program. After paying over $2 billion a year between 1980 and 1985 to buy surplus milk to help dairy farmers survive, Congress passed the Food Security Act of 1985 to reduce the number of dairy herds. Fourteen thousand farmers were paid by the government to kill their herds and stop farming for at least five years.[23] However, over the years, overproduction has continued to lower the price that dairy farmers can get for milk.

Of course, at the same time, technological advances were paving the way for a wholly new and different kind of food. While techniques like grafting and selective breeding have been used for centuries by farmers, biotechnology allowed the replication and alteration of the genetic materials of life. For the first time, changes that wouldn't be possible in nature, or that would take generations, could be performed in labs. Recombinant bovine growth hormone (rBGH), a hormone that causes cows to produce more milk, was the first of this new kind of genetically altered products to be legalized and sold to the food industry.

There was such an abundance of milk in the 1980s that the government was paying farmers to kill off their cows. Yet at the same time it was green-lighting a project that would make cows produce more milk. From a production standpoint, this project was completely unnecessary.

The United States is still the only major dairy-producing country that allows the use of rBGH. In fact, a major scandal erupted in Canada when scientists studying bovine growth hormone testified to the Canadian senate that attempts were made to bribe them, their research notes were stolen, and they were eventually removed or transferred when they refused to favor approval. Like the European Union, Australia, and New Zealand, Canada still prohibits the use of rBGH.

The issues related to the synthetic hormone center mostly on concerns about the increased risk of cancer to humans, antibiotic resistance in general, and the health of the cows being injected. Some of the potential health risks for humans and cows are interrelated. If cows develop health problems such as mastitis (a painful inflammation of the udders that is warned of as a possible side effect on every package of rBGH sent to farmers), dairy farmers will use more antibiotics on their cows. This in turn can lead to a greater immunity in the environment to antibiotics, which is an issue of concern to doctors and scientists. In one report, many farmers who began using rBGH when it was first made legal found that it caused so many health problems in cows that some had decided to stop using it.[24]

A particularly frightening potential health problem activists warn about is the increased possibility of cancer due to the way rBGH works. rBGH increases milk production because it releases a chemical called IGF-1 (insulin-like growth factor 1). IGF-1 is identical in cows and humans, and the milk that comes from cows injected with rBGH will, according to most sources, increase the amount of IGF-1 in the milk we drink. IGF-1 has been linked to cancer (particularly breast and prostate cancer) because it causes cell division in humans. While drinking IGF-1 is not known to cause cancer—pro-rBGH forces argue that it's broken down by saliva; anti-rBGH activists argue that since the IGF-1 is bound to casein (milk protein), it isn't—there is reason to be concerned.

Many long-term organic farmers have argued that the USDA Organic Standards, enacted in 2002, watered down the regulations too much. Indeed, while many agribusiness giants have upped their own organic production or bought previously independent organic companies in the last few years, the battle over organic standards offered the unique spectacle—possibly a singular experience—of a trade industry asking to be *more regulated,* with stricter standards than the government had proposed. Because of this, the US government certainly is not thought of as a friend to many of those pushing for food safety and high environmental standards in food production. Some also question the integrity of the agency that also approved Thalidomide, DDT, and other chemicals only to discover the health problems later on. Others note that rBGH was approved by the veterinary division of the FDA as an animal drug, not as a food-grade product.[25] There is no health benefit to humans or cows, just financial benefit to the only corporation that produces the drug (formerly Monsanto, now Eli Lilly and company), and to some dairy farmers.

This is one of the cultural issues that bring people together. Organic farmers, environmentalists, and lefties like me want to view the whole issue in terms of corporate profit and consolidation of smaller dairies into the hands of big business at a potential cost to humans and the ecosystem. But conservatives, the religiously devout, and many traditional dairy farmers can oppose the use of synthetic hormones with an equal fervor on completely different grounds. It can be seen as unnatural, hurtful to the animals, and against God's law just as easily as it can be seen as another case of corporate plunder.

Since rBGH cannot be used in goat, sheep, water buffalo, organic, or non-US cheese, there are some customers who avoid non-organic US cow's milk cheese altogether. Granted, I work in a natural foods store, so my perspective on this effect is somewhat skewed, but this has become an issue for the entire domestic dairy industry.

While many Bay Area dairies and milk co-ops pledged to remain rBGH-free even before the synthetic hormone was legalized, other large producers are just now taking a stand. In 2005 both the Tillamook cheese cooperative in Oregon and BelGioioso Cheese Incorporated in Wisconsin started requiring their farmers to sign pledges that the milk they provided to their companies came from cows not treated with rBGH. Both companies gave their reasons as consumer demand. In fact, Errico Auricchio, president of BelGioioso, in *Cheese Market News,* seemed downright cranky: "We don't maintain there's any difference in the milk or the cheese, but we have had pressure from the consumers . . . The customer is informed, or should I say misinformed, especially on the West Coast. It's a very touchy situation."

Yeah, sorry we are so touchy that a synthetic hormone illegal in every other serious dairy-producing country on the planet—that was designed to increase milk production in a time of a milk surplus, that gives the consumer no benefit whatsoever and causes many scientists and consumers health concerns—makes us ask questions.

It amazes me when people in the dairy industry don't get this. As long as I have been alive, dairy marketers have portrayed milk as a necessary, pure, and healthy food. Many cheese companies, Tillamook and BelGioioso included, market themselves as the keepers of tradition and connection to the land. Yet when people have a hard time squaring these timeless pro-dairy images with people in lab coats messing with *E. coli* and DNA, they are somehow "misinformed."

Despite the fact that some commodity cheesemakers in this country have pledged to be rBGH-free, there is no third-party certification of their claims. It's not that I think they are lying, but the nature of dairy milk for large production facilities is that the milk is pooled from many different sources throughout the region. Unfortunately, the 100 percent guaranteed-free-of-rBGH cheeses mentioned above—as well as goat, sheep, water buffalo, organic, and non-US cheeses—tend to cost more. As a retailer of cheese in a community-oriented store, one of my fears is that corporate-sponsored genetic engineering creates a world in which wholesome products that were once taken for granted as accessible and cheaply procured now command top-tier prices. People have to make decisions based on cost as well as their health concerns. I consider it part of my job, as a person trying to serve my community and not just to profit off it, to help ensure that cheap food can also be pure food, and to fight the trend of the natural foods industry becoming solely a market niche for people with the ability to opt out of genetically modified foods by paying more money.

Ironically, the low price of fluid milk has driven so many dairy farmers out of business that those looking to stay on the land have had to seek out ways to make more money out of every gallon of milk or suffer the same fate. Fancy cheese is many things, but it is also what is called in the industry a "value-added product." If you can create something original, you are not bound to price it at the going rate for fluid milk or commodity Cheddar. One of the biggest incentives for farmers to get in on the growing handmade cheese business is that it can, if done well, lead to a whole lot more money per gallon of milk.

Money is a culture issue, too, of course. Much imported cheese—which is, historically speaking, traditional peasant food—costs more than most people can regularly afford without a trust fund or a six-figure income. As I've mentioned, we have a lot of folks who budget for their cheese addictions. But still, there is an irony to living in an area in which so much of the rural community has been displaced at the very time the demand for the "authentic" local food of Spanish, French, or Italian rural communities is in high demand.

There is still a lot of rural land around the Bay Area and in other regions of the country, as well as an increase in demand for local food. My local cheese, even when it's priced higher than imported equivalents, sells well if it tastes good. All the Cowgirl Creamery cheese, Vella Dry Jack and Mezzo Secco, Point Reyes Blue, Humboldt Fog, Redwood Hill Camellia and Crottin, Laura Chenel Taupinière and Tome, Bravo Silver Mountain, Fiscalini San Joaquin Gold, the Andante cheeses when I can get them, are now cheese department staples. I hear this echoed at every cheese conference I've ever attended: Other cheesemongers who have a thriving local cheesemaking community, including the obvious places—Vermont, Wisconsin, upstate New York—as well as the less obvious—Oregon, Washington, Colorado, Maine, Maryland, Virginia—all rave about, and are loyal to, their locals. With the exception of Vella, and some notable Wisconsin and Vermont cheesemakers, those cheeses may be exceptional but don't have much history compared with the European ones. Maybe that's why there's a subcategory of foodie subculture that needs to reach out a few thousand miles to feel authentic.

There's a phrase and a tone of voice that informs me right away if I'm dealing with one of those folks. The phrase is, "Well, I've lived in [insert country here] and . . ." It's said with a condescending smile and a soft voice that tells me they're letting me in on a secret.

Living somewhere doesn't make you an expert on anything, obviously. For example, many of us reading this chapter have lived in the United States our whole lives. How many of you know the correct temperature for pasteurization? Or, even more cheese-specific, how many of you can describe the process for emulsification of American processed cheese? Yet foodies who spend a few months in some cheese-famous country try to tell me that my information is wrong because they have firsthand knowledge. As if they've been working in the cheese factory themselves as opposed to sitting in some café gorging themselves and reading the *International Herald Tribune*.

Shaking her head slowly, a customer called me over one day. "Excuse me," she said, "but your sign on the Chimay cheese is wrong."

"What's incorrect?" I asked.

"Well, I've lived in Belgium, and whoever wrote this is confused. It says that this cheese is washed with beer and that's not true. The monks make beer and they make cheese. But [pause to laugh slightly] they don't combine them."

"Actually, washing cheese with alcohol of different types is fairly common," I replied. "They make one variety that's washed with salt water like most washed-rind cheeses. But they also make this one washed with beer. You get a stronger flavor with this one." *What kind of person brags about living in Belgium,* I wondered to myself.

"Uh, no. . . Like I said, I lived there. You should make sure you get the buyer to change the sign."

I then pulled out the line I use whenever I'm in this situation. It's a compromise and in this case I knew it was a lie, but then there's no real winning in these types of interactions. It gently informs customers of the correct information while still allowing them to feel haughty and knowledgeable. "It really is washed with beer. But maybe it's export only. Sometimes they make cheese just for the American market, you know."

"Oh yes, that must be it."

The next day, coincidentally, Chimay cheese was written about in Janet Fletcher's weekly *San Francisco Chronicle* cheese column. The article didn't differentiate among the different Chimay cheeses, but it did include a Web site reference. Starting to doubt myself a little, I checked it out. Sure enough, the beer cheese had its own little section.

But as much as pedestalization of European foods goes on, it's still at least more interesting than the mockery of the unknown that is America's reaction to many foreign cheeses. It's notable though, that it is the French cheese that gets the most abuse. After years of thought on why that is, I've decided that it's all about homophobia. Even before the start of the most recent Gulf War, when elected government officials went out of their way to embarrass themselves and, by extension, all Americans, by changing the name of french fries to "Freedom fries," French food has never exactly been considered manly. We all know that, as far as Europe goes, France is the "faggy" country. Small portions, overly decorative servings, torturing defenseless geese to make foie gras . . . whatever the reason, there is a certain type of guy who refuses to engage with French cheese. If you doubt me, go do an Internet search for French + food + (pick your anti-gay epithet).

In fact, when heterosexual couples are shopping, the guy often will uncomfortably point to the cheese and say something like, "That looks weird." Or pretend to put it in the cart as if that would be the most absurd idea ever. We always have a sample of the moldiest, nastiest cheese behind the counter just for baiting them. "I know a lot of people are afraid to try this one . . ."

It spills over into popular culture, too. I'm from the Bay Area. I've lived in San Francisco proper for nearly twenty years. I'm a Niners fan—Forty Fuckin' Niners, as we like to call 'em here. But it's rare to watch a pro football game without an announcer making some derogatory remark about Brie, quiche, or white wine. You know, something like, "We may be near the Napa Valley, but the 49ers defense isn't playing like a team that had quiche and Chardonnay for dinner last night." Chicago Bears fans in particular like to pose 49ers/Bears playoff games as a battle between red meat and Brie. Green Bay Packers fans might be "Cheeseheads," but they're not talking about anything smelly or fragile.

Sometimes I wonder if American masculinity is deeply threatened by fancy cheese somehow, and whether the laughter is a sign of that. Because maintaining sanity while working retail demands making up stories about people, I've made a sweeping generalization about American men's feelings about cheese. Here it is: They distrust a country that carried around milk in animal stomachs (I know it was the Greeks, but I'm not trying to tell the coherent history of cheese here) until it accidentally curdled, and they have even less respect for people who hide food in moldy caves. Beef, on the other hand, is not funny. If the French were real men, they would have done what "we" did: As the need for food increases, just kill some more Indians to make room for cattle.

Now, I'm not saying this is a conscious thought people carry around in their heads or anything. But I can't think of a better explanation for why people find cheese and its eaters so threatening. Fancy cheese loving is a denunciation of the genocide this nation was built upon and an indictment of American culture.

But strangely I also don't really trust people, with the exception of cheesemakers and dairy farmers, who don't find cheese a little funny. Because really, besides them, who doesn't find cheese a little funny? Self-righteous foodies and self-righteous vegans, that's who. I find *them* funny, of course. Especially the foodies who insist on their interpretation of the "correct" pronunciation of cheese names. Someone coming in for an Ahhh-saaaaa-heee-ohhhh or a Howwww-da totally pushes my ugly American buttons. Sometimes I really can't tell that they're asking for an Asiago or a Gouda. Sometimes I just pretend I can't.

I've found that repeating the slogan "If you want it pronounced right, we'll have to charge you more" tends to maintain our customer base with the type of people we like.

Golden Bear Dry Jack, Vella Cheese Company: **Vellas have been making cheese for a long time in this country. I think sometimes that the new generation of cheese people don't appreciate this cheese enough. Throughout the years in this country when large-scale, factory-made cheese became ubiquitous, Ig Vella (and before him his father, Tom) was making distinct, hand-rolled cheese every day. When I wrote that some cheese eaters need to prove themselves by eating the strongest cheeses possible—ignoring milder high-quality cheese—this is one of the cheeses that gets ignored. Made like an old-fashioned, ten-pound Monterey Jack—lots of stooping into the vats and hand-rolling curds into cheesecloth—the Dry Jack is aged into** a milky, sweet, nutty delight. The Vellas have different ages for the Dry Jack: Regular (seven months), Special Select (one to two years), and Golden Bear (two to four years). All are good, but the Golden Bear is amazing. It never seems to get too sharp or salty; instead it's like chewing on caramel shards of milk. [$$, Similar cheese: Others produce Dry Jack, including a goat's milk copy, but there is only one Golden Bear.]

Reblochon: A French Alpine cheese that is sadly not legal in the United States because it is made with raw milk and not aged sixty days. As the story goes, these little half-kilo wheels were made possible by a time-honored rural tradition—trying to avoid paying what the tax man demanded. Supposedly the farmers were taxed on their quantity of milk, so they squeezed out most of the milk for the day, and when the tax man came and assessed what the farmer owed, they went back and squeezed out a little more milk, just enough to make these awesome little buttery, nutty, amazingly meltable cheeses. Now, this story has a number of logical holes, but I never thought about it until I went to France, met a Reblochon maker, repeated this story, and got an are-you-an-idiot look as a reply. Anyway, if you see one at a store, buy it unless it smells fishy (a sign that the cheese is too old). Real Reblochon producers are making some pasteurized versions to export, but I'm sorry to say that, during a blind tasting where the actual producer had us taste the raw milk and the pasteurized versions side by side, all eight cheese professionals in attendance guessed which was the raw milk one, and all preferred it. [$$, Similar cheese: Pasteurized Fleur des Alpes (France); raw milk Fromage de Savoie (France), which is made slightly larger so that it can be legally imported.]

seven

Rennet, What's in It?

A coworker of mine once had a punk band you never heard of. They sang a song called "Rennet," and when I started working in cheese, she sang it all the time: "Horses' hooves? Baby shoes? Pickled pigs' feet? People you meet? Rennet, what's in it?"

Man, I wish they had recorded that song.

Rennet is a coagulant. The reason Little Miss Muffet was eating curds and whey was because something had turned her milk mostly solid. Whey is mostly water, albeit high-lactose and high-protein water. Curds take most of the fat and casein (milk protein as opposed to whey protein). Most cheeses are made from curds. They are also squeaky and, if salted, very tasty.

Paul Kindstedt of the Vermont Cheese Council, one of this country's experts on cheesemaking, calls this the "selective concentration" of milk in his 2005 book, *American Farmstead Cheese*. Basically, the solids—the ingredients that make for good cheese, especially good aged cheese—are concentrated, while the nonsolids drain away. People often make cheese out of the whey, especially ricottas and ricotta salatas, but usually it's used for animal feed or human vitamin supplements.

Since I work at a mostly vegetarian store, I know that rennet is also one of cheese's most controversial ingredients. Traditionally, it is an enzyme taken from the lining of a calf's stomach, though any baby ruminant will do. Since there are no veterinary hospitals with calf recovery rooms and nurses serving trays of clover, the animals from whom stomach lining is taken are killed in the process. This is not the prettiest part of the cheese business. In fact, I once saw a cheese industry professional, who was in no way an environmentalist or liberal, almost break down while describing one of his first jobs: throwing frozen calf stomachs into an industrial grinder at a rennet factory.

There are non-animal options for rennet, which is why you may see some cheese labeled *suitable for vegetarians* or *rennetless*. While certain non-animal-produced enzymes are derived from fungus, some from mold, and some (mostly Spanish and Portuguese cheeses from the Iberian Peninsula) from milk thistle, most are genetically modified. This is done by taking the renin-producing gene out of the mammal's DNA string, placing it in a lab environment where it can produce chymosin (the enzyme that breaks down milk protein), and then harvesting the result. There is much debate regarding this process among cheesemakers, but generally speaking, the more aged a cheese is, the more reluctant a cheesemaker is to use a non-animal rennet. Some fresh cheeses, like cottage cheese, quark, some ricottas, and mozzarella, use vinegar or lactic acid to aid the coagulation process.

While I oppose genetically engineered crops and rBGH, I can see the value of the lab-created rennet. It doesn't grow in the wild, so there is less possibility for cross-contamination than there is with genetically engineered crops. Theoretically, this process prevents the deaths of baby ruminants. Also, the ratio of rennet to milk, while it varies somewhat, is about an eyedropper to a fifty-gallon vat, and most of the rennet is eventually drained out with the whey. Currently, most cheese produced in the United States is made with vegetarian rennet, purely for cost reasons. In Continental Europe the opposite is true. In the UK it can go either way, but they have the aforementioned *suitable for vegetarians* label requirement.

Labels, for the most part, are confusing in this country. If an ingredient list says *rennet,* it is probably animal-derived, but there's no guarantee. Some European companies, for example, might say *rennet* to hide the fact that they are using the cheaper non-animal rennets. Many vegetarians believe *enzymes* means "no animal," but that is not the case. Rennet is, after all, an enzyme in the lining of a ruminant's stomach. *Vegetable* or *microbial rennet* does mean vegetarian, and *vegetable* does not mean it isn't genetically modified. *Kosher* almost always means non-animal, but, theoretically at least, this isn't always true. (While all commercial kosher cheesemakers I know of use microbial rennet, I have read that animal rennet from the stomachs of kosher animals slaughtered according to the laws of kashrut would be permitted.) *Rennetless* means vegetarian, and it is the hippie way of saying it, but semantically one could argue about whether a non-animal rennet is a rennet or a coagulant.

There is also a lot of debate as to whether the type of rennet used affects the taste of a given cheese. The answer is yes, it can, but rennet is only one of many interdependent ingredients in cheesemaking. Much like the way people have eaten Gruyère or Parmigiano Reggiano for years without knowing that it's made from raw milk, it's likely that you've never had a Monterey Jack or mild Cheddar made with animal rennet.

Cheesemakers will occasionally change rennets. The most notable recent cheese to do this was the Colston Bassett Stilton available from Neal's Yard Dairy in the UK, but that is often as much an issue of texture and process as one of taste.

I should also note that while US organic cheesemakers almost never use animal rennets, my discussions with European organic producers have been almost entirely opposite. To them, using a vegetarian rennet, and especially a genetically engineered rennet, is unthinkable and against tradition.

It's no surprise there is much confusion, debate, and discussion around the issue of rennet. Rennet polarizes. It's an agent of change. Once used, you cannot go back. It's as final an action as first developing your taste for real beer or fine cheese; you find you can't go back to Budweiser or Velveeta without noticing the change in yourself.

I might bemoan the power that the new trendy cheese has, but the fact is I am now a part of the trend. It has provided a niche for this snarky punk rock cheesemonger.

I don't quite think of myself as a revolutionary enzyme in the lining of the bloated stomach of US imperialism, but I do see the work I do as part of being an agent of change. In my punk rock days I was more of a polarizing force. The Reagan years were no time for a teen to be middle of the road. I may not have caused the intended selective concentration of political forces in those years, but I was affected during my involvement just the same.

I got arrested for the first time at a Rock Against Reagan concert outside the Democratic Convention in San Francisco in 1984. I went there to listen to punk rock and to have my body counted as one of those culturally opposed to the Reagan 1980s, but I didn't count on going to jail for spontaneously marching in to protest how the corporations, and the political parties they controlled, were leading us into World War III and turning this country and world toward greed-driven, environmentally destructive, and dangerous behavior.

I'm long over the shock of my arrest, at age sixteen, for exercising the rights one is supposedly granted as a citizen in this country. But at the time the arrest changed me, hardened certain ideas even as others drained away. I began losing interest in team sports and starting attending more punk rock shows and hanging out with political activists. A couple of years later, I chose to go to a college primarily because it was having such huge anti-apartheid demonstrations.

The political punk scene helped spawn a new anarchist community, which in turn helped connect and train a generation of activists. Whether or not those people, myself included, continue to identify themselves as punk or anarchist, you can find us in just about every political movement active today. Reagan's cultural revolution, while causing massive, lasting damage, has also spawned a smaller cultural revolution of people committed to working against it.

Because of the isolation we felt while going against the grain of the Reagan Revolution, we had a self-importance and disdain for "regular people" that is embarrassing in retrospect. Some of it was necessary for survival and some of it was a bunch of teenagers being assholes. In part, we were giving in to the delusional or self-important idea that we were sacrificing ourselves, entering dangerous territory to help encourage other people to resist the right-wing culture war. Some of us, maybe even most of us, saw ourselves as the polarizing agents that society needed. *Delusional* may be too harsh a description of our state of mind, because while we didn't achieve many of our goals, not all of us made it out of those days alive.

Many of us had read radical histories of the Civil Rights Movement, and other people's movements, but we were faced with the fact that "The People" in 1985 seemed more interested in moving in the opposite direction, toward a Reagan Revolution we needed to show didn't speak for everyone.

We knew that one of the elements that made Dr. Martin Luther King's goals more palatable was the specter of Malcolm X. We understood that the Vietnam antiwar movement hadn't been successful until underground revolutionaries were bombing sites back home and soldiers were deserting en masse (and/or fragging their officers). Some of us self-righteously, and often naively, compared ourselves to what we perceived as the most revolutionary groups. While we had little right to this comparison, I think a lot of us had the good sense to believe it in a someday-we-hope-to-live-up-to-this kind of way.

Youthful and full of self-aggrandizement, many of us new to political action took to it as if it were necessary to our survival. We felt it was up to us to be the radicals. We worked with the scale we had and tried to make the most of our actions, to be the eyedropper full of change in the fifty-gallon vat. While we believed in our goals, a lot of us just hoped to make any kind of opposition possible, even if we ended up drained off like the whey dumped into the pig feed of history. I don't go to every demonstration anymore, and I am not up for street-fighting fantasies, but those years changed me forever.

Becoming the eyedropper landed me in trouble with the law in 1987. Reagan was still president, and South Africa still had apartheid rule. My college political friends and I had been planning a symbolic action for weeks that was supposed to coincide with a series of speakers, teach-ins, and demonstrations intended to force our university to divest itself from South Africa. As with any large institution of higher learning, certain influential members of the board of trustees of our college had substantial business interests in South Africa. One of the more outspoken was one of the Johnsons, of Johnson Wax, an unapologetic supporter of "constructive engagement," if not the apartheid regime. While most of the world wanted to isolate the racist state of South Africa, Reagan's policy, as well of that of many business leaders and college trustees throughout the country, was to keep the money flowing while occasionally gently making suggestions that would eventually make a violently racist minority government transform into an equal society uh . . . somehow. There was a set of principles—the Sullivan Principles—that these companies touted as more helpful in changing that society than disinvesting. Of course, most US companies hadn't even signed on to those principles by the mid-1980s, and most of the ones that had signed couldn't show that they were actually implementing them.

Both the art museum and the business school on campus carried the Johnson name. Also, in every bathroom in every school building there were soap dispensers that proudly displayed the Johnson Wax logo. This made the university bathrooms an obvious symbolic target for our wrath. As a crackdown on campus protest intensified and divestment got voted down over and over again, washing our hands with that soap was like a slap in the face for anti-apartheid activists.

We had it all planned. We had cases of blood-red spray paint. We obtained keys to as many campus buildings as possible. We had about fifteen teams of men and women ready to hit every bathroom soap dispenser, make the dispenser look as if it were dripping blood, and affix a sticker with the slogan: JOHNSON WAX PUTS THE SHINE ON APARTHEID. After all, we saw support for apartheid every time we wanted to pee; why shouldn't everyone?

As we gathered at our anarchist collective house to divide up the campus, someone who hadn't been involved in the planning had an idea: "Let's meet up at the Johnson Business School after we're done and spray paint there." Stupidly, the Business School Graffiti Fest, a risky plan at best, was left open-ended, an optional part of the larger plan.

Unfortunately, since none of us attended the business school, our intelligence was as faulty as our lack of planning. When my carload of people arrived, others in our group were already spray-painting. In direct contrast with the earlier well-planned and subtle action, more of us were arriving from every direction, and it looked like a siege. My carload was discussing getting out of there when a business student exited the building. Oops, the business school was open late that week for midterms. The business student heroically ran to the emergency rape phone and called the cops.

Unfortunately, the damages done by our efficient affinity group were enough for us to be charged with felonies. Even the cops were a little awed, not aware of how many others were involved. One officer said, "Wow. How many buildings did you people hit tonight?" He seemed impressed. I ended up with a felony diversion and a place in the Scared Straight program.

I am embarrassed to admit that while I didn't necessarily get scared "straight," I also didn't want to spend any more time dealing with legal hassles. I don't know how many times I got arrested in sit-ins against apartheid, but they're too numerous to count. A civil rights tactic that we talked about but didn't fully apply was to get enough people protesting a societal wrong so that the system would get overloaded and would have to change. Clearly, we hadn't overloaded the system.

While my first real moment of politicization came while getting unfairly arrested during the 1984 Democratic Convention, I had reached a point where I wanted to do more building than reacting. I was part of a community that was attempting to build counter-institutions, but we were finding that dealing with court appearances and legal support was taking up too much of our time.

The biggest personal lesson I learned during my years of activism was how to work collectively, and this lesson is what eventually led me to try to get a job at my worker-run grocery store. As a group of young activists, we had come up with a plan, made contingencies, and made decisions while looking out for one another. But when we deferred to the authority of a single person, we didn't give ourselves the chance to talk things over and hash out potential problems.

Though I had worked with unions, and had protested against apartheid, and against US intervention in Central America, putting together a collective zine with a group of anarchists and lefties taught me more skills than any other aspect of being a college radical. Collective process, when applied to writing, has the potential to kill a lot of spark and clever wordplay, but it also teaches you to make sure you're thinking about each word you're writing and helps you learn to depend on the people you are working with.

During the first Gulf War, I lived in San Francisco. I had been hanging out with the politicos more than the punks in the late 1980s, partly because the late '80s was a creative low point for punk, partly because my political work had become more important to me than the music. However, when I saw a bunch of crazy-looking people, my people, running through the city in the two-a-day protests while emblazoned with safety orange FUCK YOUR WAR! stickers, I thought, *Hey, those are my people!* Turns out they were a bunch of folks from Epicenter Zone, a new political punk rock community center and record store. I was curious. Then, when I went to the Bikini Kill/Nation of Ulysses show at the store, I was hooked.

That concert symbolized the political rededication of the punk scene. Or at least I saw it that way. Politically militant, outspokenly feminist, and queer-positive, with women and people of color involved, I felt that punk had finally caught up to my politics. This was a punk scene I could live with, and it felt like home, in both the good and the bad ways. It's not what Kindstedt was referring to when he was describing coagulation of milk,[26] but what is punk rock if not a "selective concentration" of people brought together through a complicated cultural chemical reaction? Certainly the punk scene is less of a controlled reaction than your average cheese, but even dairy scientists will tell you that some of the best cheeses were discovered by accident.

My history of working collectively to build counter-institutions while working retail to pay the rent got me my job in cheese. Before I had my cheese-epiphany moment, learning about cheese was an attempt to keep my job and do my part to ensure the success of our cooperative. If I had become a professional cheese worker through a love of food, I would have accepted certain cheese business concepts with greater ease (*terroir,* artisan, professional hierarchy, et cetera), though I doubt I would have understood the people—either the cheesemakers or my coworkers—as well.

Just saying "worker co-op" together with "San Francisco" is usually enough for people to make assumptions about the type of people I surround myself with. Blame it on the remnants of Red Scare paranoia or countercultural elitism, but those phrases conjure up images of an insular, left-wing bubble. However, working at Rainbow has brought me in contact with people I otherwise wouldn't know—more than any other previous political group I was in, no matter how much that group might stress "outreach." After all, who farms? Back-to-the-land organic hippies? Yes, definitely. Multigenerational farmers who inherited 1930s-style populism? A few are still left. Right-wingers, devoutly religious folks, and people I'd rather not discuss electoral politics with? Yup, them too.

In this way, as the outgrowth of a semi-obnoxious, yet heartfelt political activism, I came to build relationships with people whom I might otherwise consider my ideological opposites. Punk rock shows and anarchist collectives led me to find common ground with rural people whom I at one point had expected to attend our shows or demonstrations wielding ax handles.

Working in a large-scale cooperative with uncommon business values like workplace democracy, real profit-sharing, excellent health care, and no traditional top-down management has helped me to become less judgmental. I'm less about seeking selective concentration—I don't need to hang out with just political activists or punks—but hopefully I'm no less an agent of change.

I believe that counter-institutions, like our people-focused cooperative, can be the rennet dropped into our culture's political vat. I work with cheese because I love it. I work in a cooperative because I believe it's one of the best ways to start a cultural chemical reaction of change. Working in a cooperative supermarket, coordinating the symbiotic relationship between rural and urban, can serve as a bridge to the mutual respect that's needed for real political change.

Serra da Estrela: Only cheeses from the Iberian Peninsula are made in the style of this Portuguese cheese, but Serra da Estrela is the top of the line. Using milk thistle as the coagulant instead of animal rennet creates a unique cheese, and I often warn folks that Serra is not for everyone. Oozy, rich, sour, and pungent, a combination that is hard to match. It's a name-controlled raw sheep's milk cheese, one of the youngest raw milk cheeses we buy on a regular basis. It's so distinctive that I think of it as the gift for the cheese eater who has tried everything. Even many experienced cheese eaters haven't ventured into the Portuguese-style cheeses. [$$$, Similar cheese: La Serena (Spain), Azeitão (Portugal).]

Blue Stilton, Colston Bassett: Stilton is as equally classic an English cheese as Cheddar. There are only six Stilton producers—though, as I mentioned earlier in this chapter, it is a name-controlled cheese—but my favorite producer is Colston Basset. Stilton's blue-green veining, earthy, milky, and medium-strong pungency make it one of those cheeses that epitomizes the potential greatness of cheese. It makes you ask yourself, "How can milk become such an amazing food?" While there are many reasons people ask about the use of animal rennet, the Colston Bassett Stilton—at least the one exported to the United States by Neal's Yard Dairy—shows the importance of choosing the right rennet for the right cheese. As soon as Colston Bassett switched to using animal rennet, the cheese improved dramatically. It crumbled less, the texture became smoother and more moist, and it became the main Stilton we sell at our store. [$$$, Similar cheese: Stichelton (UK), Bayley Hazen Blue (US).]

eight

Salt in the Wounds

"S/M is adjusted to rout the microbial and enzymatic activities to those needed for proper ripening."[27]

I do my best to remain a professional at work, but when my coworker and I saw this particular slide go up on the screen, we giggled like schoolgirls. We were at a cheese conference, attending a lecture about the technical aspects of cheesemaking. That didn't prevent our "Sir, I believe I have been bad and need a serious routing, sir" comments, which the esteemed dairy science lecturer either didn't hear or just ignored.

S/M in this case, of course, refers to the percentage of salt in moisture.

Talking about salt can be daunting now that it has become trendy. Much like the sale of designer bottled water in the 1980s, salt seemed like one of those products that would never be sold for lots of money. But entrepreneurs have found a way to control and market salts. At our store we sell a selection of specialty salts—Himalayan pink salt, Dead Sea salt, artisanally dried salt from California—all of which claim minerals and flavors unobtainable elsewhere. But in general, salt is one of the most basic ingredients in the world and obviously versatile. It intensifies flavor, melts snow, and causes wars. Powerful stuff.

If you've ever had cheese made without salt, you'll understand why salt is an essential ingredient. Salt-less cheese is bland and rubbery, like diet cheese. We carry it because certain customers are under doctor's orders to eat no salt, and, really, I just can't say no to old folks. I imagine even salt-free cheese being the highlight of a restricted diet. While there are cheeses made without added salt, it should be noted that, since milk naturally contains salt, there is no such thing as a cheese totally free of sodium.

Salt is added near the end of the cheesemaking process, and it not only acts to make the end product saltier and tastier, but also facilitates the chemical process. Salt is used differently in different cheese types, but, depending on the type, it can help expel moisture, remove lactose, harden the outside during brining or dry salting, change the rate of ripening, prevent excess fermentation, help determine the cheese's texture, and prevent the growth of food-borne pathogens.

As with cheese's other ingredients—milk, rennet, and cultures— the way the salt affects the cheese is determined by the percentage of salt compared with the other elements (culture, protein levels in the original milk, et cetera) that go into the process, as well as temperature and curd size. Don't get me wrong, you could ruin a cheese by over- or undersalting alone, but to achieve the type of cheese you are trying for, whether it's a Brie, a Cheddar, or a feta, the ratio of salt to moisture must be perfect.

Blue cheeses and feta, for example, are highly salted in order to stimulate enzymes that lead to stronger flavor and smell. Small, soft-ripened cheeses like Camembert are salted after the cheese is formed, which draws moisture out through osmosis. This relatively low amount of salt is part of the reason that Camembert has low acidity and why the bacterial activity rises as the cheese ages, which is not the case with most other cheeses (and why the French raw milk version is banned in the United States).

Maybe it's because I live in San Francisco that when I read quotes about the ratio of salt to moisture I think about pervy sex, but there is no denying that there is a link between cheese and sex. I can't tell you the number of times I've been asked, "Which cheese is it that smells like come?"

To which I always reply, "Well, it depends on what your special friend has been eating."

Any cheese worker will tell you that the cheese counter is often a place of flirtation. I'm sure it has always been this way. The smells and lusciousness of cheese bring out lust in people. Cheese lends itself to hedonism and excess. During the Folsom Street Fair (the world's largest leather street fair, which starts a block away from our store) we usually pierce the nipples of the Spanish Tetillas and put the Sainte-Maure logs and mozzarella balls on sale. One of the local sex parties buys the cheese for their snack room from us.

As a witness to customer-to-customer cheese flirtation, I see many techniques. Some people try too hard by pretending to know more about cheese than they do. I overhear conversations all the time, particularly guys (and really, it is almost always guys) trying to impress their dates with lines I know they're making up on the spot. I leave it alone unless they start insulting our cheese. I won't let on that I'm listening, but if someone crosses the line and then asks me a question, I'll contradict everything he has said previously. "Yeah, that cheese is really popular. But I think it's really overpriced and over-rated. It's kinda one of those cheeses people buy to impress people because it has a name, ya know?" I don't want to put salt in anyone's game, but I will if provoked.

Sometimes couples manage to drag me into their drama, especially when I don't see it coming.

To me: "Is this a cow's milk cheese?"

"Yes," I reply.

To boyfriend/girlfriend: "See! I told you. You always have to know the answer don't you? Why can't you admit you don't know everything?"

There's some amount of creepiness one must involve oneself in when flirtation gets out of hand. That damn episode of *Sex and the City* in which one of the women hooks up with the cheese worker hit us like a sleeper wave, and we still haven't recovered. All of a sudden we were selling four times the amount of Explorateur as we had previously just because it was involved in a TV couple's *fromage* foreplay. I must admit it was a good choice. However, it led to a small subculture of cheese flirters hanging around our section looking for action.

The flirtation is bad enough, but sometimes customers attempt to use me as cover and credibility. One notoriously lonely customer hangs out in the cheese section making small talk as long as we let him. On occasion, I'll forget that he's a little hateful sometimes, but then he starts to make negative comments about the cheese he's sampling to show off for the other customers. It took me a while to realize the extent to which he was using me to flirt. Not flirt with me, mind you, but flirt with women at the cheese counter by pretending to be buddy-buddy with me, the cheese guy.

His motives became painfully obvious when a woman he thought was attractive was picking out cheese next to him. She tried to ask me a question, and he kept cutting her off, making cheese suggestions that had nothing to do with what she was asking for. She was searching for a mild goat cheese for sandwiches, and he kept saying, "Try the Raclette. Gordon will give you a sample." He went so far as to get a piece off the shelf and put it in her hands. I wish I had never given him my name.

I'm pretty laissez-faire about customer interaction. There's a certain community aspect to the store that lends itself to people helping one another out and making suggestions. Before I worked here, old ladies assumed that I did and would ask me for help, and I gave it to them without mentioning that I wasn't getting paid to do it. Of course, in this case, I needed to point out that Raclette is a cow's milk cheese and not as mild as what she wanted.

At this point his true plot was revealed. He kept inching closer to her and offering cheese advice while dropping my name as if we were best buddies. Her answers got sharper and curter. Customer flirting and customer harassment are sometimes difficult to distinguish, but when I am implicated in it, I'm much quicker to put a stop to it. I was just about to say something—I don't know what exactly, as it's a tricky subject fraught with potential bad feeling and embarrassment—when the woman's boyfriend showed up. Cheese-buying woman took control of the situation immediately. "Oh, there you are!" she said, and then grabbed him and started making out with him as the lonely guy stood only inches away.

He tried to play it off as if he hadn't been flirting by saying to her, "Try this Italian truffle cheese. Gordon will cut you a sample." But I could tell by his voice that his heart wasn't in it anymore. She ignored him. I thought, *This is a good example of acceptable PDA.*

The couple took their cheese and walked off arm in arm. The lonely guy stayed and asked about more cheese, obviously smarting from the whole interaction. At some point I described the characteristics of a cheese and he responded, "I wish I could find a girl like that." That must have jammed up some of my brain cells because I've tried to remember what cheese I was talking about and all I can come up with is Taleggio, which I usually describe as "rich and stinky."

But I certainly don't think he was looking for a "sharp" cheese, if you know what I mean.

There are the sweet folks, too. One guy came up to me and said, "I'm going to a dinner party with people who are real foodies. I have to bring cheese and I really want to impress a woman who will be there." He put himself in my hands, and I picked out a few for him, explaining some of their characteristics (milk type, region, type of cheese, et cetera) and sent him on his way. Incredibly, he sent me a letter the next week with a picture of his cheese plate (very nicely arranged, I must say), a picture of him and the woman he was trying to impress, and a thank-you letter explaining that everyone loved the cheese. While sending a picture from a first date was borderline creepy, overall it was a sweet gesture. A year later they told me they were getting married. See how cheese can bring people together?

Unfortunately, it can also pull people apart. One of the main selling points of cheese is the popularly conceived notion of the dairy farmer as the salt of the earth. There's something both quaint and powerful about that stereotype. The idea of the dairy farmer conjures images of hard work, passed-down knowledge, no-nonsense work ethic, and skill. And yet, ironically, artisanal cheese typically evokes images of art openings and the parties of the rich.

How is it that knowledge of peasant food enables one to have entrée into the cocktail-party set? The ability to travel to foreign lands is certainly helpful. As I mentioned before, the I've-lived-in-France-ers are their own subset of cheese customers, but admitting a knowledge of cheese, and the desire to eat adventurous varieties, puts one on a particular side of the class war.

I grew up with more privilege than most of my coworkers and went to a fancy college. Maybe that's why I was well positioned to become a cheesemonger, even if I never saw any fancy cheese growing up. My parents had simple tastes, and a block of Cheddar that hadn't been transformed into processed cheese was kind of a special occasion for us. Still, as the buyer for a more yuppie-accessible section of our store, I felt the daily need to keep cheese accessible, both monetarily and through demystification. There is a lot of push—not only for cheesemakers but also for cheese sellers—to become as snooty as the wine industry.

Class positioning can work both ways. Familiarizing oneself with the nuances of cheese, like those of wine, can make one appear to be a member of a different class. Cheese knowledge is cocktail-party knowledge is upper-class knowledge. When I was in college, it seemed the real reason many people attended was so they could learn how to appear smart at business dinners and client parties. Learning to appear knowledgeable about elite foods is one alternative to taking out all those loans.

I once saw a small farmstead cheesemaker at the annual Fancy Food Show (officially called the National Association for the Specialty Food Trade show) handing out chunks of his new washed-rind, soft-ripened, raw milk cheese. It was such small production that you had to be in the know to get a taste because he didn't have enough cheese to give to everyone. Among the suits, the pretension, and disposable displays, which cost thousands of dollars, he was standing in a T-shirt and dirty boots and offering cheese with a bleeding and bandaged hand, the result of a farm accident the previous day.

Now, we wouldn't let any of our coworkers handle food with a bloody hand, and he certainly wouldn't have worked in his own chee-semaking room like that, but I loved the dose of reality he was inject-ing into the feeding-frenzy bullshit fest that is the lingua franca of the show. Farmers are meant to be invoked but not seen.

Most of the folks at the show aren't rich. Most of us work for a living. Retailers are not only there to buy products, we are there to learn how to convey *authentic, traditional,* and *sophisticated* stories. Nobility, tradition, and suffering are talking-point concepts that evoke the idea to customers that they are purchasing a high-quality product. Tragedy (loss of land, deaths in family, intrafamily betrayal) moves units. Talk of whether a factory is unionized does not. The sales reps stay on message. The world is scoured for peasant food. Farmers are expected to be seen—on promotional materials—and not heard. It is undoubtedly comforting to some end-use consumers that there are still a few places where people know their place, even if it's only on packaging designed by a graphic artist. This kind of tourism-by-dinner offers a glimpse of the past and a nod to cultural roots, sometimes real, but often distorted by nostalgia.

It's times like these that I remember an apocryphal story told to me by a government professor back in school. Among the Spanish anarchists in the late 1800s, there was much debate about what to do about the rich people. Many anarchists believed in "propaganda by the deed" and had strong support among the Spanish working class and peasantry who were, let's just say, not very happy with the land-owners and the Spanish Catholic Church. The anarchists generally agreed that blowing up selected members of the ruling class while they ate in public restaurants was a good thing, but what about the working-class waiters and cooks?

Debate among those anarchists went back and forth for quite some

time until it was decided that those who served the food were toad-
ies of the ruling class and might be unfortunate victims—unless, of
course, they were unionized, in which case it would not be okay to
blow them up.

I can empathize with those Spanish waiters; I hope my status as a
co-op worker member would grant me a similar dispensation.

At the same time, I wonder what this business is doing to me.
Every food show brings out at least one Jack Lemmon moment from
Glengarry Glen Ross (or at least *The Simpsons* knockoff version of it):
a desperate salesman, stinking of booze and failure, trying to sell me
something.

One year my coworkers and I were walking to an appointment
with an Italian cheese importer at the Fancy Food Show. We were
attempting to navigate the fluorescent-lit gauntlet of booths. While
we found some amazing food, as a whole the show was too much:
the trade-show equivalent of doing LSD in Las Vegas. One booth at a
time I can handle, but if I let myself take in the big picture it threat-
ens to overwhelm me.

The show is a weird mix. It's "fancy," but not really. Marketing
terminology and business-speak are the coins of the realm. It's about
moving units and selling product. It's about vendors reading your
name badge before saying hello to make sure you're worth talking to.

And that's okay. It's a trade show after all, and I don't expect to find
utopia at convention centers. But since it's mostly for high-end products, many of the booths are meant to attract us by hinting at how we
can get that money; they do not focus on the products themselves.
An uncomfortable tension arises between how they want us to sell
things as retailers and how they sell those products to us. The booth
staff feed us crafted lines we are supposed to use on our customers:
*This is the finest handmade [insert product name here]. We've saved
a rare breed of Himalayan Mountain artisans whom we keep in small
temperature-controlled pens to retain the traditional integrity of the
product.* And then get down to real business: *You can mark this up
300 percent and still sell the shit out of it. If you commit to case stacking*

we'll set up an EDLP,[28] *otherwise we can set up a 10 percent off-invoice deal. Call me!*

Obviously, there's a wide mix of products, and it's not all hype. But the overall experience of the show? It's like fancy gold frilly contact paper on plastic trays. It's less a 2010 BMW than new-car smell in an aerosol can.

As we were navigating to the Italian section of the show, that year's Jack Lemmon moment found us. Were they lying in wait? Usually I wear my badge backward and dress punk so I can make my appointments and pass by random vendors. Unfortunately, my badge was visible, and when they saw it they jumped directly in my path: a man and a woman, dressed in sales rep garb.

"Hey, we've been trying to find someone from your store," the man said. Despite what I've written above, I always try to be friendly to people who approach me, even if I'm protecting my time. "Do you wanna try our blue cheese dip?"

I figured they were going to lead me to a table or send me a sample. No. The woman began digging through her backpack, and came out with a melty, plastic-wrapped piece of something. Any child would have rejected it at lunchtime, that's for sure.

I was taken aback. "Is it clean?" I asked this because that's always my first question and the standard way to phrase it in the health food industry. The question is asking, are there any preservatives, genetically engineered ingredients, and so on.

"Of course! What do you mean?" The woman looked like I'd shat in her free, corporate-logoed, conference tote bag. She'd obviously never heard that question before, which suggested that they were not concerned with those issues, meaning that I probably wouldn't be able to carry their product. Professional language can be elitist but can also work as a good shorthand for knowing where people are trying to position themselves and to whom they are used to selling.

I looked at the offering of sad, drippy Roquefort on a toothpick she was pushing in my face. "How long has this been out of refrigeration?" I asked.

"About six hours" came the reply.

I was a little flustered from the three-day constant schmooze endemic to trade shows. I found myself accepting what she had put in my hand. What the hell was I thinking?

I looked at the sample I held between my fingers and wondered whether I was really going to eat it. The moment reminded me of a time long ago, outside US borders, when I was drunk at an anarchist political conference. The day's panels were finished, and we had a social meeting of affinity groups and were partying and getting to know one another better. A new friend offered me a hit of acid, and before I had time to evaluate the situation, I put it in my mouth and chased it with some beer. I spent all night wandering this strange city's streets until the rips in my tight punk rock jeans cut into my skin and I was bleeding from my inner thighs. It was a furtive wander, not a mind-expanding one, because I had to spend the whole time trying to avoid the cops, who were looking for Americans to deport for anarchist-related immigration fraud. Since I was staying on the roof of a squat, by the time the acid had left my system, everyone else was waking up. I couldn't find a place to clean my wounds. The day was sunny and bright, and I would get no sleep at all.

I decided then and there that I would never again put something in my mouth without thinking it through. Would I eat this sample?

My biggest disadvantage in the food business is that I have a rather weak stomach. I get sick from food easily. Usually not cheese, because it doesn't often make anyone sick, although there were a few expired fresh mozzarellas early in my career I'd rather not think about. This nasty little cheese spread, this looking-like-it-was-made-in-someone's-home-kitchen-over-a-dirty-sink drippy morsel of death, this waste of a Roquefort's life, was not a food I was willing to risk getting sick over.

Instead I had an idea. I would communicate in a language they would understand. My cell phone hadn't rung but I pulled it out of my pocket. I showed it to them and said, "I have to take this. Call me next week." Then I walked away, looking for a trash can.

Oh, the cheese might not be hardened, but sometimes I am.

Explorateur: This is a brand name of a French triple-cream Brie. Invented in the 1950s, Explorateur has one of the best logos in the cheese business—a rocket ship streaking out of the cheese case and into your heart. Seventy-five percent butterfat makes it luscious, because fat is sexy. The fashion and diet industries may try to convince you otherwise, but anyone looking for a sexy date cheese knows you have to include a triple cream on the plate. Rich, creamy, mushroomy, buttery, with the texture of silk, this is the perfect cheese to get you laid. [$$, Similar cheese: Brillat-Savarin (France), Delice de Argental (France), Mt. Tam (US), Hudson Valley Camembert (US).]

Sainte-Maure de Touraine: I could choose a lot of good ripened French, Loire Valley, goat cheeses, but since this is the chapter that mentions cheese and sex, it seems only fair to mention the most phallic of them all. San Francisco is the kind of city where we can get away with marketing it that way; they used to be a staple of our Leather Week display. These days it is hard to find one (made with raw milk), and the difference between this AOC cheese and other "Sainte-Maure" is noticeable. The real thing is ashed, delicate, tangy, and just a touch fermented, like tropical fruit. It also has a straw running from one end to the other so that the cheese ripens evenly—think shish kebab. [$$$, Similar cheese: High-quality French ripened goat cheese like Chevrot, Valencay, Selles-sur-Cher, Pouligny-Saint-Pierre—but watch out for similarly named imitations.]

nine

Mold, Secondary Cultures, and Cheese with Stuff in It

Mold is a great divider among cheese eaters. Blue cheese is the gate-keeper of cheese love. The people who've embraced blue cheese stand on one side of the divide, sure of their superior knowledge. Though the cheese may hurt them on occasion, it also helps them appreciate the sweet creaminess they taste most of the time. A little bitterness . . . well, that's just the way those cheeses are. On the other side, the non-mold-eaters are often half scared, half grossed out by the thought of it. Why would you introduce something into your food that will just make it rot and taste stronger?

"Can I eat the rind?" may be the most common question over the cheese counter. Like many of the questions we get, people are often embarrassed to ask, behaving as if they should have knowledge of all cheesy things before they even step into the store. I hate what the cheese snobs have done to people's self-confidence, their ability to believe their own taste buds.

The fact is, I don't care whether you eat a rind or not. I DON'T CARE. Really. No judgment either way. I am neutral. I am Switzerland. Actually, I'm in the French Alps. I am a Beaufort Alpage, standing above the fray.

I have a rule about eating: Try it if you feel like it, eat it if you want.

People are afraid of looking foolish if they eat the rind or unsophisticated if they leave it behind. I am here to tell you there's no right or wrong way. The rinds of soft-ripened and washed-rind cheeses will generally add a bitter and pungent flavor, but sometimes not. Sometimes they are chewy like a crust of bread. Sometimes cheese needs that extra bit of flavor to punch it up. Sometimes the cheese is strong enough already; sometimes I'm just in the mood for a stronger or milder cheese. Think of the rind as the flavor packet in your ramen: Mix in to taste.

Different kinds of mold are used for different kinds of cheese. Blue cheeses have some form of *Penicillium roqueforti*. Many of the great American blue-makers have family origin stories of touring the caves of Roquefort, France, and illicitly scraping mold off the walls to bring back to the United States. Like any story passed down for generations, I don't necessarily take these tales at face value. "Grandpappy, tell me again how you stole mold from the French people!" Theft is unnecessary now because, like cultures, you can buy a pure form of any mold needed to get yourself started in the cheese business.

It wasn't always like that, of course, which is why many U.S. blue-makers had to start off with a trip to the caves of France and a bit of thievery. Whether it's the cheese cultures or mold, the ambient environment of early cheesemaking is not, historically speaking, something that would make a health inspector happy. Indeed, cheese would not have been possible if there were health inspectors worrying about the safety of using an animal stomach for milk transport or dirty caves to store unwrapped food products.

The best-known tale of the value of natural bacteria is the story of Liederkranz. Liederkranz, a now dead cheese, was one of the true American originals. Made in upstate New York, it was in the same family as Limburger: stinky, ugly, and strong. Demand, especially among German immigrant communities, was so great that in 1926 the cheesemaker moved his entire operation to Van Wert, Ohio, where he could have a much bigger factory and larger supply of milk. Unfortunately, as the story goes, the first batch had none of the characteristic flavor of Liederkranz. So they dismantled the old factory and, depending on which version you hear, either brought all the microorganism-loving wooden tools and shelves from New York to Ohio or simply scraped the walls for their years of built-up bacteria and then spread it on the walls of the new factory. Either way, Liederkranz started tasting like Liederkranz again, until it was sacrificed forever in the name of processed cheese and an outbreak of listeria.

What makes a cheese get that stinky and nasty and still taste good? In this case it's the *Brevibacterium linens* (commonly called *B. linens*). This is not a mold, but a bacterium that de-acidifies cheese, smells like ammonia, and turns the tops of cheeses reddish in color. You see it on various tommes, Gruyère, and washed-rind cheeses. You also find it in Schloss, a cheese made by the Marin French Cheese Company, an incredibly underrated cheese that is the closest living relative to Liederkranz, best eaten right at the "expiration date."

B. linens are a crucial part of the aging process for many cheeses. Both mold and *B. linens* are "secondary cultures"—that is, they do the bulk of their work after the cheese is already formed into shape. They are the cultures that are working as the cheese ripens.

Bloomy-rind (such as Brie, Camembert) and washed-rind (Epoisses, Taleggio) cheeses are basically the same thing, which is why they are often viewed in the same category by consumers, even though Brie is moldy and Epoisses is orange and sticky. Paul Kindstedt tells their origin stories much better than I can,[29] and with a lot more attention to the chemistry, but their beginnings are a fascinating tale of how economics, climate, and happy accidents have created the classes of cheese we eat centuries later. Historically, and by that I mean in fourteenth-century France, the acidity level in the milk controlled whether the white mold or reddish bacteria smear would predominate in the finished product, because the acidity determined which would have a better environment to flourish. The French peasants who could only afford a cow or two had to combine their morning and evening milkings before making cheese. Of course, holding on to their milk, especially in those pre-refrigeration days, meant there was a lot of bacterial activity, which led to higher acidity levels by the time cheese was made. This favored the white bloomy mold. Among the Benedictine monks, who were a powerful cheesemaking force throughout Europe at the time, herds were much larger, enabling cheese to be made much sooner after milking. This less acidic cheese favored the growth of natural *B. linens* on the outside of the cheese, giving us red, gooey rinds.

Thus, in cheese that originally was made in identical ways, the consequence of how quickly milk went from cow to vat created the difference between (white, bloomy-rind) Brie de Meaux and (sticky, washed-rind) French Münster. Nowadays, of course, this is a choice rather than a happy accident, and these cheeses are created more consistently by treating the rinds of young cheeses depending on which style a cheesemaker is trying to achieve.

So if the red, gooey rinds come from bacteria, specifically *B. linens,* where do the white bloomy rinds come from? When the conditions are right a mold such as *Penicillium camemberti,* or its more common variant, *Penicillium candidum,* creates that fluffy, damp white surface we see on cheeses like Brie. The fluffier and whiter, generally speaking, that your Brie is, the more likely it's factory-made. It was well over a decade ago now, but the first time I saw a real Brie de Meaux, I thought it was bad. Instead of being pristine and generic it looked like it had been forgotten on the floor of the cooler. The shape wasn't exactly a circle; there were yellow and brown molds, and red pustules looking like they wanted to burst. But one taste—and I don't mind admitting I cut off the rind that time—and I realized why Brie had a reputation, that it could have pungency, earthiness, and deep, complex flavors along with being rich and creamy. It didn't have to be, at best, butter with a rind.

People often want to know why some of the classic Swiss cheeses have holes. Indeed, it is cheese's most recognizable symbol: the holey Swiss. That's the work of another secondary culture. It's called *Propionibacterium freudenreichii* ssp. *shermanii,* and I have no idea how to pronounce that. I don't think I've ever heard it said aloud. People usually just say, "You know, that bacteria in Swiss cheese that ferments lactic acid and makes CO_2. It's what makes the eyes!"

There are other secondary bacteria, used to add flavor, control acidity, or create an environment that allows other bacteria to flourish, but if you're making cheese, this is not the book you should be using as a guide, so I'm going to move on to the most visible secondary culture: *Penicillium roqueforti*.

Traditionally, blue cheese was "wild-ripened," that is, pierced and allowed to pick up the mold growing in the cave or aging room. This is why the caves of Roquefort were the target of subterfuge and theft by so many Americans (and cheesemakers of other nationalities, too, no doubt). By far, most blue cheeses use a mold based on the properties on those bacteria-filled cave walls of France. A common misunderstanding with blues is that mold is injected into the cheese. People see holes, and assume that's how the mold got there. Instead, the mold is added during the cheesemaking process and only starts growing when the cheeses are pierced and air is allowed in, letting the mold breathe and propagate.

Caves have historically been very important to the development of cheese, but, unfortunately, it sometimes seems as if everyone in the cheese business has a "cave" these days. Don't get me wrong; there are still a lot of cheeses actually aged in real caves. Roquefort, Comte, many Gruyères, to name a few. In the United States, St. Pete's Blue has been made and aged in sandstone caves in Minnesota for almost seventy-five years. In California someone even bought an old gold mine in which to age their blue cheese (which is made in Wisconsin).

What's really important about a cave? In this day and age of inoculating cheese with blue mold or secondary cultures during production, much of "cave aging" isn't about the natural, living bacteria of the cave at all, but the constant environment of nearly impossible-to-change temperature and humidity. Clearly, aspiring to cave-like conditions is a goal for many people, whether they are building an aging room, digging into the side of a hill, having many small rooms suited to the needs of different cheeses, or simply building where the sun don't shine. All of these are good things, but none is really a "cave." What's the biggest thing, besides walls full of bacteria, that caves offer over walk-in coolers? The cave does not vary much in temperature from one end to the other, and the air inside doesn't exchange with the air outside at nearly the rate that it does with a walk-in cooler.

Consumers should be skeptical of any claims of "cave-aged" or fancy and expensive retailers with their own "cheese caves." They can be doing some very good *affinage* (cheese aging), and some people are (Murray's Cheese, in New York City, is just one example) but, call me traditional, I still like to think of caves as being in hills or underground. Heck, at least somewhere out in nature.

"Cave" (or "caaaaav" as it is often pronounced by native English speakers referring to their American, urban, walk-in coolers) has become a buzzword, something individuals can use in the intercheese world competition to separate rich people from their money. I still remember the day that I went into my corner store and the owner told me he was selling to someone opening a cheese shop. He introduced us, because he knew I was a cheesemonger. Evidently I didn't measure up, because the new owner immediately started dropping names and discussing how he, who'd never actually really worked with cheese before, was going to build an aging cave and sell only perfectly ripened cheese. And yes, he pronounced it "caaaaav."

"Good luck with that," I said.

He didn't respond. He wasn't listening. As it turned out, he didn't have good luck with that.

A fair amount of learning about cheese involves embracing the desirability of mold. Much about growing up punk in the 1980s was about trying to break out of the mold we felt society was trying to put us into. To me it's funny that of my two biggest tattoos, one is based around a cheese, that ubiquitous holey yellow Swiss, and the other is a person breaking out of a mold, a cog, which was the logo of our anti-authoritarian political zine in the '80s.

In cheese I found an unexpected niche. To be more precise, I found that niche in working with cheese at my co-op. At cheese conferences, unless people own their own stores, most of the retailers change from year to year as do, to a lesser extent, the distributors and sales reps. Being well into my second decade in this job was enough for a cheese acquaintance who works in a different city to come up to me at a conference and say, "So what do you do this for? Most people here seem to move from job to job but you've been at Rainbow forever. It must be a good place to work."

I explained that it was. That I walk to work, that I get paid fairly, share in the profits, have the best medical benefits in the city, work with people I like, and don't have to suck up to a boss. But I wonder sometimes if I would have stayed doing the *same job* at the co-op this long if it wasn't for the cheese.

When people say cheese is a "living food," they mean that it continues to evolve as it ages, that the chemical reactions of the secondary cultures are ongoing, and that not only will cheese taste different from one week to the next, but that some batches won't taste the same as others. Cheese can be affected by many influences over the course of its travels from birth to someone's stomach.

Working at a cooperative is like that, too. It's a living experiment and business model. I give the orientation for new workers on the history of the store and the way it is structured. My notes are filled with scrawls and slashes because, in the decade I've been giving the orientation, many of the policies and procedures have changed dramatically. Partly those changes are the growing pains of a business doubling in size; partly it's because we, as worker-owners, have the ability to change policy by a majority vote at our monthly membership meetings. This power is not symbolic; it's commonly exercised.

With cheese there are good molds and bad molds, but I wouldn't go that far with jobs. Having to fit a mold is bad. I know there aren't many jobs like mine, which combines autonomy, security, community, and a flexible, living structure with tasks that are, like aging cheese, a little different every day.

One odd coincidence between the cheese world and the punk world is that one of the ways of breaking out of a mold is having a silly nickname. I never had a nickname until I started working in cheese. The Brits, Scots, and Canadians have a hard time believing this, but I never met another Gordon until I was well into my adult life. Who needs a punk nickname when your real name is unusual?

Nope, I got my nickname when I started working at Rainbow. One day, back in the much-slower-paced old store, I was leisurely pricing some not-very-good blue that we don't carry anymore. Something was off. I looked more closely at the sticker. DOMESTIC GORDONZOLA, $5.99/LB.

It was done on purpose, a little practical joke, but it stuck right away. In fact, when Jen Angel, editor of *Clamor* magazine and many other independent media projects, interviewed me for the "100 Ways to Be Punk" series in her old zine, she assumed it was either my real last name or that I had a fascination with the Emile Zola novel *Germinal*. My cheese and punk worlds had not yet collided, though; it would take a few more years for that. I am proud of all of my coworkers' cheese nicknames. No other store can top Anarqueso, Dairryeire, and Sweet Cheezus.

Cheese people definitely try, though. Maybe it's because there is no recognized super-expert of cheese in the United States, no household name, but having a cheese nickname is very common, at least among the people who sell, not make, cheese. Off the top of my head I can think of the Cheese Dude, the Cheese Chick, Madame Fromage, the Cheese Snob, the Cheese Diva, the Cheese Lady, and the Cheese Mistress. It's self-branding, to be sure, and I suppose part of it stems from the lack of real professional certification for our profession. We end up creating our own titles. I can't think of any business outside of professional wrestling where so many people feel the need for cutesy names. Myself included.

It's incredibly common for people to yell. "Hey Cheese Guy!" at me in public. I know it's not just me. At cheese conferences, talking to other cheesemongers, it's taken as a given. I don't know if the popularity of self-given cheese nicknames is related, but people seem to love to have a cute name to call their favorite cheese workers.

Maybe it's as simple as people wanting to make something unfamiliar and seemingly complicated appear friendly and welcoming. Maybe it should be welcomed as the American embracing of a formerly foreign-tinged food. After all, no one needs a Cheese Dude to educate them about a loaf mozzarella or a Cheese Diva to sell them a commodity Monterey Jack. (Although the Cheese Diva actually does sell me commodity Jack among other, more interesting things.)

Still, it's odd. Perhaps the cheese nickname fad will die out as American cheese selling comes of age. I imagine that has to be embarrassing, introducing yourself using one of these names when you meet one of those multigenerational cheesemakers, the ones whose real last names pass as cheese royalty in our little world. Sure, on one level it's all in the name of increasing the popularity of cheese and ensuring that the cheesemakers can continue to make their livings off agriculture in a country where that's not so easy, especially as a family instead of a corporation. Until there is a recognized and independent professional certification, customers only have your word and the look of the cheeses on your shelf to know if you know anything at all. If you can't say with any kind of authority to back you up that you are a "cheesemonger" or a fromager, or whatever, you may as well make up your own title.

With that in mind, if there are any potential cheese workers reading this who would like to break into the profession with a splash, I have brainstormed the following names that are unused as far as I can tell. Be sure to do a Google search before buying stationery, however, because these are going fast: the Cheese Therapist, the Cheese Whisperer, the Cheese Marm, the Cheese Caseworker, Queso Grande, the Cheese Cop, the Cheese Cracker, the Cheese Avant Garde Performance Poet, OG Cheesy, the Cheesinator, the Cheese Molester, Mayor McCheese, the Cheese Square, the Cheese Single, and MC 40 LB Block. Your career awaits.

• • • • •

The names of the cheeses themselves are a big issue. While every handmade cheese is a little different, many cheese-producing nations make an effort to protect the identities of their most famous products. Many times, traditional methods of cheesemaking are protected by "name control designations." The French have regulated the way in which certain foods were produced since the fifteenth century. In the 1930s they set up a modern system of protecting the names of their unique products through their Appellation d'Origine Contrôlée (AOC) that, in turn, inspired the European Union, as one of its first actions, to also regulate the use of names through its Protected Designation of Origin (PDO). What these designations have in common is that the food they regulate can only be made in certain regions, under certain conditions (in some cases, certain caves), and using certain ingredients, though the designations can certainly have more emphasis on one of these factors than others. Name control designations are set up to protect the integrity of certain food names so that consumers can know they are eating the original. The regulations also help traditional producers survive by letting them be the sole producers of certain foods.

There is a certain amount of haziness over some of these name-controlled terms. No one has ever tried to claim they were making a California Roquefort, for example, but the price of Roquefort these days means that it is very doubtful that an inexpensive restaurant is using Roquefort (regulated since the fifteenth century to be made from raw sheep's milk, aged in Roquefort caves, and so forth) in their "Roquefort Dressing" instead of some cheap, crumbly US-made, pasteurized cow's milk blue.

The most common example of the name-controlled system is probably Champagne. However, it is also one of the most confusing. The use of that term for products not made in the Champagne region of France is hotly debated. Clearly not legal in France or the EU, French-owned, California-based companies stay true to the protected name, using the term *sparkling wine* for their California product made in the same way as they make their Champagne back home. However, many

US-owned California companies use *Champagne* for their products, citing an early 1900s court ruling that "Champagne could be used if it was specified that the grapes and production are Californian." Even as a not-particularly-interested-in-fancy-booze teen, I knew that "sparkling wine" was "the same thing" as Champagne. But is it?

Increasingly, the World Trade Organization, through its Council on Trade-Related Aspects of Intellectual Property Rights (TRIPS), is regulating these kinds of issues worldwide, and there are many name battles brewing if not already under way. The English threw in the towel on *Cheddar* years ago, although *West Country Farmhouse Cheddar Cheese* is protected through the EU, but the Greeks have been going through the process of claiming *feta* as their own. Rumors fly fast in the cheese world, and I remember one sales rep, who coincidentally sold Greek feta, informing me that we would have to start calling everything else we currently sold as feta, "white brined cheese."

As the financial value of having a name-controlled designation becomes more and more obvious, some cheese companies are attempting to devalue these traditional name-control designations. For example, there is an ongoing battle in France to allow Camembert de Normandie to be made with thermalized milk instead of only raw milk as it is now. I used to wonder why, if the name *Camembert* was protected, why so much cheap, tasteless, and soft-ripened cheese made outside France is allowed to be called Camembert. It's because the name *Camembert* is not protected—only *Camembert de Normandie* carries the AOC. Even cheese marked *Camembert fabriqué en Normandie* means nothing in terms of the name-controlled designation.

Name-control designations (AOC in France, DOP in Italy, DO in Spain, et cetera) generally guarantee a quality, traditional product, but, clearly, there is always pressure to "modernize" the regulations, especially when bigger companies want to get in on the, generally speaking, higher prices one can demand for a name-controlled product. The higher prices help the farmers and cheesemakers in those regions survive because they can offer something to the world's kitchens that no one else, by definition, can. The fact that there's a cheesemonger in-joke about it ("What does *AOC* stand for? Another Overpriced Cheese!") is mostly just the bitterness one develops from constantly trying to explain why some cheeses are so expensive.

Certainly some cheese, Blue de Gex for instance, which centuries ago was wild-ripened and depended on its natural habitat to supply the bacteria and secondary cultures that made it special, can still be name-controlled and not made in their original "artisanal" ways. But Blue de Gex is still a mighty fine cheese, one that I'm happy to sell.

Some name-controlled designations, though, have already lost much of their traditional meaning. The *Blue Stilton* designation does not allow raw milk versions from the Stilton regions of England to use that name even though they are actually *more* traditional than the factory-made versions since the cheese has, historically speaking, been made since before pasteurization was a concept. A cheese that is being made right now by Neal's Yard Dairy under the name *Stichelton* should, if the concept of name-control designations is to have any real traditional standing, be allowed to be called a raw milk Blue Stilton.

Neal's Yard started in the 1970s and from early on it took on the mission of selling and saving traditionally made English cheeses. As in the United States, commodity block Cheddar was in ascendance, and the traditional cheesemakers, some of whom had been family chee-semakers for a century or more, were having a rough time. Through the firm's (now) two retail stores, its aging facilities, and its domestic and international distribution network, Neal's Yard has helped create awareness and a market so that traditional British cheesemaking can survive.

Last time I was in London, I toured Neal's Yard's aging facility inside an old, bricked-up railway arch. Outside it looks like a Quonset hut, but inside the space is made up of four different small coolers (no one called them "caves") of differing temperatures and humidities, a large room filled with wooden shelves, a cutting/wrapping/shipping area, a large walk-in cooler, and an upstairs filled with offices and hundreds of thousands of dollars worth of cheese.

The highlight of this tour, since it is an aging facility, was tasting multiple ages of the same cheese. Blue Stilton, in particular, is notorious for not ripening predictably by age; younger cheeses are often ready to sell before older ones. A rough-looking outside does not necessarily mean stronger flavor inside. There's no way to tell if a Stilton is still chalky until you cut it or use a cheese tryer to take a sample. Stilton is traditionally a cheese served during the Christmas holiday, so during December our walk-in at Rainbow is filled with wheels of Stilton, sorted by our tasting, not by delivery date. Honestly, it's not an annoyance I would go through for a lesser cheese, but Stilton, especially the Neal's Yard Colston Bassett Stilton, is one of the cheese greats: big, pungent, fruity, creamy, and earthy.

At Neal's Yard we tasted five different ages, all a week apart. Tasting cheeses in the actual location where they were being aged, rather than in our cramped walk-in cooler back home, and discussing the attributes with the *affineur* (cheese ager) and other cheese professionals was a thrilling experience. Then our host told us about the Stichelton, a cheese that they had just started making themselves using a traditional Stilton recipe but using raw milk.

The Stichelton was awesome. Since it's a new cheese, and Stilton is a finicky cheese to make anyway, they were still working on their recipe and aging process. However, the wheel we sampled there had all the good qualities of the Colston Bassett Stilton, but with more intensity and, at least with these wheels, more butteriness and creaminess. It's hard to improve on one of the world's best cheeses, and you can't know the consistency of production of a new cheese for years, but this one is certainly worthy of the name *Stilton*, even if legally it is unrecognized. About ten minutes after leaving my tour I was e-mailing Debra Dickerson, Neal's Yard's American rep, and asking if she could put some on my next order, even though it wasn't technically "available" in the United States yet. Our store got the honor of being one of the few in this country to give feedback on the cheese (as the dairy experimented with different cultures and aging techniques), since it was a work in progress.

Blue Stilton is name-controlled, and only six creameries are licensed to make it. The Neal's Yard raw milk Stichelton cheese cannot be called Stilton because the PDO regulates that only pasteurized cheese can be called Stilton.

This is the kind of thing that has the potential to make name-controlled designations seem like a joke or a scam. With Stilton it's especially ironic since some Stilton makers, while claiming Stilton as "the King of Cheese," have allowed mediocre factory production, waxed-rind cheese, and that horrible White Stilton with preservative-laden dried fruit to use the name *Stilton*. You'd think that since England has only a handful of name-controlled cheeses, they would try not to dilute them. Not allowing one of the best varieties to carry the name because it is made in a *more* traditional way is ridiculous.

White Stilton in particular seems unsuited to having a name-controlled designation (albeit a different one than the Blue Stilton). Blue Stilton is a cheese that is so fabulous that many people believe it's England's only name-controlled cheese. The company, Long Clawson, that makes the White Stiltons readily available in the United States actually makes a decent Blue Stilton, my favorite of the larger production ones. If White Stilton was just marketed like any other cheese it wouldn't rile me, but it's rare that producers would make a cheese so deserving of a name-controlled designation that they feel the need to stick candied ginger and pine-nut-infused chocolate prosciutto chunks in it just to make people buy it.

I admit, that's an exaggeration. But not by much. This may be my biggest instance of cheese snobbery, but I get irrationally annoyed when people feel the need to say "Blue" Stilton. In my opinion, people should have to say "White" Stilton, and if anyone says simply "Stilton," it should be assumed they are looking for the blue. I am not annoyed at the customer. I am annoyed at a society that puts cheese designed to camouflage its own flavor on par with a classic.

Most varieties of White Stilton have either sulfured dried fruit or preservatives. That is not the sign of a good cheese. The lemon one is passable, vaguely like a lemon cheesecake, but I swear the berry one tastes like Flintstones chewable vitamins. I have been told that, as a kid, I once consumed an entire bottle of those when I couldn't find any other sweets in the house. The difference is that I didn't pretend I wanted to eat a name-controlled cheese at the time.

About a year ago at a trade show, I started in on the Brits who import the White Stiltons, loudly praising their commitment to the centuries-old traditions of English cheesemaking, the fine imperial history behind their use of mangos and ginger, their ancient family recipes for making cheese taste like multivitamins, et cetera. One of the things I love about the English people I've met is that they assume that Americans are not as sarcastic as they are. I think I actually hurt their feelings, but I felt a little twinge of previously dormant national pride at being able to beat the Brits at a game of mock-in-public.

I am not a cheese purist. There are some cheeses-with-stuff that I like. I like the Bravo Farms Sage and Chipotle Cheddars as well as the Rogue Creamery Chocolate Stout Cheddar (made with beer from the unrelated company, Rogue Brewery). The Dutch love to put stuff in their cheese, and sometimes it works out well. Certainly many soft cheeses are great mixed with herbs. Peppercorn cheeses can be really good, and truffle cheese can be really, really good. For some of these, such as Gaperon d'Auvergne, which is spiced like a salami and a favorite of vegetarians, there is actually a centuries-old tradition behind it, and you don't get the feeling that they're just throwing in whatever they find in a vat and hoping for the best.

The cheapening of the name bothers me most. If those White Stiltons had cleaner ingredients and no preservatives, I wouldn't judge them so harshly. The Bravo Sage Cheddar is clearly a commodity-style Cheddar with stuff in it. They don't add other ingredients to their serious cheese, Silver Mountain, a traditional, bandage-wrapped style Cheddar. By all means, cheesemakers should make new and "fun" cheeses; they just shouldn't share the same name as a classic.

The fact that they are name-controlled, in the same way as Roquefort or Parmigiano Reggiano is, well . . . it's just not right.

When I've railed about this over the counter, people get the wrong idea. I'm not going to begrudge anyone whatever they want to put on their cheese plate. Someone recently told me, slightly apologetically, that they had some $30-a-pound truffle cheese and—the shame—really liked it. They thought I wouldn't approve. While someone's cheese choices don't need a pure pedigree or centuries of tradition to make a tasty party, knowing the tradition of the names, the history of the region, and the steps of production can make people enjoy it more. It can make people feel like they are connecting with others across borders, time, and history. There are stories to tell with many cheeses, even commodity blocks. The key is to tell them in a way that unites rather than divides people.

Of course, not all the stuff put in cheese is benign or put there purposefully. When cheesemongers get together, the subject of things they've found in cheese will eventually come up. Hairs are the most commonly found objects, especially blond ones from Holland and dark ones from Bulgaria, but likewise I've seen little bits of metal, cheesecloth in the wrong place, petroleum-jelly-filled holes in test blocks that weren't supposed to be shipped . . . none of these things shock any of us anymore, though the cheese obviously doesn't get sold to our customers. A fingercot (a little finger condom food workers wear when they have cuts) in a baby Swiss, on the other hand, was memorable and shocking, especially since I was cutting the cheese in front of a customer when it plopped out.

Anything not alive is taken in stride. However, the first time I handled a cheese and realized it was *moving,* I jumped and squealed like a housewife spying a mouse in those old sexist cartoons. Maggots aren't very common. I've—well—not gotten used to them exactly, but every couple of years when I get a maggoty cheese, I try not to show emotion and just head straight to the compost bin at the other end of the store. *Fear Factor* and *Survivor* have made the writhing of maggots a more common thing to see, but I don't think it grosses people out any less.

Maggots eat what they are sitting on, so they tend to blend in with the cheese. A white bloomy rind means a white camouflaged maggot. There's often a split second when I wonder why the mold from the cheese seems to be moving onto my hand that is holding the cheese. When I realize that the whole crust is shifting, I bite back the bile and try to act like a professional.

I have only sold a maggoty cheese once, and our cheese department was not at fault. A customer asked for a full seven-pound wheel of Brie for a party. Unlike almost any day before or since, we were completely out of Brie aside from a few small cut pieces on our shelf. Just as I was about to send the customer away, a delivery driver showed up with a pallet of assorted cheese, including twenty cases of Brie, two per box, piled on top. I lifted off a wheel while the customer watched, weighed it out, priced it, and handed it over. Because he had already told me that he was in a hurry, I didn't show him the cheese. He was doing that tappity-tap on the cooler glass, was buying it for someone else, and clearly didn't care to inspect the cheese, so I let him go.

Within minutes I began unloading the cheese pallet onto the backstock shelves. Since the Brie was on top, I opened it first. It was moving and slightly pockmarked. The maggots had been energized by the brief warm-air vacation they had between the refrigerated truck on the loading dock and the walk-in cooler at the back of the store. It was like an aerial view of larval ice skaters on a beautiful white, snowy lake. Bite back bile. Open every box. Assess the infestation. Hold breath without realizing it. Take bad cheese to the compost dumpster. Yuck. Yuck. Yuck.

The customer called back a couple of hours later. He was enraged but, since he saw the delivery arrive and watched me having to cut the pallet wrap to get at his cheese, he was mostly angry at the distributor. If he had come in fifteen minutes later, and the pallet had already rolled past the customer area, the customer would never have believed that it wasn't our fault, even if the pallet had been sitting, still wrapped tight, out of sight in the cooler. I've never let a full wheel of cheese out of the store again without looking at it first.

When people find out I'm a cheesemonger, they often ask me what my favorite cheese is. I usually give whatever answer my whims tell me to say. I wore out my old favorite answer years ago: "If I chose one, the others would get jealous." I just can't bring myself to have an answer ready.

The biggest problem, of course, is comparing across type. Can a soft-ripened cheese really be compared with the best-aged one? Parmigiano Reggiano, Beaufort Alpage, Roquefort, and Blue Stilton all claim the title of "King of Cheese." All are righteous in their claims. The cheese world would be a sadder place without any of those choices. Obviously, the title of "favorite cheese" is entirely dependent upon what you are planning to do with it.

Surprisingly, there is a lot of debate about how to classify cheese. Cheese competitions generally have thirty categories or more, but that is usually to make judging more manageable. Traditionally, cheeses are divided in categories based on how they are made. Many sources[30] cite the categories as Soft White (fresh chèvre, cream cheese, ricotta) Bloomy Rind (Brie, Camembert), Washed Rind (Taleggio, Epoisses), Natural Rind (Ossau-Iraty, Tomme de Savoie), Pressed Uncooked (Manchego, Cheddar), Pressed Cooked (Parmigiano Reggiano, Gruyère), Blue Mold (Stilton, Roquefort, Gorgonzola), and Processed Cheese (American singles, Laughing Cow, some smoked Goudas).

There are two obvious problems here. First, many cheeses fit into more than one category. Stilton, for example, is a blue cheese with a natural rind. More important, however, is the fact that it requires people to know the cheesemaking process in order to categorize cheese. While many cheese eaters are interested in learning about cheese and how it's made, I can't even imagine asking 95 percent of our customers, "Oh hello, are you looking for a 'pressed cooked' or 'pressed uncooked' cheese today?" These classifications are great for cheese professionals, but unnecessarily pedantic for the average customer.

Juliet Harbutt, author and one of the United Kingdom's leading cheese experts, reacted to this in excellent cheesemonger fashion by creating her own classes of cheese that would be more meaningful to her customers. Harbutt places (at least 90 percent of) cheeses in these categories: Fresh (fresh chèvre, cream cheese, ricotta), Natural Rind (slightly aged goat cheese like Chabichou, Crottin de Chavignol), Soft White (Brie, Camembert), Semi-Soft (subdivided into Natural Rind— Tomme de Savoie, and Washed Rind—Epoisses), Hard (Cheddar, Parmigiano Reggiano, Gruyère, Manchego), Blue (Stilton, Roquefort, Gorgonzola), and Flavored (anything with stuff in it).[31]

I find Harbutt's classes closer to what I need on a daily basis. However, I would go even further in terms of speaking to our average customer. Again, once folks are more comfortable with cheese, the aforementioned classifications are not only useful, but also generally more descriptive. However, I would estimate that more than 50 percent of our customers ask for cheese by its function, rather than caring how it got those qualities. They want to know if it's Spreadable or Crumbly (fresh chèvre, feta, cream cheese), Meltable (mozzarella, Fontina, Gruyère), Sandwichable (Cheddar, Manchego), Stinky (Taleggio, Morbier), Good for Cheese Plates or Picnics but Not Too Strong (Brie, Humboldt Fog, Ossau-Iraty), or Good for Cheese Plates or Picnics and Strong (Epoisses, Stilton, Roquefort). Additionally, cheese eaters seem to be more interested these days in whether a cheese is raw milk, farmstead, handmade, pasture-based, rBGH-free, local, and/or organic before they ask about the cheesemaking process.

I wouldn't claim these should be the universal categories for cheese—certainly different types of stores in different locations may have their own categories—but as a first step of creating a common cheese language, categories based on function seem to me the most accessible. When the customer asks, "But why is this cheese stinky?" discussing the more traditional categories makes more sense.

Even if you are just planning on sitting down and eating it, cheese is not straightforward. The problem with all food writing is that taste is subjective. Even if I could say—and I wouldn't, really—that someone's palate is undeveloped, it's their current reality. Saying that one cheese is the best or my "favorite" is actually less true than dodging the question altogether.

Quality is less subjective. There are some problems in fetishizing artisanal modes of production, but when someone can show that good milk is used, that personal attention is given to every wheel in production and aging, and that it has been treated correctly through its distribution channel and at the retailer, I feel I can say that it would be "better" than another similar product that is missing one of those elements. But that still leaves a lot of cheese to contend for the title of "best."

There are also divisions within type. Blue Stilton, as I've mentioned in this chapter, is a great cheese. But some Stiltons are, nonsubjectively, better quality than others. For a while one producer was waxing its Stiltons before shipping them to the United States. Waxing stops the aging process of cheese, so I assume this was an attempt to increase production, and protect the cheese from large distributors and retailers sitting on their stock for too long and selling old product. The whole thing with great cheese, though, is that it is a living, changing food. Wax also holds in moisture, so these Stiltons were often moister and milder than ones I'd consider better cheeses. While some customers may have liked them better, subjectively speaking, the waxing changed the process enough that I never sampled a wheel that tasted right to me.

Professionally, one of the skills I hope I've learned—beyond knowing what to relax about and what to double-check—is to judge a cheese by what it is supposed to taste like. One of the best things about working with cheese is the happy accident. The Cowgirl Creamery's Red Hawk, for example, was an accident at first, then, through refinement and experience, ended up winning a Best of Show award at an American Cheese Society competition. There's nothing to say that one of those waxed Stiltons, through chemical reactions due to the increased heat and humidity of having a wax covering, through a fluke of aging, or through just plain mishandling, couldn't have become a one-off amazing cheese. It just couldn't have become an amazing cheese in the way that traditional Blue Stilton could.

I've bought cheese at get-this-out-of-the-warehouse-now pricing that customers still ask for years later. No matter how many times I explain that the cheese was a happy accident, a function of unstudied chemistry and secondary bacteria that just happened to work out well, they still ask for it hopefully. People love that unique cheese, the one they ate at some time when the conditions, planned or unplanned, created cheese magic.

Some of those cheeses, which I try not to sell under their usual names if their names are well known, are usually half as aged and twice the retail price. But it's the living nature of cheese, combined with the all-too-human mistakes of overbuying, mis-aging, or losing product in a warehouse, that creates the possibility of these literally once-in-a-lifetime tastes. It's a modernized, and momentary, shift on the flukes of history that resulted in almost identical recipes making cheeses as different as Brie de Meaux and Epoisses de Bourgogne. That these cheeses are now name-controlled and recognized for their unique and unmatchable flavor show that cheese is truly alive.

Rogue River Blue, Rogue Creamery: **This is absolutely my favorite American blue cheese. This seasonal Oregon cheese is made with raw milk from grazed cows, between the autumnal equinox and winter solstice, and then wrapped with pear-brandy-soaked grape leaves. This cheese is big. Boozy-sweet, rich, creamy, and assertively blue. The Rogue Creamery makes great blue cheeses in general. Originally founded by Sonoma County cheesemaker Tom Vella, the current owners, Cary Bryant and David Gremmels, still utilize his son Ig Vella's half century of cheese knowledge to help guide their operation,** making a whole line of great blue cheeses, including the first raw milk cheese to be exported to the United Kingdom. [$$$$, Similar cheese: Nothing is exactly similar, so I would suggest other great American blues like Bayley Hazen Blue, Maytag Blue, as well as the other Rogue cheeses like the Crater Lake Blue.]

Roquefort: Roquefort was France's first name-controlled cheese; that is, in such a cheese-centric culture as France, it was recognized that the name Roquefort was so special that it had to be protected from imitators. Roquefort is a strong, rich, and drippy blue developed in relative isolation in a valley with natural caves and "fleurine," crevices that allow the caves to breathe, yet not so much that the caves are sensitive to temperature changes from weather. These caves provide the perfect environment for cheese aging, and they are the reason why so many people lie to consumers about their "caves" in today's dynamic retail environment. Roquefort must be made with raw sheep's milk from the local area and aged over ninety days. [$$$, Similar cheese: Ewe's Blue (US), Bleu des Basques (France). Also, all Roquefort is good, but it is worth looking for certain producers by name. The best brands are Coulet, Berger, Carles, and Papillon.]

---

ten

None of Us Is Getting Any Younger, Especially Not the Cheese

Entering the make room of a small cheese plant, the first thing I notice is the smell: It's sour but fresh, sweet but not cloying, damp but absent of dank. It doesn't matter what kind of cheese is being made. The smell of fresh milk, fermentation, ozone, and the echo of bleach humbles me.

Aging rooms, as you would expect, are even more intense. I'd like to think the experience is different, but when I walk into an aging room, I probably feel what religious folks feel when they go to church. But aging rooms also have the controlled-environment aspect of hospitals. Instead of despair, acrid staleness, and recirculated sweat, however, aging rooms are filled with the feeling of anticipation and creation. They also have a lot more humidity. Maybe it's because I'm from the relatively dry West Coast that I always notice the humidity. There's milk in the air.

There is nothing like walking through an aging room if you love cheese. They vary in their smells, temperature, and humidity levels, but they all share the feeling that you have entered a restricted and special space. I suppose it's like a vault, but one where the money needs to be attended to every day and could become worthless if you don't treat it right. In Italy, the Parmigiano Reggiano wheels are stored in huge environment-controlled warehouses called "banks," and not just because a hundred thousand Reggianos are worth a ton of money. Because there is no way that the hundreds of small producers of real Parmesan could afford to wait two years to be paid for their work— no farmer anywhere can do that. Instead, they bring their cheese to a central location for storage. Picture eighty-pound wheels of cheese stacked to the ceiling, so high and so heavy that they need to be rotated by specially designed cheese-flipping robots. I see it in my dreams.

Probably the biggest issue relating to aged cheese is cost. People ask all the time why there are so many fresh local goat cheeses and so few aged ones. Even Mary Keehn from Cypress Grove Chevre in Arcata, California, who makes some of the best goat cheese in the country, imports aged Dutch goat cheese to sell under her company's name (after an additional aging period). Why don't more cheesemakers make aged cheese?

When you make a cheese, you get paid when you sell it. If you make a fresh chèvre, you get paid days after the milking. If you are making a hard cheese, you get paid six months, a year, two years after the milking. If anyone thinks most small farmers are doing well enough to go that long without getting paid, they haven't been paying attention to agriculture in the years since the "Green Revolution" made non-agribusiness farmers an endangered species.

Which is why, generally, when many cheesemakers start out, they produce younger cheeses: fresh chèvre, high-moisture Jack, and so on. To stay around, you have to start paying off that cheese plant you just built.

One of the best things about the growing demand in the United States for more assertive, handcrafted, distinctive cheeses is that new cheesemakers are increasingly making difficult cheeses. Estrella Family Creamery, Andante Dairy, Pholia Farm, Pug's Leap, Cowgirl Creamery, Rivers Edge, Hope Farm, and Meadow Creek, just to name a handful, are making limited amounts of amazing cheese. The difference is that they can sell it at prices high enough to survive, and they have a relatively short turnaround from milking to payment.

In fact, most of these companies have to ration out their cheese. I had to wait more than a year to be able to buy from one of these companies. Another won't sell to me until I visit their farm so that I have a chance to learn what they are all about. I don't complain about practices like these. I'm overjoyed that they are producing cheese popular enough to sustain them.

Another issue for some cheesemakers is milk availability. In many places there simply is not enough high-quality milk to go around, especially when we're talking goat milk. With less yield than a cow, goats are not a traditionally popular animal for farming in this country, and a cheesemaker can go out of business banking on a milk supply that just isn't there. The popularity of goat's milk cheese has soared in the years I've worked in cheese. In 2006 alone, goat cheese sales in US supermarkets rose 12 percent.[32] We carry a huge shelf of fresh chèvre, including cheese from six California dairies. Many people—because they believe they digest it better, or because it generally comes from smaller farms, or because they are avoiding rBGH—are looking specifically for goat cheese when they come to the store, and a lot of the Northern California dairies can sell out their entire milk supply with fresh or slightly aged (under sixty days) cheese. So why take the financial hit and the risk inherent in any new cheese, when they can't keep up with demand as it is?

The risk is not to be underestimated. Developing a new cheese means throwing away a lot of cheese. Fresh chèvre is easy and, as long as you follow certain food safety guidelines, pretty much foolproof. Aging cheese brings a lot of factors into play. There are recipes, but milk varies in composition based on what the animals eat and the time of year. How these changes will react to sitting around is not always 100 percent predictable. Sure, if you are a cheesemaker in France using a traditional recipe handed down over generations, and you're using the same aging room (or cave) with milk from the same area, you probably are going to get predictable results. On the other hand, if you are starting from scratch, there is no telling what you will get six months down the road. All you have are variables.

What's the best temperature? Humidity level? Did you use the right cultures? Enough salt? Is there mold cross-contamination from other cheese or the environment that won't show up right away? Will you get cheese mites? Will that be good or bad? Is the May batch completely different from the September batch? Will the rinds crack? How often should you flip the cheese? Will the health inspector freak out at your wooden shelves? And, after all that, how does it taste?

The consumer doesn't generally see these bad cheeses. Most of the bad cheese on the market comes from distributors or retailers holding cheese too long, not from aging room problems, which tend to be weeded out. There are some exceptions, of course. One new local dairy with a great story behind it refused to stop selling cheese that was riddled with rot and mold. Their rinds wouldn't seal right, and it resulted in some of the most unpredictable and nasty cheese I've ever seen. I bought, and returned, about three or four wheels before I just stopped carrying it altogether. I understand why they didn't want to throw it out and take the loss, but I have no idea who was buying it. Eventually, they had to hire a cheese consultant to help. The first thing that person did? Threw out three-quarters of the old inventory.

Another problem is that if someone takes a gamble on an expensive, handmade product and it isn't up to the proper standard, they aren't going to buy it again. There are too many cheese choices and too little societal push toward consuming a particular cheese.

Aging cheese also leads to a higher retail price, potentially making it a harder sell. Someone has to pay the electric bill and the wage of the cheese flipper for those months the cheese is sitting there developing. If the cheese turns out great, there's no problem. There's a market for great cheese at almost any price. There is always a market for commodity-style cheese at a cheap price. There is not, however, a very good market for mediocre cheese at a high price.

The aging rooms I've visited all have had their own feel. Vella Cheese Company was cramped and historic, sitting in outbuildings behind the cheese plant. It smelled like cocoa and oil, which are rubbed into the Dry Jack. It smelled milky and crisp. Vermont Shepherd, which I saw with only a couple dozen wheels since they sell out their stock every year, smelled woodsy from the homemade cheese-aging planks and like fresh cheese since the wheels were only a week old. Jasper Hill was spicy in the blue room and wet and almost claustrophobic in the ripened room. Redwood Hill felt refreshing, like swimming in goat milk.

Understanding the aging process and what a certain type of cheese needs is crucial. Although it happens at least once a year, it still shocks me when a new cheesemaker brings me samples that are inedible. What is even more shocking is that the cheesemaker or rep doesn't seem to know it. A certain producer of soft-ripened cheese came in once to have me test a new cheese he was making. I didn't need to put it in my mouth to know it was horrible. It was supposed to have a white, bloomy rind, but it was pockmarked with yellow. It was drippy. I hadn't gotten close to it yet, but I could smell the ammonia.

"I can't sell this," I said. "It's too old."

"No, it's perfect," he replied. It was only an eight-ounce cheese but he cut at least a one-ounce wedge and put it into his mouth. As he chewed with his mouth open, he repeated, "It's perfect. I love it like this." Surprisingly, he didn't spit any cheese out as he said this. He was practiced in that at least.

Experience counts for something, and I should have known better, but I decided to try it anyway. If nothing else just so I could describe what was wrong. Cheese hasn't killed me yet.

Awful. Bitter. Pasty. Sinus-clearing, which for cheese is saying something. I spit it out in the garbage. (That is kind of seen as an insult to a cheesemaker, by the way.) I got a glass of water, rinsed, and spit again. I broke open a bag of crackers to get the taste out of my mouth.

"If you think this is well-aged cheese, then I'm afraid I can't do business with you anymore," I said.

The opposite kind of cheesemaker is someone like Allison Hooper at the Vermont Butter and Cheese Company. On a tour of cheese plants, I spent an hour with her tasting different batches of ripened goat cheese that she hadn't yet put out to market. These cheeses were already better than most US goat cheeses I carried but had slight defects in the rind. She wasn't willing to release them until she knew they would be consistent. That's someone who knows what cheese should taste like.

Consistent means different things in different cases. For a factory-made Cheddar the cheese really should taste almost identical every time you taste one of similar age. With pooled milk and culture corrections for protein content, there should not be much variation, certainly not in texture or smell. With a small-production cheese I would expect every batch to be at least a little different, but still within a certain spectrum. For example, a crumbly cheese shouldn't be a puddle of ooze. A sharp cheese shouldn't come in so young that it's tasteless, at least not at the same price. A cheese should never have ammonia, beyond a possible initial whiff, and should never taste bitter beyond a small bite, unless it is intentionally so.

The cheese business has aged me. Cheese work is physical work. Even at a worker co-op where I can pretty much control my situation, work still hurts me. I have a herniated disk in my neck and tendinitis in my right arm from the cheese. Receiving pallets of cheese, wrapping and cutting hundreds of pounds a day, and writing funny cheese stories all have contributed to work-related injuries and pain. When I go to cheese conferences and events, the other folks I see of my generation and older all have some kind of work injury. One of my peers calls the tendinitis so many of us share "Cheesemonger's Elbow." But work is like that for many people.

The way that we are conditioned to work through pain amazes me. I know many people with physical jobs who take ibuprofen every day, despite the havoc it wreaks on their livers and the masking of pain that could lead to new injuries. I fight the urge to do the same. I was not brought up to complain about pain unless it was excruciating. Playing peewee sports taught me that ignoring physical issues and concentrating on the job was what winners do, and that people who let pain stop them were quitters and losers. Part of getting older is realizing that sometimes you need to pay attention to those aches and pains.

As they say, aging is better than the alternative. A few years back, cheese, the appreciation of other people's culture, and punk rock were tragically tied together for me. The week started well when my coworkers got a call from a Swedish freelance journalist living in Berkeley. She was trying to confirm that we carried Västerbotten cheese. She hadn't seen it since she left home and was amazed that someone in the Bay Area had heard of it. Evidently, Västerbotten is made in a town of something like eight people, all of whom work at the Västerbotten factory.

We started carrying Västerbotten because one of our favorite customers kept asking us for it. Living up to every cliché, he is a Volvo mechanic with a heavy Swedish accent. He works a block away from our store, so he hasn't weaned himself from those European shopping habits, and we see him every day. Despite his profession, he doesn't drive at all. He's actually quite a bike activist and politico. I also see him at demos cheering on the Black Bloc while drinking beer.

I brought in a wheel of Västerbotten just for the hell of it. Immediately the expat Swede community began rushing in to buy it. I even bought a bunch of wheels one weekend and we sampled it out. There were more mixed reactions than usual with this sample cheese, but I assumed there would be because it really is odd. Some loved the Västerbotten, describing it as a cross between sharp Cheddar and Havarti with an extra punch of something. Others said the taste of burnt plastic turned them off. A coworker, Anarqueso, made a sign for it that mentioned our mechanic friend and described it as "indescribable," asking for people to suggest their own adjectives. My distributor began calling me the "Västerbotten King," since they were only bringing it to the West Coast for our store.

A reporter came into the store and interviewed me, the mechanic, and a coworker who spoke fluent Swedish. That coworker had called her mother earlier in the day to ask if she had ever heard of the cheese, and her mother immediately demanded she bring some the next time she visited. The reporter also brought a photographer who took pictures of Americans eating Västerbotten and of the display, which we had made extra pretty for the event. A surprising number of other customers and workers also spoke some Swedish.

Everyone was gathered around the cheese laughing loudly, and speaking Oingie-Boingie like the Swedish chef on *The Muppet Show*. The mechanic started rousting other customers, demanding they try the cheese and saying, "It's good, no?" The cheese counter became a Swedish party spot for over an hour.

Later that week, I went to a memorial for my old friend Ron who had just died a stupid punk rock death. He was almost exactly my age and was an ironworker and punk rocker. He was a little guy but stronger than almost anyone I knew. He could do the sweetest, most thoughtful things, and he could be scary. He helped build the new parts of the San Francisco International Airport and rebuild City Hall. During the work on City Hall, a decade before his death, he fell from a scaffold and broke I don't know how many bones. He was lucky to live at all. He couldn't work, but when he was well enough, more than a year later, he made a limping tour through Europe.

He met his wife, Victoria, in Sweden and they visited her family often. Eight or nine Swedes came for the funeral, and they sang a Swedish hymn that had been sung at Victoria's grandfather's funeral. Ron had told his wife how much he liked that song at the time.

They stood up in front of a crowd filled with ironworkers and stiffly funeral-dressed old Californians. They stood close to each other for support and sang the hymn while crying. It reminded me of movies of the Old West where the new ethnic group wins the respect of the other settlers because, though they have their strange ways, suffering and respect for traditions of mourning are universal. At the funeral one singer let out an uncontrollable yelp of suffering as they finished and he made his way back to his seat. It was an unmistakable sound of pure pain, part wounded animal, part loss, part awareness of how fucked up it is for a thirty-six-year-old to die so young for no good reason.

In a ceremony that was mostly about a Ron I didn't know, that sound alone bashed me over the head with the reality he wouldn't be back. That sound by itself made me sob.

I told Victoria that I would bring some cheese and bread to her house later in the evening for a small gathering. I of course brought way too much and, when I got there, I saw that most of the uneaten buffet from the ceremony had been brought as well. No one was really eating. I put most of what I brought in the fridge so she and her relatives could eat it later. When I greeted her, her eyes were pained and unfocused. "I brought some Swedish cheese," I said for lack of anything better. She likes good food and she looked dubious and a little disappointed. Obviously, I wasn't really expecting it to make her feel better; I was just trying to be thoughtful and struggling for words. "Västerbotten?" I continued.

I wouldn't say her face lit up. There was way too much grief to be lifted by anything that night. But she did get a little animated. "Västerbotten is like our Parmigiano Reggiano," she said. "You have to tell her you brought it," pointing out a tear-soaked friend with bleached-blond hair.

I went over to where that friend was sitting and introduced myself as an old friend of Ron's. "Victoria wanted me to tell you I brought Västerbotten," I said. As if it were a party or something or the reason we were there wasn't tragic and full of pain. I immediately felt stupid. She just looked at me not knowing exactly what to say.

There's a confusing aspect to memorials and grief. They're part reunion of the living and part pure suffering. At Ron's memorial, with so many of the people I grew up with returning home to attend his funeral, there were moments when I was just happy to be with people whom I hadn't seen in years. People who were important to me even if we were no longer in each other's daily lives. But then I would remember why we were together and that sadness would come back with even fuller weight when I realized I had escaped it with a disloyal moment of laughter.

Montgomery Cheddar: Made from the milk produced on a five-hundred-year-old family farm, this is the traditional English Cheddar to which all others are compared. The Montgomery is a "farmhouse" Cheddar, which means that it is made in a large cylinder shape (unlike the US-popularized 40-pound—or even 640-pound—block), wrapped in cheesecloth and aged by someone who cares for the cheese as it ages, flipping it, cleaning the rind, rubbing in oil or fats to keep it moist, and so on. Montgomery Cheddars are big and earthy. They shard, may have visible blue veining coming from the rind, and, while not as sharp as some block Cheddars, have a much bigger, more complex flavor. Neal's Yard Dairy, the exporter of this cheese to the United States, has helped sustain the traditional English dairy farmers and cheesemakers by not only creating a market to sell their high-quality products but also building aging facilities in which cheesemakers can mature their products, freeing up money and space for other needs. [$$$, Similar cheese: Keen's Cheddar (UK), Lincolnshire Poacher (UK), Fiscalini Bandage Wrapped Cheddar (US), Flagship Reserve (US), Cabot Clothbound Cheddar, made at Jasper Hill Farm (US).]

Aged Cheddar, Widmer's Cheese Cellars: One of the common threads running through any discussion of cheese is that many producers come from a long line of cheesemakers. It's certainly no requirement, but some of the great American cheese names are third- or even fourth- generation cheese people. Joe Widmer, of Widmer's Cellars, is a great example of this. Though his family is Swiss, he makes some of the best block (as opposed to bandage-wrapped) Cheddar in the country: fairly priced, sharp, sweet, and honest. When I visited him in Theresa, Wisconsin, he and his family had just moved out of the eighty-year-old cheese plant so they would no longer be aging in the same facility as the cheese. Widmer also makes real Brick Cheese, a lightly pungent, brined, square cheese the size of—you guessed it—a brick. [$, Similar cheese: Other good, sharp, honest American Cheddars include Grafton, Cabot, and Bravo Farms, but there are many, many more.]

eleven

What Did I Buy Into?

Cheese wasn't really in the original plan. Even if someone had asked me in my first months as a cheese worker, I would have been noncommittal about my feelings for the cheese. Sure, we were seeing each other every day. But it wasn't like a committed relationship or anything.

If there was anything that made me wary when I started my relationship with fancy cheese, it was that I believed cheese was a little stuck up. There is a snob culture surrounding cheese, so getting involved felt at first as if I were dating outside my clique. Being pretentious about food does not come naturally to me. True, some of my tastes had "matured" by the time I began working at Rainbow. Even though Denny's coffee still tastes like the freedom of being a teenager at 2 a.m. after a punk show, once I started getting a regular paycheck and working at a high-quality grocery store, I began buying better quality for home consumption.

Don't get me wrong—there are still some factory products that are mighty tasty and satisfying when used correctly. There's nothing wrong with a $3-per-pound Rumiano rBGH-free Monterey Jack to bulk up melty cheese dishes without going broke. There are a few factory Bries that satisfy a craving for fat, and there are times I simply don't want to feel challenged by my food.

Though I've been a cheese buyer for over a decade, my cheese authority is still questioned at times by the cheese snobs because our store, like any store that doesn't want to cater just to the rich, has a variety of products. All grocery buyers sometimes have to choose price over quality, local over traditional, or one company over another because there is only so much room on the shelves. Also, we don't cut cheese to order but, rather, precut and wrap it to keep the prices lower and create a less intimidating environment. All these things bump up against cheese-snob culture.

While it is just one element of my work, and in many ways the least important, the attitude surrounding cheese can be so intimidating to some folks that they stay away from it or treat it with contempt. There is a part of the cheese world—not the cheesemakers—who enjoy that and want to see the world of cheese become even more status-oriented than it is. Since I had to overcome this tendency in order to become a cheese buyer and cheese lover, I've spent a lot of time thinking about these people.

Snob culture in food has three main traits: entitlement to the "best," judgment about what others eat, and competition with other foodies over who is the first to discover something "authentic" and about who has the most refined taste. Most of our customers at Rainbow don't fall into this camp, and neither do most of the professionals I deal with, but there are enough of them around that they have influence.

I grew up watching a lot of war movies on TV. No matter how lefty I am as a grown-up, those images have become default metaphors for me, more than I would like. And sometimes I do feel as if I'm holed up in an abandoned, bullet-scarred apartment as a house-by-house battle rages on in the food world. There's Snobbery and Pretension on one side and Crass Consumerism on the other. I'm huddled with a lot of other folks in cheese selling and distribution, just trying to survive the day.

I'm in the middle because retail is an inexact science. The people I'd like to surround myself with all are generally on the side of truth, education, and demystification. But they also recognize that telling the whole truth is impossible in short interactions. Declaring oneself a freedom fighter for honesty can easily end up putting you in the camp of Pretension by default, because there's a limit to how much you can do while working a retail floor. If you're not careful, or if you're extremely jaded, being "truthful" becomes just another lie or cynical marketing strategy. There are too many cheeses, too much unverified gossip, too much uncertainty about what people really want to know. Plus, the whole truth is a little subjective because taste is subjective. Once you move past cheese type, milk, location, cheesemaking process, size of operation, and taste characteristics, it gets fuzzy. And people want to know more.

There are some very fine lines between things I believe in and things that are self-deceptive. I believe in asking about farm conditions, working conditions, integrity of milk, hazard analysis in the cheese plant, and how people learned to make cheese. I love to know whether their families have been on the land for generations or whether they are guided by the desire to make a better world by improving the way food is produced.

But you can't buy a completely transparent political relationship with your food, even if you are using your dollar to support practices that are good for the planet. Does a San Francisco liberal foodie want to support family farms? Of course. Does the same person want to support a business that contributes money to the Republican presidential candidates? No. Well, sometimes they're doing both.

While I believe supporting a small farmer over a bigger one is a worthy political stance no matter who they vote for, the point is that simplifying the issues too much can lead to creating other untruths. This is why my real enemy is snob culture, which, in heralding some foods as worthy and others as affronts, sets up a number of false equations. Too often exclusivity and expense are treated as morally good, and disdain is leveled at anyone who would consume a factory-made cheese or a pasteurized copy of the real thing.

We have a variety of choices for most types of cheese. The nature of retail in a busy store is that sometimes in matching cheeses to customers, you have to start out with a guess. If someone wants "Brie," there are many choices at any given time. As I write this, in the Brie family we have three French factory-made cow's milk cheeses, a factory goat's milk cheese, and a factory sheep's milk cheese. We also have handmade ones like Brillat-Savarin, Explorateur, Fromage de Meaux, a French Camembert, a French goat Camembert, two Italian Robiolas, Vacherin du Jura, local favorites like Redwood Hill Camellia, Rouge et Noir Yellow Buck and Triple Crème, and other American choices like the MouCo ColoRouge, Sweet Grass Dairy Green Hill, and the Hudson Valley Camembert. About thirteen options in all, and then about half as many again in the soft washed-rind category.

We have to start somewhere, and guessing is part of the job for anyone working retail. But the wrong guess can lead to loss of credibility in the eyes of some people who take these things too seriously. One unseasonably warm and sunny San Francisco day, a heterosexual couple walked up to the counter. "We need a picnic Brie," the man said. It was clear from his tone that he was going to do the talking.

Now, when I hear *picnic Brie,* I think, similar to the phrase *picnic wine,* of something pleasant but not challenging. This looked to me like a date, so I further assumed nothing too stinky because no matter how stinky and sweaty people are planning on getting later in the privacy of their own homes, many daters are smell-phobic. I recommended the Fromager d'Affinois, a factory-made French soft-ripened cheese that is fatty and oozy, but also mild and inoffensive. It's a cheese with no story or pedigree; I buy it myself for large parties at my house because, like flystrips around dairy cows, the d'Affinois draws the casual cheese eater at parties away from the expensive stuff. Why? Because many people love it.

It was the wrong guess.

One of the many cheese books I own is *The Specialty Cheese Shop Manual.* Published in 1981 to encourage people to open cheese stores and increase business for Gourm-E-Co Imports, the publisher, it actually has many helpful tips. Unfortunately, it also contains some who-the-hell-wrote-this gems like, "The major customers of specialty cheese shops are the higher-educated, more affluent and better traveled members of the community—in short, the leaders."

Now, I don't attach status to cheese eaters, but some snob culture folks clearly do. The "picnic Brie" customer flinched as if I had slapped him. Moreover, it was as if I had taken the cheese out of the case, unwrapped it, pissed on it, and then tried to sell it to him. Clearly he was insulted that I offered him a factory-made cheese instead of a handmade one.

"No, I think we'll go with the Brie de Meaux," he said. He stretched out the words with disdain. Clearly I had not recognized him as a community leader. I questioned his status in front of his date no less! He grabbed the cheese and walked away.

The punch line is that while he was showing me, and his date, his sophistication level, he was actually wrong. There is no legal "Brie" de Meaux sold in this country, despite the fact that many other stores still sell it under that name. He was buying the Fromage de Meaux, a handmade version made for the US market by the same company as Brie de Meaux, but made with pasteurized milk and therefore given a different name by the company, which still finds it important to differentiate between traditional and nontraditional methods.

I didn't point this out, however. I let him walk away.

The problem with buying for snob culture is that sometimes "the best" is not available. Sometimes it's the best we can get. Sometimes the airplanes are grounded, sometimes importers misorder, sometimes Europe is on vacation because workers there have a reasonable amount of paid time off, sometimes trucks get stuck in the snow, and sometimes pallets get left on unrefrigerated loading docks. Combine that with the fact that cheese in its natural habitat has specific temperature and humidity guidelines as it ages. Most imported cheese sold in this country gets its *affinage* in the cargo hold of a boat crossing the Atlantic.

Cheese, historically speaking, was developed as a way to extend the life of milk. On a taste level I am not a purist who demands that cheese needs to be eaten only in its place of origin. Part of the original mission of cheesemaking was that, unlike milk, cheese could travel. Certainly those originators weren't picturing cargo ships and jets, but one can over-fetishize the "tradition" of local cheese. Back in the day it wasn't shipped farther because there was no infrastructure for it. We should all appreciate how well something designed before modern transport actually does when traveling so far from home.

That doesn't, however, take away from the fact that many cheeses originating in far-off lands weren't designed to be shipped thousands of miles before being eaten. Like many modern foods, new versions and factory-made copies of the old originals are designed to take abuse. That's one of the reasons most Cheddar is made in forty-pound blocks these days. It fits nicely on a pallet and is really hard to damage. What one sacrifices, of course, is flavor and uniqueness.

While we can get some pretty damn good cheese here, expectations need to be realistic. Sometimes the best product just may not sell. Because of its perishability, I have to constantly make buying decisions based on size. If we can sell a wheel a week, we can almost always carry it. But wheels vary from two pounds to two hundred pounds, and some cheese just doesn't move quickly enough.

Generally, I don't have to take the most committed cheese snobs into account when buying because they'd rather pay more at some other store, where pretension is figured into the markup. However, while most cheese is steady, trendiness has to be accounted for in any store that serves the urban foodie demographic. For example, we might have a perfectly good cheese in stock, say a ripened French goat cheese like Chevrot—flaky, tangy, fruity, and moist. A cooking show or a newspaper recipe may suggest using a cheese like Chèvre d'Or, which is a different shape but shares the same flavor and texture qualities. Often that's great because it lets all of us who work there taste new (to us) cheese, too. There are an uncountable number of cheeses in the world. One of my life goals is to taste them all.

I went to a food show recently that summed up something important in the promotional logo they were using. It was a regular shopping cart with a globe inside. That they were promising to deliver the world to anyone who could pay for it at checkout wasn't a new concept—many importers promise something along those lines—but the image of something as common as a shopping cart highlighted the belief that we, as Americans, should be entitled to anything we want, available at any time, and easily accessible to our whims.

Those of us who appreciate fine and crafted foods of course want the "real" thing. But even our wanting it can change it, turning it into a commodity instead of a regional specialty, an everyday item instead of a seasonal treat.

There have been a lot of trends in the fancy cheese world since I started buying. Some are half-understood words like *artisan* or *terroir*. Other times it's "raw" cheese, cheese from a certain region, or cheese from the milks of "pastured" mammals. There is nothing wrong with any of these ideas. Indeed, these are the things that make cheese great. But in the end it always comes down to the taste, not the concept behind the taste. Fetishizing these concepts is a disservice to one's own taste buds.

Years ago I used to make a bold statement. One highly regarded American cheese expert even agreed with me but made me swear I wouldn't tell anyone she said so. I believe that the mass-produced, no rBGH-free claim, Stella-brand, black-waxed Asiago is superior to most Italian ones.

This statement is risky. Right now, cheese people reading this book are zooming in on the previous paragraph in order to discredit this whole work. I can hear them saying, "You can't take anything in that book seriously; he said Stella Asiago is one of the greatest cheeses in the world."

I'm not saying that, of course. What I'm saying is that for the money and flavor, the black wax Stella is going to be more satisfying to more people than the usual Asiago Mezzano available in this country. Partially, it's because Asiago here is considered a sharp grating cheese and most imported ones are milder. As a retailer, sometimes you have to give the folks what they want.

I don't make that statement much anymore. Not because it isn't true, but because better Asiagos are being imported to the United States. That black wax Stella Asiago is clearly not better than the Italian Monti Trentini Asiago Vecchio, which is still a mostly traditional cheese with complex, sharp, fruity, sometimes even tropical-fruity flavor. However, often the quest for authenticity in the case of Asiago might lead you to pay more for a less interesting cheese.

There are also times that brand names become bigger than they ought to be. Romano, for example, is a type of cheese. It's made from sheep's milk, is hard like Parmesan, and is both sharper and saltier. It gets its name from Rome. These days, though, most Romano is made in Sardinia. While there are some great Sardinian cheeses, these Romanos are large-production, less subtle, and less interesting than the "true" Romanos from the region around Rome. Some are so dried out and abrasive that they would be best used as salt licks during deer-hunting season.

True Romanos are fabulous, though. They're still too intense to be table cheeses for most folks, but they amp up anything they are added to without overpowering it. Locatelli was the first import to market itself as the real thing, and it is a great cheese. However, most other Romanos from that area are just as good, even if they don't have the reputation. We carry the Fulvi Pecorino Romano Genuino, and I consider it an equal of Locatelli, but many customers dismiss it out of hand, assuming that there is Locatelli and then there is cheap crap. On a related note, I should state that despite my praise of Stella Asiago, Stella makes a "Romano" that is too young, made from cow's milk, and that I can't bring myself to call "Romano" without quotation marks. It's like a cheap American Parmesan, but even younger, and I would avoid it unless the only other option was a Kraft green shaker can.

While most of my cheesemonger work is done at our store, I also get to visit farms and meet cheesemakers. The first few times I did this I didn't know what to expect. I figured there would be urban/rural cultural differences and that I'd have to build trust, especially when

I was younger and dressed more punk rock. What I didn't expect to find was a type of bonding with the cheesemakers, similar to the other subcultures of which I've been a part.

Back in my younger days, I used to be enough of a political activist to travel around the country and stay at the houses of relative strangers for a Good Cause. I've done some punk rock travel, too, which involved harder, but not dirtier, floors and less sleep. Imagine my surprise to find out that the cheese world offers a similar travel plan. The big difference, as you might guess, is that the food is a lot better.

A cheesemaker whom I'd met a few times at conferences and trade shows offered me a bed in his house if I visited his farm. I didn't want to impose, so I replied, "That's okay. I'll just get a motel or something."

He laughed. "You haven't been to the Northeast Kingdom before, have you?"

Growing up in a populous place like the Bay Area, I didn't really comprehend how isolated some dairy farms are. Sure, theoretically I could picture it. But it wasn't until I went on a tour of dairy farms in Vermont that I really got the picture. It would have taken about a three-hour drive to find another room near that farm. I couldn't imagine a whole state with fewer people than San Francisco until I saw it for myself.

Staying with a cheesemaker is not just a convenience, though. There isn't the kind of outcasts-banded-together feel of punk travel. There isn't the righteous mission of the political activist couch surf. There is, however, a similar community feeling that goes beyond a business relationship, a feeling of doing something important, and a we're-all-in-this-together air that all these groups share. Not to mention the real community-building exercise of gossiping about shared acquaintances.

It's a big country and a big world, but meeting people at conferences every few years makes it a lot smaller. Just like other subcultures, the common connection lets you meet people with less guardedness and with some obvious topics of mutual interest. During one weeklong tour of the Northeast, I felt comfortable enough to share my fetish over old dairy equipment, strategize the remaking of the Grange as a rural social force, talk politics of small farming, and drink beer not in a bar, but in a barn full of cows.

One of the endearing things about cheesemakers is that few really have any idea that to a lot of our customers and other cheese workers, they are rock stars. Franklin Peluso, for example, is a third-generation California cheesemaker who was honored at the founding meeting of the California Artisan Cheese Guild for lifetime achievement.

Franklin is known for Teleme. It's a soft oozy cheese with the best rind in the world—a thin, chewy crust that is rubbed with rice flour. The cheese itself is mild, sour, tangy, and milky. It's one of the few cheeses that has the smell of fresh milk at the dairy. It's most similar to an Italian Crescenza, taste-wise, but you could also think of it as a Taleggio without the ugly and the stink.

I've always felt that this cheese has never gotten the recognition it deserves. One of the things about American specialty cheese fans is that they tend to want strong cheese, as if to prove they can take it. There is a cultural lack of confidence with fancy cheese, as if the harder a cheese is to eat, the better it must be. Teleme is easy: It goes with almost any fruit, any bread, any cracker. It makes an amazing fondue. When it's at its ooziest, it'll be the first thing gone from the cheese plate, guaranteed.

One of the best parts of being a cheesemonger is getting unhurried time to spend with masters of their craft. I feel privileged to have spent a day with Franklin while he made one thousand pounds of cheese. He has someone helping him flip cheese in the aging room, but basically he does it all himself. At 8 a.m. he draws the milk into the vat and at 1 p.m. he has one hundred wheels ready to age. At one point I commented on the stream of whey he was making by pulling the curds up on the sides of the vat, saying it looked like the California Aqueduct.

"Yes," he said, "It's like an aqueduct . . . the Roman aqueduct."

I love the Italian American cheesemakers for remarks like that. But I also love being able to visit anyone who leaves me in awe with how much they know about cheese. As a cheesemonger, I can know more than 99 percent of the customers I'll ever talk to. But watching cheesemakers do their thing is a humbling experience. Buying their cheese takes on a deeper meaning when I actually get to see the people working their hearts out at a sometimes risky and frustrating task, one with potentially great but not necessarily lucrative rewards. The way this society works, these creations are assigned a fixed monetary worth, but watching them being crafted makes it impossible to see them only as products I need to move.

Being an ambassador for this kind of cheese is part of what gives my job meaning. But I'm still not sure how I ended up pushing cheese for a living.

Franklin's Teleme (not Peluso's Teleme): **Franklin Peluso is the third-generation cheesemaker of this California classic. I worked an event for Franklin once and was amazed. Every Italian American coming up to the booth and a few years older than I am said almost the exact same thing, "Teleme! I grew up on this stuff!" Similar to an Italian Crescenza (or, if you can imagine, an unwashed Taleggio), this cheese is milky, sweet, and a little sour. Wannabe cheese snobs will not be impressed by this cheese because it is not strong in any way. But what it does have is integrity and presence. Amazing for cooking, great with fruit, often the first thing gone from a cheese plate. You can't pretense it up with this honest cheese, but I always have a quarter wheel in my fridge. [$$, Similar cheese: Bloomy-rind Robiola (Italy), Crescenza (Italy and US).]**

Bonne Bouche, Vermont Butter and Cheese Company: **Ripened goat cheese made in Vermont using a traditional French technique. Very similar to the French name-controlled Selles-sur-Cher, Bonne Bouche (which translates to "good mouthful") is pasteurized but incredibly flavorful, and is fast becoming** one of my favorite US-made goat cheeses. Covered in ash, the black-rind cheese can scare off a lot of customers, but the inside is mild, tangy, acidic, and fruity. Hand-ladled and aged in specially designed aging rooms, this may be the US cheese that convinces Americans that other Americans can make great French-style cheese. [$$$, Similar cheese: Raw milk Selles-sur-Cher (France), pasteurized milk Tradition Jacquin (France).]

twelve

Terroir, Trucking, and Knowing Your Place

There are many things I will never know about rural life. Hell, there are lots of things I will never know about urban life outside my own city. I wouldn't lie and tell you San Francisco isn't a bubble. And a worker-run natural foods grocery store is a bubble within a bubble. But that is much of the reality of modern urban life. *Bubble* is another name for community. Certainly other stores create their own bubbles, sometimes simply by their pricing.

Cheese has traditionally been one of those travel-the-world-without-leaving-home foods. Though undoubtedly many people with the privilege of traveling to Europe were introduced to cheese there, many others use cheese as their personal Eurail pass. Geography is my weakest cheesemonger skill, but even I know that you can learn about a place from eating its food. Food, like someone who wants to buy it, doesn't arrive at the store without a history.

Formaggio di Fossa is a cheese that the locals of Sogliano sul Rubicone, in the Emilia Romagna region of Italy, make and bury underground, which gives it a distinctive flavor that *earthy* only begins to describe. It's spicy, perfumy (not stinky), and often bitter. A sales rep told me that historically Formaggio di Fossa was buried underground because of frequent pirate raids on the village. Burying their cheese was the way that villagers could run for their lives and not lose all their food supplies. Now, it doesn't *really* matter if that story is true or not, and it certainly made my bullshit detectors go off the more I thought about it. But the story does tell me that the cheese is made by the ocean in a village that, at least historically, was remote. It tells me that, like many cheeses, the particular flavor was discovered by accident and necessity—when you're starving, you eat what's there. You might even develop a taste for it and turn it into your hometown delicacy.

Cheese can also tell you about history. Valencay is a ripened French goat cheese, covered in ash and mold in the shape of a pyramid with its top cut off. Valencay has competing origin stories, but all have to do with Napoleon being mad at his failed Egyptian campaign. Did he chop off the top in a fit of pique? Or did the cheesemaker, fearing his wrath, do it himself? Either way, it created a new cheese shape that would live for centuries. From this I learned that Napoleon was irritable and that it was probably best not to get too close to him when he was eating. Many of our customers—and remember that I work in a store founded by health food hippies in San Francisco in 1975— buy Humboldt Fog, a goat cheese made by Mary Keehn in Humboldt County, California, for the first time because they assume an implied connection to another notable crop of that region (marijuana) rather than to the fine goat's milk produced there.

The point is that food can make us imagine worlds beyond our own. It can make us want to learn more about history. It can make us want to try to understand how someone could come up with such an absurd thing and then actually put it in their mouths. It makes us realize food has a relation to the area in which it is produced.

There's a word for this concept in French. It's called *terroir*. It means having a sense of place. In its native language, *terroir* highlights the regionality of food developed over centuries, and indeed, if you're really committed to the experience you can taste, for instance, the different grasses dairy animals eat in different regions and understand why certain foods developed to accompany each other in different places. Stinky French Münster and Alsatian wine or beer pair perfectly. Why not? They grew up together over the centuries.

Over my cheese years, there have been many articles proclaiming some sort of US cheese *terroir*. But can anything be more pretentious than using that term in this country? Even more surprisingly, *"Terroir"* was the theme of the first American Cheese Society conference I attended. I'm not against using foreign words; it's just that choosing such an obscure one draws boundaries around the type of people you are catering to. And, ahem, it is the *American* Cheese Society.

What is especially wrong about the term is that the United States simply doesn't have this tradition. Certain cheeses might be more popular in certain regions, but that, most likely, has to do with the immigrants who settled there. And while that might not be unrelated to the climate and environment, it's not as if there is, historically, a thriving regionality to the cheeses people eat in the way that there is in Italy where cheese from the mountains simply isn't eaten in the lowlands.

The one obvious reason that the United States has such a bad reputation with regard to quality dairy products is that the US's biggest contribution to the world of dairy is American cheese. Those little orange squares are ubiquitous. Except for maybe a cartoony piece of Swiss being munched on by a cartoony little rat, those squares are the representative face of cheese in this country.

You make American Cheese—a type of pasteurized process cheese— by heating, mixing, and emulsifying cheese, usually a Cheddar variety or curds, "into a homogeneous plastic mass."[33] Mmmmmmmm. On its best days, the Food and Drug Administration has a way of describing the romance out of food, but in this case it's very fitting. Pasteurized process cheese food, a cheese product even further removed from traditional cheese, can contain even less actual cheese by weight and more filler ingredients than regular processed cheese.[34]

American Cheese is what I grew up on so it's not like I'm above it, even if I don't really eat it anymore. But the United States once had many varieties of traditionally made cheeses. Immigrants from cheesemaking countries, at least the ones who settled in rural areas, brought their cheesemaking skills with them. The Swiss, the Italians, the Germans, the French, and others all made the traditional cheese of their people, and many tried to find areas of the US that were similar to their homelands agriculturally. The cheeses were produced on a local level, but cheese factories started appearing in the US by the 1850s, especially on the East Coast and in the Midwest, particularly in Wisconsin. Wisconsin still produces the most cheese in the nation, even though the state is no longer number one in fluid milk production.

For good or ill, many "advancements" in technology are found in times of war, and this is true of cheese production, too. James Kraft, according to my 1954 booklet by the Educational Department at Kraft Foods, supplied millions of pounds of pasteurized process cheese in tins to soldiers in World War I before distributing it nationally in the 1920s. Unspoilable cheese is a functional food. If one's top priority is trying to extend the food supply as long and far as possible, it makes a lot of sense. Like housing in the old communist bloc, the cheese might not have been the best, but it served an important purpose.

Clearly the cheese that people are interested in talking about when they come visit our store is not the feed-the-masses type. Today's food enthusiast is looking for "artisanal" cheese. Cheese that is interesting is more difficult to make, more difficult to predict the outcome of, more controversial in taste, and more expensive.

While one can mourn the lack of character in American Cheese, or its slightly more respectable cousin, the forty-pound block of commodity Cheddar or Jack, mocking it is part of the elitist foodie culture that led me to reject my role in the food world for so long. There's a fine line between pointing out why American Cheese betrays the art of cheesemaking historically and saying, "Let them eat cake."

I'm torn by this. It is a foodie truism to sell or buy a product because of its "story." How many generations of farming tradition does the product have? Are there anecdotes with historical figures? Do I have a personal relationship with the producers? Is this food born out of a retailable tragedy?

It's the truth, too. Telling tales works. Anyone with a perceptive nature can see which of these buttons to push in order to move product. There's a fuzzy line in a retail setting between explaining and manipulating. I'm sure there are times that I've crossed it. But the whole food movement that came out of the 1960s and has its home in the San Francisco Bay Area has made it so that some people expect a story with their every meal.

There's nothing wrong with that, in theory. The lives of farmers *should* be talked about. In urban areas, food not bought at farmer's markets comes to the consumer invisibly. Learning about where our food comes from and the struggle to produce it can be political. The act of buying certain foods can be a small act of solidarity.

But when the consumer starts expecting a story, the story can quickly become marketing. The story one hears, obviously, cannot encompass the whole individual, family, or business. A struggling family farm is a good story to sell in a liberal city. That they are conservative Christians and voted for Bush, like most of rural America, isn't. Much of the time both are true, but if I mention the latter, the customer likely would not only not buy the cheese but might even question why I sell it. It's worth noting that the farmers, who usually have a less conflicted relationship to capitalism, don't care so much who buys their products as long as it sells.

What is true, though, is that in this country, where urban and rural communities have become increasingly polarized, if one believes that blue/red election results are indicative of people's true feelings, food is one of the few remaining avenues of contact. This exchange isn't much, but I try to do my part to build solidarity by not being an elitist jerk.

There is simply no denying that America loves its processed cheese food and forty-pound blocks of commodity Cheddar. These, my friends, are the truly American forms of the art. The real American originals. Developed here and loved here more than anywhere else. Yet you are unlikely to hear the word *terroir* used to describe the combination of, say, cheesesteak and beer in Philadelphia, even though that would probably be more accurate than using the term to describe an obscure, high-priced, handmade cheese that has a history of less than ten years and is sold only to a certain segment of the population in specialty shops.

The most depressing thing about the state of cheese and dairy farming in this country is that making expensive cheese is one of the few ways left to survive as a small dairy farmer. It doesn't make the news in big cities, but wholesale fluid milk prices have been so low at times over the last few years that many dairy farmers dumped their milk in organized protests. Big agribusiness dairies can survive just fine on low wholesale prices and buy up the farmland from independent farmers once they decide they just can't make it work anymore.

One of the responses to this is for small dairies to try to make and sell cheese, which is what you call a "value-added product." That is, you can charge what you want for it and whatever the "market" will bear. Fluid milk prices are tied to the commodity pricing of the Chicago Mercantile Exchange, so by making noncommodity cheese, these dairies are less at the mercy of super-big-time capital; instead, they are, depending on their scale, at the mercy of slightly smaller-time capital. That breathing room enables them to survive.

As a cheesemonger selling everything from $3-per-pound rBGH-free commodity Cheddars to $30-per-pound American handmade cheeses, am I helping independent and family farmers survive, or paving the way for their destruction? What does it do to farmers to only be able to sell products that most people in their own community cannot afford? (Though the barter system is alive and well at every farmer's market in the country.) Why can't small-scale dairy farmers make a living selling milk or cheese when it's such a basic food?

There are competing thrusts in specialty handmade foods right now. Some want the finest, smallest, and most authentic traditionally produced cheese possible, and want someone to travel the earth to find it for them and bring it to their grocery store. Others want local products only—"local" being arbitrarily set up as within the hundred-mile radius of a city.

Local is a funny concept, though. Humboldt County, for example, is

250 miles away from San Francisco. Where is Mary Keehn supposed to sell her amazing Cypress Grove cheeses if she can't even hit up the biggest city in her area? Here she is supporting small dairy farmers and being a fairly large employer in her rural community, but somehow she isn't local enough to qualify for "Eat Local Month," during which "locavores" challenge themselves to not eat anything produced outside their self-defined area?

Of course, Cypress Grove is a horrible example to pick for the preceding paragraph. I chose them for that reason, to show how tough it is to really know what's local and what isn't. Though Mary has always been upfront about the fact that, along with her locally made cheese, she ages some cheese made to her specifications that she imports from Europe, many retailers and restaurants don't read promotional information carefully enough to know which is which. With the best intentions, and with all the integrity in place, sometimes messages get garbled.

In addition, many local companies may need to supplement their cheesemaking by buying frozen curd from elsewhere. There simply isn't enough fresh goat's milk to meet demand in the United States.

Further complicating things is the fact that, traditionally, co-packing is common in the cheese industry. This is where a cheese company may supplement its product line by buying cheese made by another company. For example, a company may make all sorts of fresh dairy products and even a feta, but it doesn't have the milk or ability to make Cheddar, so it contracts with another company, possibly in another state, sometimes even another country, to sell it cheese that it then sells under its own label. Today's foodies, upon learning about such an arrangement, feel as if they have been betrayed, but in fact it has been standard industry practice in the cheese world for decades—not meant to defraud, but to provide products to customers that might otherwise be unavailable.

The thing is, though, I love telling stories. It's one of my favorite parts of selling cheese for a living. Retail gets so rote sometimes that having a long, detailed conversation with a friendly shopper makes my day. My problem as a cheesemonger is that I sometimes forget the marketing and tell too much of the story. I've been working in the same store at the same job for quite some time, and I've retained some nonmarketed facts over the years. I remember who had Bible quotes on their cheese labels before someone told them that this wouldn't fly in the national market. I remember who has been shut down for listeria. I know more than I want to about nasty divorces, who may have a substance abuse problem, and whose facility is not especially clean. I know who's in the industry as a hobby and has tons of money from inheritance or some other business. Politically, well, don't forget that Oklahoma City bomber Terry Nichols's brother was an organic farmer; don't assume that working the land organically makes someone a lefty.

The stories that people want to hear tend toward the nostalgic. There's a reason that the word *artisan* is probably the most common word used to describe fancy cheese. It harks back to a day when people actually made things, when craft mattered, when commerce was family business and trade secrets. In a post-industrial US economy, where production jobs are exported overseas and service work, like cheesemongering, is a bigger and bigger part of the workforce, there is a sellable fetish for craft.

Craft is good. Craft is your $20-per-pound story cheese and Kraft singles are your $4-per-pound pseudo-cheese. There's a whole spectrum of scale: from one-person operations to the Hilmar cheese plant, which chugs out a million pounds of cheese a day. No cheesemonger can visit them all. We rely on the stories we get told, and part of the job is distinguishing the reality from the marketing.

Cheesemaking and dairy farming are hard work. I know that the cheese world is not the only place where the old joke, "How do you make $1 million in the cheese business? Start with $2 million," is heard. It seems to resonate with cheese folks every time I hear it said out loud, which is usually five to six times per cheese conference.

When I'm behind the cheese counter I hear a lot of assumptions about what farming and cheesemaking are all about. Much of it is weepy-eyed for a time when America made things. A simpler time when people could farm and earn a living. An idealized view for sure. I'm a nostalgic person by nature, so I have a hard time telling where my love of cheese fits into the way I see reality. To some extent, I want to believe in the simple honest farmer. It evokes justice to me, no matter how rigged I think the game is intellectually, to believe in small farmers making a life out of cultivation and creation.

Rustic, handmade cheese is greater than the sum of its parts (milk, culture, rennet, salt . . .). A handmade cheese is imperfect; it is similar, but not identical to the others of the same batch. Imperfection allows it to transcend, to capture the imagination of history in a way that a pallet of forty-pound Cheddars just can't. Sometimes, when visiting an aging room I try to unthread the reasons why it looks so beautiful and so impressive. Other times, when I'm not trying to be analytical, I just let the view flood me with memories, some precise, some half formed, and some elusive. It might be a longing for a world that never existed, but there are moments when I can see why that nostalgia is seductive. Cheese like this jars the brain because its existence brings into question the dominance of the individually wrapped "homogeneous plastic mass" in the stores with which most of us grew up.

Obviously I am not a proponent of processed cheese. It is not because it offends my artistic and nostalgic sensibilities. Unless you're buying it by the can to prepare for the Bad Times, it's an inferior product not worth the money. If you cost the stuff out, it is often more expensive than regular mild Cheddar and has less nutrient value, added fillers, and sometimes contains potentially imported and mysterious "milk protein concentrate."

Milk protein concentrate (MPC)—mostly a product of new technology that can superfiltrate milk, breaking it down into smaller component ingredients than used to be possible—has become so controversial that I've heard it referred to as the potential killer of American dairy. That may be overly dramatic, but it is a concern for large dairies and anyone worried about tracking where our food actually comes from. Processed cheese food companies began adding MPC to their products even though it was not allowed as an ingredient by the FDA's definition, and it has never been approved as a cheese food additive. The legal definition of MPC is still being worked out as I write this, but so far it has mostly been defined by the World Trade Organization as a dry blend of dairy ingredients, ranging from 42 to 90 percent protein.[35] This high-protein, nonperishable, cheap mix of ingredients is quite attractive to large-scale processed cheese food producers looking to easily bulk up their products.

It's ironic, but hardly surprising, that the US claim to cheese fame is now being filled with cheap imported ingredients. Why the FDA has allowed this is up for debate. They did send warning letters to the big processed cheese companies, including Kraft, but did not follow through with any enforcement actions.[36]

It is fitting that the only working definition for MPCs that we had while they were being introduced to American processors is from the WTO because "free trade" is what is hurting small dairy farmers in this situation. Imported MPCs are replacing domestic milk by undercutting the price. It's hardly unusual in this era, but most people don't imagine that a good portion of the ingredients in their Kraft single come from New Zealand, Australia, or India.

While it's slightly amusing to watch some American dairy farmers recoil in horror at the idea of water buffalo milk—even if these water buffalo are from India and not Italy—being turned into MPCs, their opposition is real. It's one thing to import a finely crafted cheese like Mozzarella di Bufala that is impossible to reproduce in the United States. It's quite another thing to transport dairy ingredients ten thousand miles to make a product that would taste exactly the same if made with milk from a few miles down the road.

The other American standard in the cheese business is the factory-made, forty-pound commodity block Cheddar. I may carry snobby cheese, but the forty-pound block is the staple of any US grocery store cheese department. It's simple, affordable food that feeds a lot of people.

Not many people outside the cheese world know this, but the price of forty-pound Cheddar is set at the Chicago Mercantile Exchange. That's why it's called a commodity cheese, because, even though most cheese isn't actually bought through the exchange, it sets the price that everyone uses as the baseline. The price I buy for a wholesale block from a distributor is an exact markup from the CME price and changes weekly.

The price fluctuates somewhat, but it remained incredibly low through the early 2000s. This led to protests by small dairy farmers and others. The pricing of cheese and milk has always been controversial to small farmers. In fact, there used to be a National Cheese Exchange in Green Bay, Wisconsin, that set the price until an exposé by two University of Wisconsin–Madison agricultural economists revealed what some would call "thin trading" (0.02 percent of purchases set the price for the whole country) and others would call "price rigging" by large dairy corporations. Though a class action lawsuit was eventually dismissed, the NCE was dismantled and cheese trading went to the CME. The CME is not without controversy, either. It is such an important factor in the lives of dairy farmers that there are often calls for investigation. As recently as 2006, US senators have asked questions about the CME on the Senate floor, once again worrying about the possibility of price fixing at the expense of the small farmer. These images of commodity cheese, which along with factory-made loaf mozzarella is by far the most common cheese in the United States, differ dramatically from the types of cheese people want to talk about in our store.

So where does the romanticization of cheese come from? Visiting farms, I am often struck by the amount of things you don't tell the casual consumer. I don't mean dirty little secrets. I mean the emphasis on which part of the story to tell and which to leave out. Earlier, I mentioned the emphasis on discussing cute goats and permaculture over goat hides drying in the wind. Another thing I wouldn't mention to people who haven't spent time farming is the flies.

While the rooms where cheese is made should be kept clean on a level beyond obsession, farming itself is a dirty business. I mean, there's a lot of dirt on a farm. Dirty clothes, muddy boots, and insects buzzing around your head. There's a mistake that nonrural folks like me make exactly once when dealing with dairy farmers. No matter what the weather is like, don't leave your car windows open on a visit to a dairy farm.

Very early on in my cheese days I visited a wonderful cheesemaker and goat farmer. I went on a tour of the pasture, watched the cheese being made, looked in the aging rooms, and had a lunch of goat cheese and salad: an all-around fine day of professional dairy work. I said my good-byes, to both the goats and the people, and walked back up the road to my car. As I approached, something seemed odd. It looked like one of those cardboard sun visors was inside my windshield, but I didn't have one. As I got closer, I realized that the "visor" was moving.

I don't know what to call that many flies in one place. They were on every window and though there was no more prime fly real estate, they kept cruising through the open window to join their friends. It wasn't a rural fly street gang but more a gathering of all fly gangs in the area like in the beginning of *The Warriors*.[37] My windows were tinted like a crazed entomologist's SUV. If it's a "herd" of cows and a "gaggle" of geese, then this was a "monster movie" of flies.

Herding flies out of your car is harder than it might seem. Sure, most will go out the open window, but a number fly right back in and decide they like the view out the back window. And when you think they are all out and you are driving on the rural roads back toward the highway, you'll find a number of them are sneakier than you thought, buzzing your head in a fly fury as if they were willing to bet that they can survive a head-on collision with the tractor in the opposing lane better than you could.

Driving is another way that the bubble of our little post-hippie, punk-positive, urban, organic grocery world is pierced—by a steady influx of truck drivers. Most of our regular delivery drivers are locals of some sort, an ethnic mix that may reflect the food they are delivering or may not. But there are definitely a few drivers who seem to resent our worker-run store that's filled with commies, freaks, and homos. Our store that is closed on Labor Day; International Workers Day; Martin Luther King Jr. Day; Cesar Chavez Day; and Lesbian, Gay, Transgender, Queer Pride Day.

I can tell what drivers think of me by the way they park their hand trucks. Sergeant Cheese was parking his too close. One day he penned me in behind his stack of Italian Asiagos. He was dressed in camouflage like always, topped off by a camouflage baseball hat with his sergeant stripes sewn on the front. Like always.

My coworker in the walk-in fridge gave him that nickname. After the driver dropped off his load one day, the produce receiver walked over to me and asked in his So Cal accent, "Dude, what's up with Sergeant Cheese?"

Sarge had something on his mind. "So I've got a bone to pick with you. Why does that sign say WORKERS ONLY?" he asked, pointing to the sign demarcating the retail floor area from backstock.

"Well, you're working, right?" I replied. Make him say it, I thought.

"Yeah, but when you write it like that, it looks communist."

There's something so quaint about the Red Menace these days. So much simpler than those terrorists. Much more European and comfortable. It's only us old folks who can really remember it anymore. Luckily I can spar with anti-communists in my sleep because I had a lot of practice in those days when we communists were doing things like trying to end apartheid in South Africa.

"Why doesn't it say EMPLOYEES ONLY?" Sgt. Cheese continued.

"Because we're not employees. We all own and run this place."

"Then maybe it should say SHAREHOLDERS ONLY."

"Well, that makes it sound like we just sit around and count our money all day."

"Well, why not WORKER-OWNERS?"

"Hmmmm, that's probably the most accurate. But it's kinda long. So we shortened it to WORKERS."

"Grumble," grumbled Sergeant Cheese as he grabbed his hand truck and gave up.

I guess that sign, four feet long in black and yellow, is really visible to people on opposite ends of the political spectrum. Amusingly enough, we usually get the other side of that argument from customers. "I'm a worker. I should be able to come back there. Wanna buy a newspaper?" Still, most customers don't see it at all, walking into our food prep area and dodging hand trucks and pallet jacks.

But they're some of our most loyal customers, wanting to support the largest worker-run grocery store in the country. Although I am often out of context to folks I see, I pass by many of our customers' apartments every day as I walk to work. I love being that close and, until I get evicted from my rent-controlled apartment, I'm not going anywhere. My walk to work—and I've been walking it over a decade now—gives me a sense of place, even in a place that changes rapidly.

Our store, now thirty years in the same neighborhood, is already an institution. In this small city, gentrification can change a neighborhood incredibly fast. A decade ago, the building where I go to work every day was a St. Vincent De Paul thrift store, the office supply chain store was a junkyard, and the electronics chain store was a discount grocery store, the type that would have pallets of about-to-expire food and products in the language of countries that, for whatever geopolitical reason of the moment, food wasn't being imported into. One of my favorite urban pastimes is using the storefronts and streets as a way of remembering the history of "unimportant" things. Unimportant when taken individually, but when taken as a whole, they are the untold history of our city, the unspectacular moments that represent the way we lived more accurately than our flashy memories or the official histories of the newspapers.

A friend once described me as the most nostalgic person she knew, but acknowledged that I can get just as easily nostalgic for last week as for last decade. In a city like this, where knowing what store occupied a building five years ago makes some people treat you like an old-timer, keeping a record in my head of these little tidbits of time is something I need to do while walking the streets. It doesn't really matter that few people remember what I remember, and that no one will have the exact same triggers.

That I have a soft spot for the poignant *terroir* of urban living might make me susceptible to the lure of that term for cheese, but too much of it smacks of marketing and manipulation for me to feel comfortable using it myself. One can also become so enamored with oneself and one's surroundings that one can forget that many other things are in the mix.

On my walk to work, filled with these memories of people who don't live here anymore and things that no one else remembers, I saw the most poignant graffiti ever, one that summed up a truth about urban living, modern society, and the expensive, exile-producing city I call home.

Within a block of my workplace, in a place only pedestrians and homeless campers go, someone wrote, in letters big enough to see half a block away, YOU ARE NOT ALONE!

It seemed kind of hokey. I could almost envision this being the signature of a new, groovy city social service agency, kind of an Up With People make-work program for the urban poor. I could imagine a presentation given to one of the mayor's lowest-paid aides. "Our vision is to raise the self-esteem of housing-challenged individuals. Through our Street Talk (registered trademark) program, we empower unrealized clients to end substance abuse and obtain employment and homes."

It turned out, though, that wasn't the case. As I got closer to the writing I saw, in all lower-case letters almost too tiny to read, but definitely in the same handwriting: but i am.

Humboldt Fog, Cypress Grove Chevre: No, that's not blue, it's ash. Really. I swear. Cypress Grove in Arcata, California, makes this delicate ripened goat cheese with the layer of ash in the middle because it looks awesome that way. This may confuse people who think this will be a pungent blue, but it actually also creates an opportunity to tell them about the cheese. The Humboldt Fog is probably the number one suggestion I make for people looking for a California-made cheese to impress their out-of-town relatives. Why? It's a goat cheese. It has a layer of ash, which you can now explain is not blue mold and look smart. It has a bloomy rind like a Brie. And it tastes great—tangy, fruity, and just barnyardy enough to acknowledge you're eating a goat cheese. [$$, Similar cheese: Sofia (US), Leonora (Spain), handmade Bucheron-style (France).]

Comte: Generally fatter than Swiss Gruyère, Comte wheels are eighty to a hundred pounds of dense, wide, hard-to-handle cheese. Gruyère and Comte (often called Gruyère de Comte) are basically the same cheese, just made on different sides of the border. At similar ages, the Comte tends to be moister, more buttery, and often nuttier. The Swiss Gruyère tends to be sharper, firmer, and more pungent and oniony. Both the Swiss and the French will point to these differences as symbolic of character flaws of the people across the border. But you, you don't have to choose. You can love them both. Comte is great for any kind of cooking and also good to snack on right off the block. If you don't know it, and your budget will allow it, substitute it or mix it in with mozzarella in any recipe. Mmmmmmm. And with potatoes? Double mmmmmmm. Comte is also remarkable because of its name-control protections. It must be made with cooperative milk. Villages all have small cheesemaking facilities called fruitieries where all the milk from the area goes so that they can make such big wheels of cheese. The one I visited only makes about twelve to fifteen wheels a day. The name control also limits the amount of cheese individual fruitieres can make, keeping large-scale international agribusiness out of the picture. [$$, Similar cheese: Gruyère (Switzerland), Beaufort (France), Appenzeller (Switzerland), L'Etivaz (Switzerland).]

---

thirteen

Withstanding the Cuts of a Thousand Cheese Knives

"Thanks for representing us. I'm a crammer, too."

The retailer form the Midwest came over so quietly I didn't even notice her until she started to speak. I could tell what she had to say was heartfelt.

A few months before the 2003 ACS conference, word got out there would not be a whole day of workshops just for cheesemakers as there had been every year in recent memory. Some dissident cheesemakers discussed having their own one-day conference somewhere else in the Bay Area to coincide with the first day of the American Cheese Society's convocation. I would have helped organize that alternative day, but there were too many obstacles, so the idea was abandoned quickly. However, word had gotten around, and I received a call inviting me to be on a panel at the ACS on the day in question. Knowing the other event wasn't happening, I immediately accepted.

"Oh, what's the topic?" I asked as an afterthought.

"Cheese display."

Oh my nonexistent God, I thought. *How do I make this not boring?*

But I had already committed myself. Amusingly enough, when the program came out, I saw that the session had been titled, "Making Cheese Move: Three Styles of Retail Display."

A friend helped me brainstorm ways to make the talk a little political. The other mongers, who, for the record, I respect immensely, gave perfect-world scenarios about practices that don't really happen at stores with any real volume: examining every cheese before accepting delivery, giving every cheese its own clearly defined space, et cetera. I went the cheese-for-the-people route, actually mentioning commodity cheese, the fact that being a co-op keeps our worker turnover very low so we don't need as much retraining, and that cheesemakers sometimes price themselves out of our store.

When I said, "We don't have a cheese museum. I don't wanna see any white space. If we pay to refrigerate it, I wanna see cheese there," one fellow panelist looked as if I had slapped her. That statement made me a hero to my fellow crammer. My cheese display philosophy stems from the fact that I'm a messy person. But it's also true that I work at a store that needs to actually sell some volume of cheese because, as a community-based store, our margins are lower than those of my fellow panelists.

I didn't know how the audience would take it. As I mentioned, I was pretty nervous about my talk. That was the first time I'd spoken publicly about cheese to such a large gathering of cheese industry people. I could hear the knives sharpening in the audience as we got ready to start. *Clackity clackity.*

The people who felt they should be on the panel, the cheesemakers whose cheese I don't carry very often, and the distributors I don't buy much cheese from all are used to being the experts in their own domains. At these conferences, other cheese professionals seem to be waiting to pounce on any mistake a panelist makes. I've done it myself. In the evenings the hotel bar is always full of cheese pros whose grievances get louder as the beer and whiskey flow. Plus, at this panel, a national grocery chain required all their available members to attend. The room was packed.

Luckily, my cheese peers laughed at my not-a-museum declaration. In being nervous, I'd forgotten how low the bar is set for panelists at a trade conference. But I'd also hit some kind of nerve for the folks who felt inadequately fancy among the retailers who were so upscale, they proclaimed that telling a cheese's story allows you to sell it at any price. For the rest of the week people whom I hadn't seen during my panel came up to me and offered thanks and support. Many told me they felt like they couldn't speak on certain issues because their stores weren't glamorous enough.

Most cheese work isn't glamorous. Cleaning drains, shivering in walk-ins, listening politely to sales reps trying to sell you products that customers would never buy: not glamorous. Pest control, kicking reps out of the store: definitely not glamorous.

Cheese injuries aren't glamorous, either. The Parmigiano Reggiano that put the toothpick through my finger was only playing fair. After all, I spend all day cutting cheese. Clearly it was self-defense.

Wielding big cheese knives? Well, okay. That feels a little glamorous.

When I traveled to my first cheese conference, I brought my own cheese knives. I knew I would be cutting samples and, like a chef, nothing bothers me more than using substandard equipment. I walked around that conference with knife handles sticking out of my messenger bag; they were held safely in place by a cardboard sleeve I had constructed the night before I left town.

At the store, customers love to watch us cut big wheels of cheese. Everyone loves big cheese. We've discussed having a posted time to cut the big ticket items so everyone can gather 'round. It would be like feeding time at the zoo. We could throw the too-small-to-package chunks into the audience and watch them fight.

People can be particular about the shape of their cuts of cheese. A well-known East Coast cheesemaker stopped by the store one morning to drop off some new samples. We were chatting in the cheese-cutting area when a customer came up. Observing the proper rules of store visits, the cheesemaker and her handler (a local rep) stepped back and stopped talking so I could help the customer.

An older woman with an accent, German Swiss I think, held up a piece of a Dutch cheese that is actually called "Prima Donna." Because of the price of the cheese, we cut it through the middle and then wedge it so we can sell pieces between $3 and $6. If we cut a piece at its full height, the cheese would have to be razor-thin to get that kind of retail price.

"You have ruined this cheese." The customer declares.

"Uh, what do you mean?" I ask.

"When you cut it in half, you ruin the flavor."

"Uh, what do you mean?" I ask again.

"All the flavor is in the middle. When you cut it down the center, all the flavor runs out. I know, I come from a cheesemaking family."

"Okay," I say, not knowing what else to say. Eventually we agree that we will cut her a two-pound piece with an undefiled middle the next time we cut that cheese. She goes away mollified. Well-Known Cheesemaker says nothing, but I can see in her eyes that she has just gained more respect for retailers.

We run a high-volume cut-and-wrap cheese department. While we do cut cheeses to order, our program is set up like a typical American grocery. Customers come to the cooler, pick out a cheese, and put it in their cart. We offer samples and help, but we also give the shoppers the right to shop in peace if they want. We don't assume everyone wants a cheese experience. Some people just want to get their shopping over with, not embrace cheese as a lifestyle.

While we sell off everything we cut fairly quickly, we make some aesthetic cutting compromises due to price. We cut and wrap ahead of time because it helps us handle our labor-to-sales ratios and keeps our margins lower than other specialty cheese retailers in the area. While a cheese might look better in a thin, top-to-bottom wedge, some cheeses are impossible to cut that way without cracking, so in order to make cheese affordable to most people we cut down the center. Mathematically speaking, you get the exact same amount of middle as you would in a tall piece, of course.

An artist who worked for the store for a while designed a beautiful illustration of cheese cutting that hangs over our cutting area. On one side was an evil creature in a top hat and a crazy grin and a handlebar mustache. The figure loomed over an innocent and scared creature that looked as if it were trying to get away. The first figure was labeled RIND; the second was labeled CHEESE. Underneath it said, AVOID BAD RATIOS!

Bad ratios, old dates, and obvious imperfections like cracks and unwanted mold are what you should look to avoid as a cheese customer. Of course, occasionally you will buy a bad cheese from almost anywhere and, as every cheese book before me has said, you should not feel shy about returning it. You may want to have a conversation with the cheese workers about what exactly is wrong with it, though. I will happily give out credit, but there are times when I really want the consumer to know, for example, that the Cowgirl Red Hawk—an organic, soft-ripened, washed-rind cheese that won the American Cheese Society's Best in Show award in 2002—actually is supposed to be red and sticky.

We named our area where cheese awaits return or credit "Cheese Jail" because that's where the bad cheese goes. Without getting into a discussion about the prison industrial complex ("Why does California rank forty-first in the nation in education spending? It's the prisons."), or a debate about whether the cheese is really bad or whether the social conditions make the cheese do bad things, let's just say that Cheese Jail is not a pleasant place.

At the 2004 ACS conference in Milwaukee, I thought I might get sent to real jail because of my cheese knives. I awoke, somewhat hungover, on the last day of the conference to help cut cheese and plate samples for the beer and cheese tasting panel. "Plating" in this case meant that we had to cut about ten cheeses and arrange them in the exact same order on about 125 plates so that Mark "The Cheese Dude" Todd, an expert on craft beer and handmade cheese, could guide the audience through each combination at the same time. It's not a complicated task, especially to those of us who cut cheese for a living, but it does take a fair amount of time and a system.

Another volunteer and I showed up in the auditorium where the tasting was supposed to take place and found it filled with luggage.

Hmmmm. We started moving through the bag maze to the table that was supposed to be our work space. Suddenly a big, beefy guy approached and blocked our way. He questioned us: "Who are you? Why are you in this room? Don't you know this room is off limits?" He eyed us warily as if daring us to go for our cheese knives. It probably didn't help that my pirate-style eight-inch bladed knife was handle-out in my bag, ready to draw in an instant.

It turned out that John Edwards, candidate for president, was making an unexpected Milwaukee appearance on his way to the Democratic Convention. We had breached security, and the room started to fill with Secret Service. The luggage was part of the Edwards traveling party and no one was supposed to enter before noon. No one had told us that, of course, so we were causing a mini commotion. Suddenly an interaction I had the night before made perfect sense.

I had walked up to the elevator and someone—short, stocky, and unmemorable in a three-piece suit—was already waiting. He appeared to be in great pain, looking away and holding his head with one hand. "Are you okay?" I asked.

He looked up and glared. I saw he had an earpiece and had his hand was clamped on it so he could hear better. Bothered, he said, "Yes," and looked away again. I figured he was hotel security—rather well dressed for hotel security in a relatively sleepy, urban midwestern hotel, but I figured maybe he was one of those overachiever types.

Back in the luggage/tasting room, the hotel manager and the, by now, five Secret Service agents negotiated a deal so we could be in the far end of the room cutting cheese while they guarded the luggage. This was almost derailed when four French cheese guys showed up to help. The French seemed to put the Secret Service on edge again. Since this was not too long after that whole "surrender monkey" embarrassment when France wouldn't support the US war on Iraq, they seemed to be proof that we were up to something.

We started cutting at the other end of the hall. There were no hand-washing facilities, but heck, we were only serving trade. We tried to explain pirate jokes to the French guys. "What's a pirate's favorite cheese? Hav-arrrrrrrrrrrr-ti," but there was a language barrier. The Secret Service dudes stood across the room, hand-on-ear, waiting for trouble.

Edwards was, of course, staying in the presidential suite. We had stayed there the night before he did, putting on a cheese event. I wondered if they had managed to get the beer smell and cheese stink out in time.

As an alternative to the $125 not-included-in-the-conference-fees "Dine Around Milwaukee" event, cheese educator Sheana Davis and beer writer Lucy Saunders had gotten cheesemakers and brewmasters to donate products for free. Renting the presidential suite at the top floor of the Hilton was cheaper than renting a conference hall and a room for the night, so for the first time in my life I stayed on the top floor of a Hilton Hotel. I felt like American royalty.

Royalty has been in decline, thankfully, for centuries, and the presidential suite was a weird mix of super-fancy and broken down. The two main rooms were paneled in dark hardwood. Piano, banquet table, pretentious books on the shelves, everything a president could need. The entryway was marbled and the main bedroom huge. The bathroom was all black, even the toilet and whirlpool bath.

But the bathrooms off the entry were classic dorm room, with cheap-looking tile, and the doors to the toilets had been removed. I wondered if anonymous blow jobs in the presidential suite had historically been a big problem. The kitchen simply didn't work at all. The fridge, the biggest single reason why'd we rented the room, didn't work and leaked a constant, dangerous, slippery puddle over the slick floor. The staff, undoubtedly sick of the demanding ACS people, at first told us refrigeration wasn't included in the rental, and then grudgingly brought up coolers and ice, which they then billed us for. (It was eventually taken off the bill, to be sure!)

Like speaking at a cheese conference, putting on a cheese event is rife with potential problems. As I mentioned previously, cheese people are used to being the authority and being in charge. This may be true at other business conferences, too, but I have no way of knowing. I do know that cheese folks hate to RSVP, and they hate even more to be told an event is sold out. Many don't really even like handing in a business card in exchange for admittance.

There is a large degree of don't-you-know-who-I-am at every cheese event. One cheese professional that I talk to regularly flat-out said he wouldn't attend events anymore unless he was a panelist. "Who are these people?" he asked while looking at a speakers list for a local event.

I went through and pointed out people's qualifications, showing that everyone speaking had been in the business longer than he had. That shut him up, but it clearly still wasn't sitting right.

I'm not immune to it, either, I must admit. Every food profession lends itself to self-promoters. There are a couple of people I keep my eye on because they came from nowhere, speaking as cheese authorities with no apparent qualifications other than their ability to get put on panels or try to push in front of me at trade shows. At those times I try to channel the counterculture founders of my co-op and mellow out. After all, I didn't get a job at a worker co-op to compete for authority and titles with folks like that.

Despite all the potential for bad feelings, the Milwaukee event was a success. Beer was drunk. Cheese was devoured. Shit was talked. Gossip was exchanged. An obnoxious distributor was kicked out for being a jerk. This is exactly what I want out of a cheese party. Even though the cheese world can be small and intensely competitive, the conferences are full of people sharing all types of information. As an independent retailer not looking for a new job, I'm fairly untouchable, and the drama tends to pass me by. But there are some days when I fear I will wake up with a cheese knife in the back.

Cheese conferences are an odd mix of trade event and community gathering. I've been told that back when the American Cheese Society first started, it was a small group of people with the then-absurd idea that great small-production cheese could be made in North America. There's a lot of money to be made from cheese right now, and the

events are exploding exponentially with attendees. The spirit of sharing and solidarity is still there, but the specter of business-speak and
deal-making is getting bigger and bigger. The business of small-scale
cheesemaking is changing. Even so, I find it reassuring to know I will
always find some "crammers" amongst the self-proclaimed experts
and the would-be Brutuses.

Red Hawk, Cowgirl Creamery: Cowgirl Creamery uses only
Straus organic milk to make its fabulous cheeses. Straus
was the first organic dairy west of the Mississippi, and the
Straus family has been instrumental in preserving farmland
in Northern California. The Red Hawk is my favorite of the
Cowgirl Creamery cheeses, a firm triple-cream cheese with a
washed rind. Red Hawk is sticky, stinky, rich and pungent, and
won the Best of Show at the American Cheese Society compe-
tition in 2002. [$$$, Similar cheese: Any washed-rind cow's
milk cheese—Livarot (France), Brescianella (Italy)—though
the Red Hawk has more butterfat and is generally a firmer
cheese.]

Gran Canaria, Carr Valley Cheese Company: Some cheese
snobs look down on Sid Cook's Carr Valley cheeses because
he makes so damn many of them. For example, Franklin
Peluso—also a third-generation cheesemaker—finally added
a second cheese to his product line seventy years after his
family started making Teleme: Teleme with ground pepper. Sid
Cook, meanwhile, has probably developed a new cheese in the
time it is taking you to read this paragraph. Carr Valley makes
well over fifty different varieties using cow's, sheep's, and/or
goat's milk. The Gran Canaria won the best of show at that
2004 American Cheese Society Conference in Milwaukee, and
it is a blend of all three milks, aged for two years and cured in
olive oil. The Gran Canaria is sweet like ripe fruit, nutty, tangy,

and rich as only oil-cured foods can be. [$$$, Similar cheese: Finding similar cheese is difficult because of the oil curing and the mixed milk. Manchego cured in oil (Spain) would probably be the closest one. But just try any of Carr Valley's originals if you can find them.]

---

fourteen

The Salesman Smiled, The Salesman Lied

The art of retail is maintaining your self-respect without *directly* insulting the customers.

As a retailer, I'm never supposed to admit this. There's a myth of American capitalism—that while we are all equal partners in a transaction of goods, somehow the customer is always right. Obviously that equation doesn't make sense, but if one doesn't abide by it from the retailer side, license is given for the customer to be angry or even act out.

There are exceptions to this. The "Soup Nazi" on *Seinfeld* is a type, the abusive retailer with arbitrary rules whom people go to because first, their product is good, and second, people like to pay to be treated badly if they believe they are in on something special. I'd say this archetype even extends to a few other personas, accepted differently depending upon where you live. The Sassy Waitress is another role, as is the Eccentric Old-Timer. At my first-ever cheese event, I was seated next to a man who did most of the customer work at a small store. He admitted playing a character while at work. "Honey," he said, going into that character, "I just tell them what to buy and they buy it. Everyone likes to be told what to do by a big queen."

Of course, there are all kinds of customers, too. Most people who buy cheese in our store are great. I've made friends with people over the counter, and there are a lot of people I look forward to seeing every week even if I will never hang out with them socially. Though we are worker-owned and not consumer-owned, we are part of the San Francisco community. We workers aren't all alike, either, but what we share with our customers is the fact that we work for a living, we live in the Bay Area, and we all have to eat.

It took me years to figure out how to avoid the traps of cheese retail because there are many. Since our store isn't a cheese-only destination, we get a wide variety of folks across the cheese counter. There's a very quick window in which to read someone before deciding how to talk to them and what cheese to recommend.

Some types are easier to spot than others: If customers ask where the mild, familiar Monterey Jack is, don't try to sell them the— pungent, stinky, and likely strange to them—Epoisses; it just makes everyone cranky. If they show interest, I might try to step from Jack to Teleme to Taleggio to Epoisses, but there are very few folks who want to take such a big jump all at once. Three dollars a pound to $30 a pound is also not an obstacle to ignore.

Figuring out what customers want is mostly about identifying what they already eat and suggesting something familiar, but with a few different characteristics. This cheese journey and experimentation is based on consent, of course. If you want to eat Fromager d'Affinois every day for the rest of your life, I'll be happy to sell it to you. It's a wonderful factory-made, mild Brie that will never challenge you, but will be consistently satisfying. A not-so-famous ex-punk-rocker buys only a $1.50 piece of Domestic Muenster every week, and he's one of my favorite customers.

I try and gauge people's cheese tastes by asking them what they generally eat. If someone says "Saint-André"—a French, soft-ripened, factory-made, triple cream—for example, it means they have higher-end mass-produced cheese taste. Nothing wrong with that, by the way. It tells me that the person likes mild, fatty cheese. It tells me that he is somewhat adventurous, but probably hasn't discovered more handmade products, or he can't afford them. If the customer is asking for an if-I-like-this-what-would-I-like cheese, I would suggest a similarly textured, but handmade, Jean Grogne or the local Cowgirl Creamery Mt. Tam. Or maybe the oozy handmade triple creams like Explorateur (our Explorateur sign actually reads, THIS KICKS ST. ANDRE'S ASS) or Brillat-Savarin. If the customer was trying to break out of a rut but still wanted soft, I would suggest Taleggio (stinkier, but with less butterfat and just a little more pungency), a goat Brie, or one of the gentler washed-rind stinkies like Pont-l'Evêque.

What I look for in a customer's answer to my question of what cheese they usually eat is whether they are eating a factory-made or a handmade cheese. The problem, however, with looking for that answer is that such a distinction is the great social divider, even if people don't know it when they answer the question. I try to avoid putting customers in a permanent profile, but questioning them on their regular cheeses lets me know where to start. Mostly I let the cheese sell itself, but offering samples near a person's stink-and-strength-comfort zone makes for a much happier retailer–customer relationship.

I would assume that my coworkers and I make less money than most of our shoppers, based on a basic knowledge of San Francisco demographics. As a store that carries ingredients that range from the most basic (bulk rice and beans) to the most snooty and awesome (five-hundred-year-old balsamic vinegar), we have a diverse customer base. Parmigiano Reggiano might be our biggest-grossing cheese, but the Rumiano rBGH-free Monterey Jack we get in forty-pound blocks has the biggest volume.

The only time the shopper-versus-worker tension got really bad was during the plague of the dot-coms. During the late 1990s the "boom" hit. Weekly, friends and coworkers related how they got eviction notices and would ask if anyone knew of an available rent-controlled room. Crappy apartment houses turned into million-dollar buildings overnight. Longtime businesses, art spaces, and nonprofits seemed to disappear every month. In the 1849 Gold Rush, it wasn't the gold prospectors who made the real money; it was the people who sold supplies to the gold diggers. In this late-twentieth-century gold rush, one of the most needed and valuable supplies was space. Real estate speculators made lots of money and, truth be told, a lot of native San Franciscans made good money that way, too, by selling their homes—usually at the price of leaving the city for good, of course. Once people lost their foothold, it didn't seem like they could ever afford to come back.

Our worker-owner turnover tripled, mostly from people leaving town. We hired people who worked for six months and quit to move away because they hadn't been able to find apartments. It felt like a siege, losing friends to other cities every time you turned around. But even worse was the feeling of losing. Losing to the rude and greedy.

Certainly, I'm not saying that everyone who worked at a dot-com was rude and greedy. But gold rush was in the air. An attitude started permeating the city that if you weren't getting rich, you were just plain stupid. And people working in a grocery store aren't getting rich, so . . .

I don't want to sound like I'm complaining. I work at a great job with great benefits, a job that pays me to eat and talk about cheese all day long. Our store was founded on the concept of Right Livelihood, and though I am not a spiritual person, the idea of working a job that serves the community and does good in the world is certainly one of the reasons I love my workplace. The new attitude took me a while to name, but all of a sudden, when the fourth person of the day asked me if I knew how much money they were losing while they talked to me, I knew it was for real. Reagan had finally won.

This attitudinal shift reminded me of a conversation I had while eating in a restaurant with my parents once. Teenagers at the next table started talking on their cell phones. My parents got a little huffy. They started going off about how uncivil and impolite society has become in their almost seventy years of existence. After venting for a while, they asked me what I thought. You know, for my midthirties "youth" opinion.

"It's just generational," I said. "They're not being any louder than if they were talking to each other."

They didn't like my answer. "It's just so selfish," my mom said. "Why are the kids today so self-involved?"

"Reagan, of course," I responded without thinking.

It's such an obvious link that I forgot that it would be a controversial statement. And I mean an obvious link in that overgeneralizing, pop-political kind of way, of course. But with a large grain of truth, one that is easily defendable while drinking Guinness over lunch. At least one of my parents had voted for Reagan in 1980. Though, if memory serves, they voted for Bush Sr. in the primary because he was more liberal.

"What?" my dad said.

"You don't see a correlation between the 'greed is good' philosophy of trickle-down economics and the fact that there is less feeling of community responsibility?" I asked in mock disbelief. "That somehow in the 1980s when it was not just okay but fashionable to destroy communities and sell worthless stock to make as much money as possible, there would be no long-lasting effect on people's public behavior?"

In a volatile and gentrifying city like San Francisco, a lot of a neighborhood's character, for better or worse, isn't held together by neighbors, but by the neighborhood corner stores and local businesses. I might not know my neighbor who has lived down the block from me for a decade, and I might resent my closer neighbor because I know how much he paid for his house, but all three of us will probably know the guy at the corner store.

One of the things I've learned to love about retail in the last decade is being part of a community. I love going into shops in my neighborhood and being greeted by "Hey Cheese Guy!" as long as the next line isn't some kind of fart joke. I even loved it one day when anonymous fans yelled "Cheese Whore!" at me out of a speeding car window on my way home from work.

My view of being a cheese worker is colored by the fact that my mom always had a favorite clerk at the local Alpha Beta. His name was Brad. He would always recommend things for my mom to buy. Weirdly, I never met him, though I often went shopping with her. I don't think he was fictional, though. For one thing, my mom's imagination doesn't work like that. While I would happily create a fictitious person to blame my impulse buys on, especially if they turned out bad, my mother would never do such a thing.

No, based on my more recent real-life experience, I believe my mom probably really enjoyed her weekly social interaction with Brad. Maybe she even subconsciously flirted with him, in a harmless way in the nice, safe, and unthreatening environment of a well-lit retail store. He became forever enshrined in family lore one Christmas dinner when my mom unveiled a new ice cream called "Holiday Fruit." Basically, it was like fruitcake ice cream. Yes, that is a bad idea, which is probably why I had never seen it before, nor have I seen it since. But Mom had been hyping it all evening, saying that Brad had recommended it and that we needed to save room. I remember even then being unsure why she was so excited by her store-bought dessert at the expense of her huge home-cooked dinner. And why Brad's word carried so much weight.

When it was time to eat the Holiday Fruit, everyone gagged. Hard, rum-soaked fruit pieces in nasty, cheap vanilla ice cream. It hurt my teeth, and my teeth weren't even bad back then. I still remember the horror more than twenty-five years later. No one finished more than a bite or two, and my mom had generously given everyone at least two scoops.

Brad is my grocery work hero.

I both want to be him and hate to be him. I can carelessly ruin a dinner or betray a trust with ill-chosen words. Certainly, the pressure there is not that of a school bus driver or nuclear power plant operator. My mistakes are relatively low-impact.

But I know that what I recommend to folks can make their meals, that I can provide a nice respite for someone in an otherwise hellish week, a source of stability in an uncertain world. I can inspire loyal defenders, perhaps even followers. I can even be a subversive symbol while appearing to be a source of ridicule.

Brad also taught me that taste is subjective. Many times I will refuse to answer a customer's question about which cheese is better. Sure, if the question is about a factory-made Brie versus a handmade Fromage de Meaux, I will tell them that the handmade cheese is better quality, but make sure that they actually want better quality. If you're feeding an art-opening crowd of a hundred strangers and grazers, the factory Brie might well be the better choice.

Punk rock changed my life. I listened to those records over and over and really believed in them. I still believe in many of them. One lyric that has haunted me throughout my life of working retail was by a great San Francisco band called B-Team, which unfortunately has been pretty much forgotten. In a song that was more about how to live one's life than how to shop, the singer, suddenly alone in an instrumental pause, sings in a pained croon, "You bought what you thought was pride. The salesman smiled. The salesman . . . lied."[38]

Obviously those lyrics are not directly about cheese selling. They are about taking control of your life and not having other people sell you a bill of goods. They imply that other people may have ulterior motives about having you think a certain way. They say that someone who claims to be your friend may not be. Still, as a cheesemonger, I am a salesman. And I am concerned with what I am selling people besides cheese.

Consumer purchases come with societal baggage. Fancy cheese, more than many other items, comes with class and cultural meanings. There is always a way, as a retailer, to flow with and reinforce societal pressure. I can imply that certain cheese is more highbrow than others, look disdainfully upon certain questions, and mock cheap cheese. I could sell snobbery and judgment fairly easily.

I don't work in a vacuum, so in some ways many people assume that is exactly what I sell. Our store doesn't carry meat or fish, but the cheese area is usually where people new to the store come and ask for it because we are working behind a service counter. I learned early on that it was an extremely delicate question and that the answer would often make people angry. One customer came up to me on a busy Saturday asking about the politics of farm-raised versus wild salmon and the concept of organic fish. I told her what I knew, but after a minute or two was out of answers.

"You know, since we don't sell fish, and I don't buy it for myself, I don't know enough to answer your questions," I said, and gave her a couple of stores to try.

She walked away and a few minutes later a coworker came up to me. "What did you say to that woman?" he asked.

I told him and he laughed. "She said that you sneered and said, 'We don't carry fish and I certainly don't buy it.' She was really upset."

The reason he laughed is that it is well known in the store that I've never been a vegetarian and that the reason I don't buy fish is because I get it from my dad who goes fishing as often as he can. He also owns a local hunting and fishing store. Though I haven't hunted or fished since I was a teen, I'm sure I have killed more animals than the average meat eater. I am the last person to give customers attitude about their meat eating.

But it's an expectation that people who don't eat meat will give attitude to those who do. Just like it's expected that someone who knows cheese will mock the plebeian palates of those who don't. It's one of the reasons we avoid using wine industry terminology to describe the tastes of cheese. Many of the people I meet, especially those not in the foodie comfort cities, will be unabashed about their love of cheese. When someone says to me, "I love cheese! Mmmmmm, smoked Gouda," even if I know they're talking about the processed log version that we won't sell, I'm not going to scold them and tell them they shouldn't love it. I may make suggestions for other things they might like, but that love is real. Who am I to be disdainful?

There is also often a fear of judgment at the cash register.

Sometimes for good reason, mind you. The act of hip record store clerks sneering at musical choices is so standard that it's a cliché. God knows I used to judge people for the records they bought when I worked at Epicenter. I kept it to myself, but other volunteers didn't even bother. This didn't help our reputation for being a bunch of mean music snobs.

I remember buying a copy of the Afflicted's "Good News About Mental Health"—which does not have the world's most sensitive cover—before I worked there and wondering if I was going get any crap for hating on crazy folks. For years I put off buying a hip-hop CD by a local cop that I knew would be unintentionally hilarious because I couldn't face going up to the register with it.

I was quite embarrassed to buy it actually, pathetically making excuses to the cashier, even though I knew that was the wrong thing to do when buying a questionable product. Call no attention to yourself. Act casual and confident. Try to give off the air that you don't care that the person behind the counter is judging you, even though they are and should be. I'd likely be embarrassed by buying an album by any white rapper. But when it's an album with a big white cop prominently displaying handcuffs and badge on the cover, I just couldn't even try to pull off "too cool to care." I opted for "I have a reason, don't hate me" instead. The cashier gave me the uncomfortable laugh and a condescending sneer I deserved for trying to explain my purchase.

Because, after all, judgment helps pass the time, and passing time is the primary goal of almost all retail workers. When I worked retail at a photo lab I hated, I wouldn't even remember most of the things I said about customers to other workers by the time I got home. In retrospect, I loved the busy days at the photo lab because not only did the day go faster, but the customers were more stressed and more likely to do something really classic, like threaten to get me fired or sue the store over the fact that they didn't load their roll of film into the camera the right way.

When I tell anecdotes to friends, I usually talk only about the customers I hate because, let's face it, that just makes for better stories. It is also the fatalism of punk to embrace and find humor in the worst things because it takes away some of their power to hurt. But there are quite a few people whom I look forward to seeing in the store every week whom I know only through selling them cheese. The goth-punk mortician, the teacher who looks like Ray Romano, the chef guy who always has a big plan and dubious "inside information," the sweet older lesbian couple who offer to set me up on dates with friends of theirs, the old woman who grew up on a farm and special-orders gallons of raw milk. There are many more.

The customer interactions I've mentioned throughout this book, good or bad, were all in the range of what is considered normal behavior. But when I argued with my parents about Reagan causing a generation of greed, I made the connection to another Reagan-era paradigm shift. The defunding of mental health services and the crumbling of traditional communities are taken as givens in today's urban environment. However, there is very little discussion of the people picking up the slack on the front lines. The people who have to deal every day with the victims of post-industrial capitalism and privatization-fetish. That's right: retail and service workers.

Advertising has always promised that you can buy your way to freedom, happiness, and a better life. Now it seems that, without many other alternatives, those with little money increasingly must come to the business temple of their choice to get their social needs met. They just, by necessity, come to those businesses that will put up with their type, whatever that type is. For example, someone not dressed well enough to be welcome at a Lexus dealership might be able to linger at a Walgreen's for hours. And while it's a cliché in some circles about gangs of senior citizens haunting malls near retirement communities, I see little written about how the nature of some jobs now covers care and friendship, or at least a facsimile.

Of course businesses are only set up to deal with these social needs in certain ways. The object of any business, even a post-hippie store like ours, is to sell things. Meeting the social needs of people is generally only viewed as valid if they can be seen not as people but "potential customers." I'm not saying that business owners never give away free food or that none of them care about the community they live in, just that there are increasing numbers of people without support networks who end up getting themselves semi-adopted by retail service workers because they lack other alternatives.

Is it just a coincidence that there is a rise in a "philosophy" of customer service coinciding with the less-caring government mandated by the Reagan Revolution? It's hard to tell from the retail-worker front lines. A good chunk of my work is social-service-oriented. I don't mind it—I even enjoy it at times, and I think of my workplace as partly a community service institution anyway—but it's sad that we can't apply for government funding. It's a standing joke in our store that we should have a category on our time card for our social service work so that it doesn't get counted against our sales categories when we review profit-and-loss statements.

One regular at our store I call the Senile Socialist. He's been coming into the store as long as I've worked there. With unblinking eyes, open mouth, and rice paper skin, he appears, ghost-like, every few months. The first time he saw me, there was a calendar on the wall and Ernest Hemingway's picture was on that day's date. He waved me over and in a quiet but gruff voice said, "Hemingway was a communist. Died in Cuba." Over and over. Every time I tried to get back to work he'd wave me back and repeat those words. Eventually, over the next couple of years, our conversations expanded to topics like, "Father ran for mayor. Socialist. Beaten up by thugs. From Milwaukee." He even brought me a present one day: CDs of the Soviet Red Army Choir *and* the Chinese Red Army Orchestra singing traditional revolutionary songs. I always made time for him, but he is only one of my many "clients."

Though they are mainstream now, natural foods stores historically attracted a certain type of needy customer, and though I work with cheese I am not immune. People are concerned, perhaps too much, with their health. It could be because they have had cancer or other illnesses. It could be that they are athletes trying to burn the most efficient fuel possible. It could be that they have a credible or incredible philosophy of nutrition. Also, while this is not true of most of our customers, there are definitely some who come to the store just to talk to somebody.

Retail, at least our kind of retail, is the place that allows everyone in as long as they are dressed and aren't visibly armed upon entry. I just take it as part of my job to give those folks a little time. Certainly this is made easier by the founders of our store, who did not predict natural foods becoming a billion-dollar industry and who started our store partly as a community service—indeed we donate to many community organizations, schools, and food banks. We have even worked out deals with certain customers we had banned from the store so that they could return, albeit sometimes with mental health officials or a minder, so that they don't repeat their previous behavior, like biting every apple and putting it back on the shelf.

While we certainly get the stereotypical loony hippie, our customers with special needs come in all forms: government workers, the homeless, aging rockers, "artists," and, most poignantly, senior citizens. For the seniors, the city has moved on without them. They might have some form of subsidized housing, but their friends and family don't, so they are stranded alone on some high ground of San Francisco. Or maybe they were jerks their whole lives and didn't make any lasting friends, or they have family who can't stand to be within a thousand miles of them. I don't know. I just work behind the cheese counter.

But what I do know is this: I have been called upon to look at pictures, to help read official government letters, to admire new purchases from nonfood stores, and to offer my opinion on numerous subjects of which I know little. It's part of the responsibility of being located in a community to give everyone a little time no matter how much they are going to purchase at the end of the interaction.

The government has privatized social service into unacknowledged places. It helps retail workers stay sane if we start looking at the bigger picture and see ourselves as front-line social service workers. Not because we want to be there, or because it's a good thing for society, but because people have and will put us in that position anyway. We end up doing a lot of the things necessary for these people to remain more or less functional: provide human contact, help with basic survival issues, and help them navigate the world. We might as well acknowledge it.

Even though some folks would be better off talking to a case manager than an untrained service worker, retail always has a community aspect to it. Some retailers certainly will define their community according to who they sell to. Since we sell food, our community is everyone.

Minuet, Andante Dairy: **Soft-ripened, triple-cream cylinder of goaty goodness enriched with Sadie Kendall's (cow's milk) crème fraîche. Kendall is a California dairy legend, making only one product—crème fraîche—since the 1980s but making it so traditionally and precisely that it rivals the product from Normandy. Soyoung Scanlan—a biochemist turned cheesemaker—makes fabulous French-style cheeses at Andante Dairy, but this is my favorite since it combines the tang of the goat's milk and the rich sourness of the crème fraîche into something completely special. [$$$, Similar cheese: The goat's milk/ crème fraîche combination makes this cheese unique enough that I don't know what to compare it to. Texturally it is similar to any high-quality, ripened chèvre like Chevrot (France), but it also has the rich taste of a cow's milk cheese like Jasper Hill Farm's Constant Bliss (US) or Chaource (US).]**

Monet, Harley Farms: **This beautiful fresh chèvre is covered in edible flowers, making it one of the prettiest cheeses around. The difference between a really fresh goat cheese like this and one that's packed in plastic to sit around for months is incred-**

ible. It smells like the milking parlor; it's tangy and tart and fluffier than almost any other "fresh" chèvre. It is also a farmstead cheese, made only on the Pescadero farm from cheesemaker Dee Harley's herd of goats. It was one of the biggest honors of my cheese career when Dee asked me—because she couldn't get away from the farm—to accept for her any awards she might win at the American Cheese Society (even if really it was just because I was the closest cheesemonger to Pescadero in attendance). I was up on that stage all night and even accepted an award for the Monet in the farmstead cheese category. Amazingly, I don't get to sell this cheese anymore because Dee has become successful enough now to sell all her cheese off her farm. No more wholesaling is great for the farmer but no fun for this retailer. [$$, Similar cheese: I don't know of any other cheese with edible flowers like the Monet, but another great fresh farmstead goat cheese producer is Pure Luck Dairy (US).]

fifteen

It's Not *What* We Eat, It's *That* We Eat

A customer came in one day who knew her cheese pretty well. She asked smart questions and was looking for good cheese. She was intrigued by the new (legal) French raw milk cheeses we had in— Dome Saint-Estèphe, Brique des Flandres, Gaperon au Torchon— but rebelled against their insanely high prices. I couldn't blame her, though I bought a half of one of the Domes myself at about $9 for about 3.5 ounces. I didn't do the math to get a per-pound price—it was just too good. She decided on a half of the Jasper Hill Winnimere: my favorite American cheese. Not cheap, either, but cheaper than the French alternatives.

As knowledgeable customers often do, she started off a little wary, but our mutual trust grew over the five minutes of cheese talk. I actually appreciate when I have to earn it.

When she finished her cheese selections, she asked, "You don't carry foie gras, do you?"

Despite knowing the potential pitfalls that we have in our store around meat questions, I felt as if I had developed a trusting relationship with this customer and that she had a sense of humor. I figured we had bonded enough that I couldn't offend her. I went for broke.

"No, ma'am, we don't carry any meat or fish so we certainly don't carry the torture meats."

She heard the "no" immediately, but the rest took a second to sink in. She did a slight double take. "Well, okay," she said, "but I don't share your opinion." She looked back at me, challenging me to go off on animal cruelty, PETA, or a description of shoving feeding tubes down the throats of geese. Retail workers aren't supposed to snark about touchy subjects.

"I'm sorry for the way I phrased that," I replied. "How about if I say, 'We don't carry the torture meats that are extremely tasty'?"

"Okay, I can live with that," she said, pushing her cart off to finish her shopping.

When I say that punk rock made me a cheesemonger, I don't mean there was some kind of clear linear path from buying my first Clash album to selling Brie and Cheddar. Indeed, from the number of vegan punks who wanted to send me to reeducation camp after hearing about my job, it would almost seem the opposite.

What I am saying is that when people ask me how I got started working in cheese, they expect some story of apprenticeship or restaurant work or culinary school. Instead, I trace a lineage that includes listening to punk, and becoming involved with a political punk scene, following that scene on its logical path to political collectives, to becoming interested in workplace democracy and alternative institutions. That the job opening happened to be in cheese was very good luck (for me).

I got to learn about cheese in relative isolation, so my early mistakes (getting talked into carrying the Swedish cheese with vodka; buying bland, mass-market cheeses thinking they were more special than they were; believing the dubious promise that "the cheese looks ugly but tastes great" without a guarantee of return) weren't noticed the way they would be now by today's more cheese-savvy customers. In my first couple of years, our old store was slower-paced and didn't have customers with grand cheese expectations. Certainly they didn't expect details about the farms or cheesemakers.

Even through the 1990s there was a lot less customer knowledge and interest. It wasn't as if I was leisurely thumbing through *The Cheese Primer* while waiting for customers to ask questions. Most of those years were spent cutting and wrapping forty-pound blocks of cheese as fast as I could and hustling to fill empty spots in the cooler. But it wasn't until recent years that interest in cheese exploded.

I was lucky to have that buffer period in which I could learn. No one in the store had any kind of fancy cheese experience when I started, so there was no training program. I just tried out a lot of ideas I got from reps or stole from other stores until we figured out what worked. Through trial and error, we developed a system and figured out which cheeses we could handle.

Learning about cheese is basic for a cheesemonger on some level. You taste every wheel of every cheese that comes in. You have sales reps bring you samples even if you know you can't buy them all. You suck info from cheese salespeople and correct it when you realize who is a liar, who is an exaggerator, and who is usually a good source.

Identifying the good sources of information is important because stories are the very basis of selling cheese. We're constantly urged to "tell the story, tell the story, tell the story," which can, in less honest hands, mean, "tell the pretty, romantic story that will separate urban people from their disposable incomes." One cheesemaker even said to me, while setting a price for his cheese far in excess of what he would set in his local area, "I've seen the house prices in San Francisco. You people can afford it." I tried to explain that I live in a city of renters and that many of our customers (and workers) are just barely hanging on. They may prioritize certain foods for political, environmental, taste, and/or health issues, but it doesn't work to treat them like a personal ATM. Indeed, though I brought his cheese in for my own reasons, we ended up selling it near cost just to get rid of it. A decade and a half later, I still make mistakes.

Even though that cheese was a failure at the price he wanted, there is some truth to what this cheesemaker said. Cities often have a lot more money flowing through them than rural areas. Sometimes such money can call the shots in faraway places.

Paul Haskins of the Wisconsin Sheep Dairy Cooperative told me that "in general, the urban population tends to believe there are right and wrong answers in agriculture. There is a growing trend toward consumers to support a particular type of agriculture or take sides in some sort of good-versus-evil food battle. What they don't understand is that there are no right or wrong practices in agriculture, only compromises. In farming, you can have a belief system concerning practices and the environment, but that system only holds up if it's actually profitable. Many times, farmers are forced to compromise their beliefs just to stay in business."[39]

I cross these battle lines often in my role as urban interpreter of rural life. When I sell agricultural products, the training from every retail job I've ever had pushes me to sell it the easy way: talk about family farms and bucolic settings. Discuss the exotic (to city folk) things like cows, grazing, milk collection, and getting up at 4 a.m.

And I do support, theoretically at least, one type of agriculture over others. My initial understanding of farms came from an emotional distance. The beautiful rolling hills of my Northern California youth, political radicalization, tasting that first amazing Gruyère: all huge influences on my life and my cheesemongering, but, just as clearly, not the same thing as living on a farm and working with the animals. From this distance it is easy to think I can supply the remedy to problems that have been with us as long as industrial capitalism. Abstract concepts of environmental health and "traditional farming practices" are easy to get behind from this interested distance.

The reality of making compromises to stay on the land is not quite so obvious to an outsider like me. But it should be. For example, I don't own a house. I live in San Francisco and it just isn't realistic on my wages. But I understand the struggle farmers face because I've watched my friends and neighbors get swept away by evictions and the high cost of living. I've watched people work more than they want to in order to stay in an expensive city that just happens to be their home. I've watched people do their best and get forced out of their communities anyway.

In the same way, the romanticism of "artisan production" seems almost inevitable to people, like me, who haven't had to create something handmade every day to make a living. Some fetishists of handmade products would be upset at some steps cheesemakers take. Is it still "artisanal" if someone goes to an automatic system of cutting curds as opposed to spending hours hunched over a vat? My chronically aching elbows and shoulders, earned from years of cutting and wrapping cheese, tell me that some mechanized production, if chosen wisely, is better for everyone.

"Tell the story" is good advice if we try, in the ways that we can, to tell as much of the story as possible, and not just the pretty bits.

Before I started on my poorly marked trail to becoming a cheesemonger, punk rock had taught me some things. I knew before I started on that path that you can become your own expert if you want to. And that experts don't need to be pretentious or snooty.

The woman shopping for fancy cheese and tasty torture meats represents one type of cheese customer, the type the pretentious and snooty purveyors often cater to, but treating her like a regular person, like someone in your community, works just as well. There are many folks who won't shop at our store or take us seriously because we aren't a cheese-only specialty store, because we have products at cheaper prices than elsewhere, or because we are a worker cooperative.

The 1980s made American punk what it was: a time when a group of people felt an obligation to go against the grain. I don't have as much energy for in-your-face protest as I used to, but that's more likely a function of age than one of era. If anything, things are even worse now, but time and tactics change. So, while it's a great time for artisan cheesemakers in America right now, it's an awful time to be a small dairy farmer.

I help build cooperatives and support small farms, and those beliefs come from experiences I had as a punk rock teen. I don't deal with only the greenest dairies or the smallest producers, though. People need a range of choices in taste and price. Sometimes people need familiar products as a contrast, so they can ask questions about the things they don't know about. For example, one might ask why anyone would buy a more expensive Gruyère or Brie than the one they can buy at the nearest supermarket chain. I support a diversity of tactics. Punk taught me to examine everything I consume and to see what it really supports in the end, but being a polarizing force taught me that there are times when getting along with all sorts of people is harder than alienating them.

But I love cheese. That was unexpected. As I moved through the obstacles to becoming a cheesemonger—kicking reps out of the store, bleeding on cheese, et cetera—there have always been those times when I couldn't believe I was getting paid to eat and talk about cheese all day.

Don't get me wrong: Being shoulder-deep in a cooler on Saturday night at midnight cleaning cheese gunk out of drains, trying not to cut off my fingers in the fans or electrocute myself while standing in puddles of water that flooded out of the bottom of the cooler— that always feels like work. Talking to the customers who contradict themselves with every confused sentence and then talk to you like you're stupid? That's work. Even schmoozing unfamiliar crowds can feel like work when you'd rather be hanging out with the freaks and weirdos at your own bar than the professional freaks and weirdos at a fancy hotel. Being "on" when you're mourning the death of a friend or nursing a freshly broken heart? That's the hardest part of retail work, one that is rarely, if ever, acknowledged.

A lot of punks say they hate everyone, but a wise friend once said to me that punks are basically nice people pretending to be mean, whereas hippies are mean people pretending to be nice. A working-class anarchist whom I went to college with once interrupted a group of punks talking about the stupidity of "normal people" by saying, "You're talking about my family."

Subculture is elitist, but it's how some of us survive. I have a broader tent now. I had to admit that, really, I like people. That's why retail is okay for me, at least as long as I don't have a boss. It's a one-on-one performance, really. Crowds make me nervous; the cheese doesn't.

It's often said that food brings people together. That's becoming a trite-ism because it just as surely sets them apart. Organics, kosher, halal, vegetarian, vegan, artisanal—some people can choose food as a lifestyle or as part of a belief system and be every bit as elitist or wall-building as any snarly teen punk rocker could hope to be.

But there is a power in the love of food and in sharing the experience of tasting a cheese that can change the way you think. The realization that possibility doesn't end at the rind. Whether it's that a Cheddar doesn't have to come from a forty-pound, untouched-by-human-hands-and-vacuum-packed-in-heavy-plastic block, or that you may be illegally arrested at a peaceful protest, these experiences can lead to seeing the world in a different way. That reality is not exactly what you've been taught, or that whole avenues of experiences you've never heard of can help you see that another world is possible.

Unfortunately, in a society as bound to consumer culture as this one—especially in an expensive city like San Francisco, in which cultural centers of all kinds get moved out of the way for projects that can pay more rent—the store where people shop becomes a center of human interaction. Retail workers have a place, whether we want it or not, as part of this new commons.

One of the reasons I wanted to become a cheesemonger, rather than just some dude who works behind the cheese counter, was that I saw the potential of cheese as an eye-opener. I came in with a background of Kraft singles, retail schmooziness, and direct-action politics. Even though snobbery and trendiness repulse me, that first taste of Antique Gruyère let me know that there was something real there, something transformative. In the end, the cheese always does the talking.

Loving food can be a sensory experience that brings people together, so long as you don't use language or attitude to set up boundaries.

Demystification of bands and how records are produced is one of the main underpinnings of punkness. Clearly, you can describe such a basic activity as eating in terms understandable to everyone.

Food has to be a unifier. After all, we all have to eat.

One of the biggest issues in US urban settings is access to grocery stores that sell nutritious products, not just alcohol and processed food. Indeed, in many areas of this country it is easier to find cheap booze than fresh produce. I am lucky to work in a store that has always been in a working-class to mixed-income neighborhood, and has always operated under the assumption that everyone should have access to healthy food. And not just healthy to the end consumer. One of the reasons we have always pushed organics is that industrial pesticides are a farmworker issue as well as an environmental and consumer health issue. Whether it's dairy or produce, California agriculture depends on mostly immigrant Latino labor. Rural communities and our food should not come at the expense of their cancers and poisoned water. That our neighborhood, the Mission District, is the most Latino-populated neighborhood in the city only brings home the awareness of the food–farmworker connection. People need food to be healthy on both sides of the food chain.

Near the start of this book, I mentioned the battles lefty activists in the 1960s and '70s fought in the no-man's land between "the masses want Twinkies" and "we must educate people about healthy food." To make a rhetorical point, healthy food advocates sometimes declare that food in this country is too cheap. What they mean is that the prices Americans pay for certain foods are cheaper than the actual cost of production, that workers throughout all stages of food production are not paid enough, and that the (historic) power of the United States allows food producers to get raw materials from other countries at unfairly low prices.

To use just one example, through water deals given to certain growers and the use of industrial fertilizers developed through public moneys, lettuce may actually cost less in the grocery stores than it would cost to produce if large farmers had to pay the same costs as small organic farmers. It's true that small farms find it hard to compete not only with the scale, but also the hidden benefits that large-scale corporate agriculture gets in the form of research, water, tax breaks, government programs for the poor, and direct subsidies.

All of this is true: Locally grown, organic food costs more in stores, and small farmers, of any kind, can have a hard time recouping the money they put into their work. But it is still a huge mistake to call, even just rhetorically, for food prices to go up, even if that reflects "reality." The problem is that the wrong agricultural products are (directly and indirectly) subsidized. The goal of anyone in the system of growing, distributing, and selling food should be to make healthy food as attainable as possible while still making a living. Food is one of the basic necessities of life. Food workers, therefore, have a greater responsibility to their communities to figure out how hungry people can get fed and how small farms can survive. Declaring that food should be more expensive, rather than deciding that it's a community duty to make sure there is healthy, affordable food, is not the way to develop support for alternatives that will be better for the environment as well as healthier for the farmworkers and consumers. Saying food is too cheap is a slap in the face to people throughout the country who only have minimal access to healthy, natural, and unprocessed foods.

I would have a harder time working in a cheese store that wasn't a full grocery. We may have some of the most boutique grains, which sell at extravagant prices to foodies who don't care about the cost, but we also have the cheapest organically grown rice. We might have some amazing small-production fancy-schmancy cheeses at over $40 a pound, but you'd be hard-pressed to find cheaper rBGH-free Monterey Jack or mild Cheddar. There are walls of bulk foods that are actually functional and full of shoppers (unlike the ornamental bulk bins in some natural foods chain stores), huge amounts of produce (almost all organic and from California), and a cheese section where people work hands-on with the cheese every day. All of these departments have food you can imagine being grown or being made. This is one of the ways to demystify eating.

The fact that all these foods can be under one roof is one of the things I love. All sorts of people come together in our store partly because both the cheap and the expensive are available, partly because it's part of a neighborhood and a community, and partly because those of us who work there and own the business also live close enough to get to work every day. Of course, when I started at Rainbow a greater percentage of folks lived in the neighborhood. Like family farms, high costs of living have forced a number of our worker-owners to move, not only to outlying counties, but also out of the Bay Area altogether.

When cheese people are told to "tell the story," it's supposed to be a story that makes people feel good, one devoid of the messiness and nuance of real life. One incident early on in my cheese days really crystallized my view of the cheese-selling world, and I think back on it often as I work the retail floor. A customer was picking through the cut pieces of Parmigiano Reggiano. Finally she found one she liked and tried to hand it to me over the counter. "I'll take this one," she said, "but can you cut off the rind? I don't want to pay for the rind."

I immediately shifted from the open palm, I'm-here-to-help-you position to the hold-it-right-there, talk-to-the-hand one. I wanted to make sure I understood what she was saying. I told her that our prices reflect what we pay for cheese and that we pay for the rind. I explained to her that Parmigiano Reggiano rinds are great additions in soups, as well as their perfection as doggy snacks. But nothing I said would sway her. "I don't see why I should have to pay for something I don't want."

"Ma'am," I said in an ad lib that I have now been using for a decade, "we all share the rind."

It was a reflex response, but truer than most things I've ever said. Our pleasures and our trials are interconnected in this world. Without preserving farmland, you won't be able to go to an urban store and buy fancy cheese. Without affordable housing, there will be no people to milk the cows and no cheese workers to cut and wrap your cheese choices. Without a safe, healthy, and accessible food supply, that piece of fancy handmade cheese will become even more of a luxury. And even more rare.

Sometimes you can't have the good cheese without taking home some rind, too.

Dante, Wisconsin Sheep Dairy Cooperative: **Aged more than six months, the Dante is one of my favorite American cheeses. Nutty, caramel-sweet, smooth, but with enough sharpness to invoke a Wisconsin Cheddar; I buy this by the pallet because I believe in this cheese so much. The Wisconsin Sheep Dairy Co-op, now made up of fourteen dairies, was set up to support and help market sheep milk for dairy farmers who were too small to make it on their own and too dependent on the fleeting whims of other cheesemakers. The WSDC now supplies a great deal of the sheep's milk made into dairy products through-out the United States. Unlike cow's or goat's milk, sheep's milk can be frozen with little damage to its cheese- or yogurt-making prowess, so this fine Wisconsin sheep's milk makes it—in one form or another—to supermarkets on both coasts. I hope they will forgive me when I say that they have the ugliest label in the cheese business—a version of Rodin's The Thinker with the head of a sheep on a bright orange background—but I have made it my personal goal to turn that into a market-ing benefit. People may not remember the name Dante, so I tell them, "Just remember, it's the cheese with the ugly label." They never forget that. [$$, Similar cheese: Vermont Shepherd (US), Ossau-Iraty (France).]**

Winnimere, Jasper Hill: **Cheesemakers of the United States, please don't hate me, but I think this is my favorite American** cheese. Winnimere is a seasonal, raw milk, spruce-bark-wrapped, washed-rind cheese that is pungent, rich, meaty and earthy. It's smoky, too. My coworker Anarqueso and I decided that the pleasure of consuming Winnimere is like eating your way through a bacon forest in autumn. Usually we are not so wordy and pretentious, but this cheese deserves some hype. It's also a farmstead cheese made from only the small herd (thirty-six the last time I was there) of Ayrshire cows on the property. The Kehlers—back-to-the-landers for the new millennium—not only make great cheese, but also have recently finished a huge addition to their farm: aging rooms in which they plan on aging the cheese of other Vermont cheese-makers, freeing them to concentrate on herd management and making cheese rather than the expensive cheese-aging aspect of the job. This type of partnership has already borne fruit: a Best of Show for the Cabot-made/Jasper Hill–aged Clothbound Cheddar at the American Cheese Society conference in 2006. [$$$, Similar cheese: Most often compared to Vacherin Mont d'Or (France/Switzerland), it is actually more like the Forsterkase (Switzerland) because of its washed rind.]

Cheese lovers contact me from all over the country asking for cheese tips. As I mentioned in the *"Terroir"* chapter, cheese availability can be very regional. While I can point folks toward some cheeses local to them, it's hard to know what other brands will be available there, or, if they are, whether they will be a good value for the price.

People who live in the cheese cities, big metropolitan areas with specialty cheese shops and good distribution, have no real problem finding a good place to buy cheese. San Francisco, New York, Boston, Chicago . . . if you can't find a place to buy cheese in those cities, you aren't really trying. Unlike in Reaganomics, there *is* a trickle-down flow of information and cheese desire in big cities, so even smaller stores and local grocery chains tend to have decent cheese options.

But what about other folks? A lot of the time people who e-mail me through my Web site have no obvious options. While cheese love is spreading, it hasn't oozed into every town yet. Some places it seems like your only option is still the rock-hard, identically-sized-to-all-the-others piece of French Brie.

So, how do you find good cheese? Here are some ways:

Where to Go

Farmer's markets: These generally give you the best prices and the best opportunity to taste cheese. Often, depending on the market, you can meet someone who actually works directly with the cheese or the animals and build an actual relationship with a person who helps produce your food. The only downside here is that the range of cheese will be limited.

Cheese shops/specialty stores: This is your best option for high-quality, usually cut-to-order cheese. If a cheese shop or small specialty store is any good at all, it will provide the biggest range in options of fancy-schmancy cheese. These stores will cost more; you are paying for added labor in a cut-to-order program, generally higher overhead, and (theoretically) a more knowledgeable staff. These stores can be snobby. Don't try to buy your mild Cheddar or block mozzarella here or you may be the object of sneers.

"Ethnic" stores: Though limited to the country of origin, you can find a depth of types of cheese. For example, Italian cheese at an Italian deli will often be more varied than you can find at any other place. Perfect for exploration or a specific menu. Plus, they generally know its use and character better than any other store will.

Co-ops: We are one of the few worker-cooperatives, but I have love for the consumer co-ops, too. The great thing about consumer co-ops is that, since they are owned by the consumers, once you join you can, depending on the co-op, have a say in what gets carried or even get to work with the cheese. Working with the cheese on an occasional basis is great because you get to taste a lot but not get tendinitis in your forearms and elbows!

Independent grocers: Selection here can vary, but I find independent grocery stores to have the best balance of price, selection, and knowledge. (Of course, I would, wouldn't I?) First you have to find one that actually highlights its cheese selection. Independent grocers tend to have staff that stick around, so if you can become a regular, you can benefit from having workers learn your cheese tendencies. It's also possible to give input here with the likelihood that the buyer might actually pick up a cheese you want to try. Be nice about it though, okay?

Chain groceries: Of course, these will vary. Some do a good job and some just buy large-scale production cheeses with good price points and a marketing department. Most stores in a chain are limited in what they can buy, so suggestions are less likely to be heeded. The non-union stores in particular tend to have extremely high turnover, especially among their buyers. So trying to build a cheese-based relationship can be tricky. However, sometimes, like a Borders in a town with no other bookstores, they can be beacons of hope.

Internet sites: Wow, talk about disadvantages! No tasting in advance, no examining the actual cheese, super-expensive (if you include the shipping costs), and it's going to be shipped through many differing weather patterns on its way to your home. The disadvantages can cut both ways. I know that, for example, Cowgirl Creamery in Marin County has taken returns for their awesome Red Hawk just because it was "all red" (as the name would imply)! However, if you are in the middle of nowhere and you know your cheese, this can work for you. Make sure they have a good return policy, and beware.

What Should You Look for, Assuming You Can't Get Cheese Cut to Order?

Does anyone seem to care about the cheese? If individual pieces of cheese are moldy when they are not supposed to be and the displays are thin without evidence that the store has recently been busy, it's probably not the place you should be buying cheese. Still, maybe it's your only option. Even in these places, if you can find one worker who is interested in cheese, who can help steer you to the gem in the pile of manure, you can do all right.

Contrary to what you may be thinking, nice tall, orderly cheese displays may not be the best thing. Sure, if you are the first customer in the store in the morning, that's fine. But on a Saturday afternoon, displays can sometimes be falling over due to customers Jenga-ing for just the right piece. The signs may be on the wrong cheeses. Some cheese may be in short supply. If this is what you see—but there are also numerous cheese-cutters clearly busting their asses trying to cut, wrap, price, stock, and answer questions—you know you're at the right place.

If the people behind the counter care, and the customers are buying at a rate that depletes the displays, you can be assured that the store is selling cheese in volume. Volume is a good thing in this situation because that means that the same piece of cheese you bought last week isn't still there this week. Which brings me to . . .

Check dates

Don't look for "sell-by" dates on cut pieces of cheese, look for the day they were cut. Sell-by dates, except for very young or soft cheeses, are really beside the point. Even with young cheeses, especially French ones, sometimes the sell-by dates are misleading. Our regular Camembert often isn't even worth eating until it hits the sell-by date. I like to imagine that it's a French protest against the ridiculousness of requiring arbitrary time lines instead of inspecting the individual cheese for ripeness.

What you want to know is how long the cut cheese has been in plastic. The softer the cheese, the less time it will survive in plastic. Depending on your options, you can draw your own conclusions about what is acceptable to buy. Every cheese book in the world gives you advice to look for discoloration, inappropriate mold, and pooling liquid. That is also good, if obvious, advice.

Taste the cheese

Most stores that take cheese seriously at all will let you taste at least some cheeses. Go ahead and ask. Taste a few. But if you want to taste everything in the case, you probably need to go to a cut-to-order store.

Often there will be one cheese out for sampling in a store that doesn't necessarily have anyone around to give you other tastes. The best thing about that is, besides knowing what you're going to get, you know they are going to be moving through that pile of cheese. Cheese in big piles generally implies a fast mover.

Be daring, but not too daring

You can get all the advice in the world about how to buy cheese, but you have to adapt it to your environment. Like the "no, thank you" helping that many parents have forced on their children, you may be surprised about what you like. Try something new even if it's a leap of faith. Don't try something new that looks as if it may kill you, but if you're an American looking to expand your cheese love, you've gotta push that comfort zone.

If you get a bad cheese, return it. Every grocery store sells some bad cheese sometimes and they will take it back unless they are really trying to ruin their own business. However, know that they probably know more about cheese than you do, so ask them if the cheese is supposed to taste that way before you assume that they are selling bad product. About half the time someone returns a cheese, they simply didn't know what they were buying. I, like Cowgirl Creamery's mail-order department, have taken returns on Red Hawk from people who said, "It smells strong," and "The outside is red and sticky." Retailers and producers can try to avoid these things by having good signage, but it's important for customers to know the styles they like.

What Should I Look for That May Be New to Me?

Local cheese: Whatever is local to you is what you should try first. Get to know it, because there are quality cheesemakers almost everywhere in the United States. The more local, the better the chance that the price and quality will be at its best. Especially for soft and young cheese.

Goat cheese: Fresh chèvre is popular enough to be in most grocery stores these days, but you should look for firmer cheeses also. Young Goat Gouda is a good gateway goat.

Sheep cheese: Most people have heard of it, but once you know that *pecorino* means "sheep" in Italian, you will see lots of new options. Italian pecorinos are relatively affordable; they can range from young (*fresco*) to aged (*stagionato*). Another type to try is any Basque sheep cheese. We sell more Ossau-Iraty than any other sheep cheese. The brand can vary around the country, but they are almost all high-quality and good. Once you try that, you can move on to seeking out the raw milk varieties that may be a little stronger and more interesting.

Whey cheese: Ricotta salata is a great salty, smooth alternative to feta that, because it is whey-based, tends to be affordable.

Feta: If you have a choice, stop buying cow's milk feta. Get sheep or goat. You will be amazed at what you have been missing.

Parmigiano Reggiano: Always buy this. It's the real thing. Even the best domestic Parmesans are just sad imitations. Grana Padano is good, too, and good ones surpass over-aged Parmigiano Reggianos, but if you stick to name-controlled Parmigiano Reggiano you will be happy. Some Reggianos are better than others, but all are top quality. For the sake of Sweet Cheesus, don't buy it pre-grated unless you are doing a large event.

Cheddar: Okay, you grew up on Cheddar. Now try seeking out one made in the traditional way. It might be sold under the not-tasty-sounding title of "bandage-wrapped" Cheddar or maybe just "farmhouse" Cheddar, but, while often not as sharp as, say, a two-year-aged block-style Vermont Cheddar, it will be much more complex and interesting.

Blues: There are lots of amazing American blue cheeses: Rogue Creamery, Point Reyes, St. Pete's, Maytag, Jasper Hill, et cetera, but most Americans have never ventured beyond whatever kind of generic Danish-style blue (or American "Gorgonzola") was cheapest at the grocery store. There's a whole world of good blues out there, and you don't have to go too far beyond the $10-per-pound mark to find some, even if the best (Rogue River Blue, good Roquefort, and the like) are closer to the $30-per-pound range.

Gruyère: If you haven't tried a Gruyère aged more than nine months, you haven't tried Gruyère. Not all great Swiss cheeses need to be aged that long to be fabulous; the seventy-plus-pound wheel of Gruyère needs that time to start achieving its greatness, but smaller wheels don't. Once you start appreciating real Swiss cheese (as opposed to domestic factory copies or Jarlsberg/Maasdammer/Madrigal/Leerdammer Baby Swisses) there are a lot to choose from.

Aged Goudas: Everyone knows the mellow, rich, and soft young red wax Gouda. By now, thanks to the mass marketing of Parrano, many people know the great flavor of aged Gouda when it starts to become sharp and sweet. Parrano, though, is just the beginning. Ask for the most aged Gouda you can get. The more it ages, the more it tastes like hard cheese candy.

Hard cheese: Hard cheese in general is the hardest thing for any store to mess up. It's difficult to do damage to a cheese that can drive nails. The aged Goudas and the Parmigiano Reggiano are good examples of this, but there are lots of good hard cheeses out there: Piave Vecchio, Dry Jack, aged Mimolette . . . see what they've got.

Mozzarella: If you've never had fresh mozzarella that comes in water, you're in for a treat. During tomato season, cutting these into bite-sized pieces, topping with an heirloom tomato, drizzling olive oil, and adding salt and pepper . . . It's a meal. Basil and balsamic vinegar are optional. Try finding some made from water buffalo milk (Mozzarella di Bufala).

Soft-ripened: Factory-made Brie has its uses at parties. It draws people away from the more expensive cheese. There is a reason that soft-ripened cheeses have always been seen as special. Finding a non-factory-made triple cream will make you happy as only eating fat can. There's a world beyond Saint-Andre and Cambozola.

Stinky: It's not an endurance contest. You don't have to like stinky cheese. But there is a reason that people do. Start off with Taleggio. It's a rich, mild, nutty, and stinky cheese that is a good gateway into cheese that makes scaredy-cats mock and gag.

Ask for their favorites: Look, if you walk into a fancy cheese shop and ask for illegal raw cheese, they'll think you're an agent. They probably don't have any anyway, but you will be marked as suspect from then on. Talking to cheese workers, especially if you tend to come the same day to shop every week, will build a relationship where they will let you know if exciting new things are in stock. They will likely have tasted everything in the case, so something new will be exciting to them. If they sound like they are reciting a push-this-quick-it's-going-bad list that someone handed down, beware. On the other hand, if they sound excited, it's a good bet you will be, too. Especially if you have told them what cheeses you usually like.

Prepare yourself: Cheese workers will do a much better job if you can communicate with them. In fact, experienced ones can probably figure out the cheese you can't remember the name of if you give them some hints. We keep a card file for customers, writing down the cheese they buy, but usually with information about a country of origin (that may or not be remembered correctly), an animal (that may or not be remembered correctly), and a texture (that may or not be remembered correctly). An experienced cheese pro can make some good guesses.

What should you know if you plan on talking to a cheese person? Here is a list of questions that good cheese workers will ask. You will get cheese that will make you happy if you anticipate these questions:

What cheese do you like and why? What cheese don't you like and why? You don't need brand names necessarily, just types. "I like sharp cheese," "I like soft cheese," "I like fatty cheese," are all good answers. "I hate goat," and "Don't give me stinky!" are good, too. Someone who says he likes Saint-André may well get a different recommendation than someone who says she likes Delice de Argental. Both are soft-ripened triple creams, but the former implies you are used to mass-produced cheese, the latter that you like the highest-quality, small-production, and expensive stuff.

Do you want the usual or something different? Your answer could be "I hate goat" but that you want to learn to love it. A good cheese person can steer you to the right gateway goat cheese that won't make you feel like you stuck your nose in a goat's crotch.

What do you want to spend? How much cheese do you want? If you're on a budget, you will get a different answer than if you want to impress some foodie friends. If you're on an unlimited expense account, definitely let the cheese person know.

Why are you buying cheese? A party? A picnic? A date? A potluck? There are different cheeses for different occasions. There aren't hard-and-fast rules, but if the person isn't bringing a variety of knives on a picnic, it might change the cheese assortment I'd recommend. If there are other considerations (you can't refrigerate the cheese for the next twenty-four hours, your friend thinks he or she is lactose-intolerant, you want your cheese to be unusual . . .), you should mention these, too.

Does your cheese have politics? Buying mostly local products, trying to support small businesses, and caring about the treatment of animals are all valid goals. Trying to find a cheese seller who knows about these particulars can be tricky. Finding retailers who admit when they don't know something, as opposed to making up an answer, is trickier. If you can't find one locally, you may have to do this kind of research on your own.

With these tips you should be able to find good cheese if it exists where you are. Remember that flavor is somewhat subjective and it's okay to like or dislike whatever you like or dislike. Don't let anyone give you a hard time for that, whether it's because they are snobby or they think you might be. Cheese is food, not a status symbol. Push your boundaries, but buy the cheese that makes you happy.

NOTES

1. Jean Buzby, "Cheese Consumption Continues to Rise," *Amber Waves* (official publication of the USDA's Economic Research Service), February 2005.
2. Ibid.
3. Ibid.
4. Crowley Cheese Company also claims the title, but its own Web site dates the history of the cheese plant to 1882 (www.crowleycheese-vermont.com/history. html). The family has been making cheese in Vermont since 1824, but their cheese plant is only the second oldest in the country. Sorry, Vermont.
5. Linda McGraw, "Grazing Cows Produce More Cancer-Fighting Compound in Milk," USDA Agricultural Research Service, April 7, 2000.
6. Second International Congress on CLA from Experimental Models to Human Application, September 19–22, 2007, Tanka Village Resort, Villasimius, Italy. Summarized by UK Dairy Council at www.milk.co.uk/page. aspx?intPageID=283.
7. Duckett, S. K., D. G. Wagner, et al., "Effects of Time on Feed on Beef Nutrient Composition," *Journal of Animal Science* 71, no. 8 (1993), pp. 2079–88.
8. Alice Beetz, "Grass-Based and Seasonal Dairying," ATTRA Publication #CT079, National Sustainable Agricultural Information Service, 1998.
9. www.farmland.org/resources/fote/default.asp.
10. Farmland Information Center, "Agricultural Conversion Easements," Fact Sheet, June 2008.
11. www.farmland.org/resources/reports/NationalView.asp.
12. US Environmental Protection Agency, Emission Facts, EPA420-F-05-004, February 2005, p. 2.
13. FDA, "Risk Assessment Reinforces That Keeping Ready-To-Eat Foods Cold May Be the Key to Reducing Listeriosis," October 21, 2003.
14. The FDA reprinting the USDA advice is in many places, including here: www. cfsan.fda.gov/~dms/fttmilk.html.
15. FDA/Center for Food Safety and Applied Nutrition/USDA/Food Safety and Inspection Service/Centers for Disease Control and Prevention, *Quantitative Assessment of Relative Risk to Public Health,* from the section "Foodborne *Listeria monocytogenes* Among Selected Categories of Ready-to-Eat Foods," September 2003, chapter 5, "Risk Characterization."
16. *Food Science & Technology Today* 12, no. 2 (June 1998), pp. 117–122.
17. Robert W. Hutkins, *Microbiology and Technology of Fermented Foods,* Blackwell Publishing, 2006, p. 160.
18. Commonwealth Club Panel, "Cheese in the Raw: Evaluating Risks and Rewards," May 19, 2008.
19. www.realmilk.com/asthma-brucellosis.html is one example.
20. Robert Kunzig, "The Biology of . . . Cheese: Safety vs. Flavor in the Land of Pasteur," *Discover* magazine, published online November 1, 2001.

21. FDA/Center for Food Safety and Applied Nutrition/USDA/Food Safety and Inspection Service/Centers for Disease Control and Prevention, Quantitative Assessment of Relative Risk to Public Health, from the section "Foodborne *Listeria monocytogenes* Among Selected Categories of Ready-to-Eat Foods," September 2003, chapter 5, "Risk Characterization."

22. The band name *Jodie Foster's Army* was a reference to John Hinckley stating that he shot Reagan to impress the actress Jodie Foster.

23. Robert Pear, "Handouts of Cheese, Milk and Rice Face 50% Cut Next Year," *New York Times,* November 17, 1987.

24. Mark Kastel, "The Real BGH Story: Animal Health Problems, Financial Troubles," Rural Vermont 1995, A Project of the Rural Education Action Project.

25. FDA press release, November 5, 1993, available at www.fda.gov/bbs/topics/NEWS/NEW 00443.html.

26. Paul Kindstedt, *American Farmstead Cheese,* Chelsea Green, 2005.

27. Dr. Moshe Rosenberg, professor of dairy science, UC Davis. But please do not blame him for my juvenile interpretation here.

28. *EDLP* stands for "everyday low price." It means that you get an ongoing discount in exchange for lowering your retail price.

29. Kindstedt, *American Farmstead Cheese,* pp. 6–11.

30. Two well-respected ones here: Bernard Nantet, et al., *Cheeses of the World,* Rizzoli, 2002, pp. 64–70; Steven Jenkins, *Cheese Primer,* Workman, 1996, pp. 11–13.

31. Juliet Harbutt, *Cheese: A Complete Guide to Over 300 Cheeses of Distinction,* Willow Creek Press, 1999.

32. International Dairy Foods Association 2006 report on US cheese consumption and production.

33. Food and Drug Administration, Department of Health and Human Services, 21 CFR 133.169 (1999).

34. Ibid., 133.173.

35. "Kraft 'Cheese'?: Adulterated Food? FDA: Don't Ask! Don't Tell!," *Agribusiness Examiner* i.115 (May 7, 2001).

36. *The Milkweed,* October 2002.

37. *The Warriors* is a classic 1979 movie. It starts with all the gangs of New York City gathering to plan working together to take over the city. Things happen quickly after that, but the main point is that if the gangs unite they will outnumber the cops three to one. *Can you dig it?*

38. Lyrics by Todd Stadtman, "Right," Love Factory Publishing (BMI), B-Team, 1983.

39. Private correspondence, March 27, 2008.

GLOSSARY

Affinage/affineur: Affinage is French for the process of skillfully aging cheese to its peak of ripeness. An *affineur* is someone who works in that profession. Some cheesemakers do *affinage,* but many producers in the cheesemaking countries with lots of tradition have professional *affineurs,* a skill that, like cheesemaking, is often passed down from generation to generation.

American Cheese Society: Set up in 1983 as a place for cheesemakers to meet one another, share information, and promote smaller-scale, handcrafted cheesemaking, the ACS is a trade organization that puts on a national conference every year, holds a cheese competition, and has helped lobby to prevent the banning of raw milk cheese.

Artisan/artisanal: Buzzword meant to imply handcrafted products. If this ever meant anything real in relation to food, the Jack in the Box "artisan ciabatta bread" commercial ruined that forever. When words with no certification guarantee are used to sell things, they soon spin out of control.

B. linens: Brevibacterium linens is the bacteria that gives washed-rind cheese its reddish pink hue. *B. linens* is a sign that the cheese will probably be stinky and pungent.

Bandage-wrapped: I know it sounds like something you do to a wound, but it refers to a cheese that is aged in cheesecloth. Cheesecloth, as opposed to plastic, is the traditional way to make cheeses like Cheddar, so that the cheese can breathe, mature, and develop a hard rind. Usually bandage-wrapped cheeses need to be flipped and treated with oil or lard so they can ripen evenly and stay moist.

Bikini Kill: A great punk band of the early 1990s, one that arguably became the most important and famous of the riot grrrl bands. Bikini Kill was extremely political, feminist, and self-described as "worse than queer." The 1991 tour they did with the Washington, DC, band Nation of Ulysses reenergized political punks and galvanized thousands of teens (especially girls) to form bands, make zines, and become politically active.

Bové, José: French anti-globalization organizer and sheep farmer. Some of his milk goes toward making Roquefort cheese. Helped dismantle a McDonald's restaurant bolt-by-bolt in order to protest American fast food encroaching on French traditions.

Bovine somatotropin/rBGH/rBST/: Recombinant bovine growth hormone (rBGH) is a lab-created, genetically engineered hormone made by a company until recently owned by Monsanto; it is used to make dairy cows increase their milk production. Not legal for use in the European Union, United Kingdom, Australia, New Zealand, or Canada—in other words, all the big milk-producing nations besides the United States. Very controversial among consumer advocates and environmental groups because of human and animal health concerns. Nonrecombinant bovine growth hormone occurs naturally in cows.

Cohn-Bendit, Danny: Onetime French anarchist and symbol of the 1968 student uprising. Once known as "Danny the Red." Later became a Green MP, but I preferred his street-fightin' anarchist persona.

Commodity cheese: Technically, cheese whose price is set on the Chicago Mercantile Exchange. Most cheese is not sold through the CME, but all Jack and mild Cheddar pricing is affected by that market. Among cheese professionals, the term *commodity cheese* is often used less specifically to refer to any large-production, factory-made block cheese as a way of differentiating it from specialty cheese.

Cooperative, agricultural: Cooperative owned by farmers. The farmers pool their resources so that all members thrive in a way that would be impossible otherwise. Cabot Creamery and Organic Valley are examples of dairy farmers pooling their milk and marketing under a brand name. However, some US agricultural co-ops are incredibly large corporations themselves, run with traditional management structures and not necessarily in the interest of small farmers or environmental sustainability.

Cooperative, consumer: Cooperative owned by the shoppers. Examples: REI, Park Slope Food Co-op, or any member of the National Cooperative Grocers Association.

Cooperative, worker: Cooperative owned by workers with the ultimate decision-making power in their hands on a one-worker, one-vote basis. This describes my workplace, Rainbow Grocery Cooperative, members of the US Federation of Worker Cooperatives, and others.

Culture: A culture is bacteria added to the milk to create a chemical reaction beneficial to the cheese. The culture determines the acidity level of the milk, the way the milk coagulates, the texture of the curds (and therefore the cheese), the taste, the moisture level, and the way the cheese ages.

Culture, secondary: Not the culture responsible for determining the main formation of the cheese, but one that is added to give the cheese a particular flavor.

Epicenter Zone: Collectively run punk rock community center in San Francisco from 1991 to 1998. A record store, venue, meeting place, and a place to hang out if one had nowhere else to go. I worked there from 1991 to 1996.

Factory-made: Definitions are a little elusive depending on who is using them. *Factory-made* generally means that the production is fully, or almost fully, automated. In some factories the milk, curds, and cheese are never touched by human hands. Handmade cheesemakers derisively call cheesemakers who work in big factories "button pushers."

Farmstead: This term indicates that a cheese is made on the farm using only milk from the farmer-cheesemakers' own animals. This is one of the only descriptors that guarantees a consumer knows exactly where the milk comes from, but it makes no claim as to the farm conditions or growing and production methods.

Food security: The idea that everyone deserves access to healthy food. If a neighborhood is said to be "food-insecure," it might mean that the only food stores in the area have lots of liquor and processed foods, but very little, if any, produce. These areas are also known as "food deserts," and they can occur in rural America just as easily as in low-income or inner-city neighborhoods.

HACCP: Hazard analysis critical control points. It's an industry term that basically means a company/cheesemaker has done a systematic overview of anything that can go wrong in its operations, especially around food safety, has figured out the potential weak points, and has addressed those issues to make a better, safer product. (Pronounced hass-ip.)

Handmade: (See *artisan* and subtract pretentiousness.)

Milk, raw: According to US regulatory agencies: milk that is not pasteurized. According to raw foodies: milk not heated above 116 degrees Fahrenheit.

Milk, thermalized: Milk that is not heated to a high enough temperature to be pasteurized, but that is heated high enough to kill off a good deal of its bacteria (good and bad). For importation purposes, thermalized milk is considered the same as raw milk since it has not been pasteurized.

Name control: If you see initials after a cheese name (AOC, DO, DOP, PDO, et cetera), there's a good chance these stand for that country's protected name designation. This means (usually) that the region, ingredients, aging conditions, and type of milk are regulated by the state (or European Union) because it has been decided that those protected aspects produce a cheese that cannot be duplicated in any other way. No US cheeses are name-controlled.

Pasteurization: The heating of milk to a certain temperature to kill off unwanted food-borne pathogens and bacteria. Generally, this is either done at 145 degrees F for thirty minutes or 161 degrees F for fifteen seconds. "Cold pasteurization" means irradiation, just so you know.

People's Food System: Radical attempt by Bay Area people in the

1970s to link natural food collectives, distributor collectives, and producer collectives together as an alternative to the corporate-controlled, processed-food-selling system that predominates in the United States. It didn't last long, but it's where Rainbow Grocery Cooperative, my workplace, got its start.

Rennet: A necessary enzyme for most cheese, used to coagulate the milk and give us the curds from which cheesemaking begins. Can be from a ruminant animal's stomach, plant-based, or lab-created.

Rind: The outside of the cheese. It could be edible and moldy, or bitter red and sticky. It could even be brined and hard as a rock. Eat it if you want to and if you can.

Ruminant: A mammal that digests its food in two steps. Cows, sheep, goats, and water buffalo all chew their "cuds," semi-digested food they regurgitate, which ensures thorough breakdown and digestion of plants. All cheese milk comes from ruminants. Mmmmmmm.

Situationists: French revolutionaries from the 1960s who created some of the best graffiti ever and helped almost topple the French government in 1968. My personal favorite Situationist saying: "Those who talk about revolution without referring to everyday reality have a corpse in their mouth."

Specialty cheese: A loose US cheese industry term referring to any cheese that is higher-priced than a big block of Cheddar or Swiss and that generally needs some attention or hand-selling by the retailer. For example, even though Saint-André may be a large-production, factory-made cheese, because it is somewhat delicate and not known to Americans who haven't thought much about cheese, it would be considered "specialty."

Terroir: A very useful French concept that means "sense of place." This, going together with the concept of name control, highlights the importance of the rationality of milk: What animals eat determines the taste and makeup of the milk. It is, however, often used to make those people using it sound smarter than they are, sometimes with hilarious results. Beware the utterance of this word and assume you are about to be conned. If you hear it used in relation

to a nonfarmstead dairy, ask how the user knows where the cheesemaker buys their milk.

Thermalization: The heating of milk to temperatures short of
pasteurization. This kills some food-borne pathogens while also
letting some bacteria survive, retaining some of the flavor of raw
milk cheese. For retail purposes, thermalized cheeses, not being
pasteurized, are still illegal to sell if they are aged less than sixty
days.

INDEX

ABOUT THE AUTHOR

Gordon Edgar loves cheese and worker-owned co-ops and has been combining both of these infatuations as a cheesemonger at Rainbow Grocery Cooperative in San Francisco for more than fifteen years. Edgar has been a judge at cheese competitions, a board member for the California Artisan Cheese Guild, and, since 2002, has blogged at www.gordonzola. net. Surrounded by his vast and decaying collection of zines and obscure punk 7-inches, he lives in San Francisco with his girlfriend and their imaginary white miniature schnauzer.

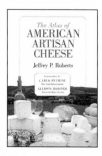